THE
CORINTHIAN
CHURCH
—A BIBLICAL APPROACH TO
URBAN CULTURE

WILLIAM BAIRD

THE
CORINTHIAN
CHURCH
—A BIBLICAL APPROACH TO
URBAN CULTURE

ABINGDON PRESS • NEW YORK • NASHVILLE

THE CORINTHIAN CHURCH—A BIBLICAL APPROACH TO URBAN CULTURE

Library of Congress Catalog Card Number: 64-20519

Scripture quotations unless otherwise noted
are from the Revised Standard Version of the
Bible, copyrighted 1946 and 1952 by the Division of Christian Education, National Council
of Churches, and are used by permission.

Passages marked WB indicate translations by the
author.

SET UP, PRINTED, AND BOUND BY THE
PARTHENON PRESS, AT NASHVILLE,
TENNESSEE, UNITED STATES OF AMERICA

For my wife

ἡ σύζυγός μου ἐν Χριστῷ

ACKNOWLEDGMENTS

For some time I have been concerned with the relevance of First Corinthians for the problems of the contemporary church. However, it was the invitation to present the M. T. Burt Lectures which encouraged me to express these concerns in written form. To Dean Raleigh J. Peterson, Jr., the faculty and students of Cotner School of Religion, I remain grateful for the warm hospitality extended me in Lincoln, Nebraska, in January of 1962. The lectures have been considerably enlarged for publication.

Biblical scholars will readily recognize my dependence on the standard commentaries. No effort has been made to cite these in every instance; explicit reference is offered only where unique interpretation or direct quotation is involved. Almost every element of exegesis in the book might have been documented by some commentary. Those which I have found most useful include: Archibald Robertson and Alfred Plummer, *A Critical and Exegetical Commentary on the First Epistle of St. Paul to the Corinthians;* James Moffatt, *The First Epistle of Paul to the Corinthians;* Jean Héring, *The First Epistle of Saint Paul to the*

Corinthians; Johannes Weiss, *Der erste Korintherbrief;* Hans Lietzmann, *An die Korinther;* and Heinz-Dietrich Wendland, *Die Briefe an die Korinther.*

The completion of this work has been encouraged by the assistance of many. Roscoe M. Pierson, librarian of The College of the Bible (soon to be known as Lexington Theological Seminary), made special efforts to secure bibliographical material. The administration of the seminary, under the leadership of President Riley B. Montgomery and Dean Ralph G. Wilburn, granted a leave of absence wherein the final stages of research were completed. The generosity of my aunt, Miss Clara M. Watson, provided the opportunity for firsthand study of Corinth and other Hellenistic sites in the summer of 1962. Miss Marilyn Rae Williams typed the final copy, and assistance in proofreading was offered by Mr. B. Lee Brummel and Mr. Loren A. Broadus, Jr. Without the many sacrifices of my wife, this book would not have been possible.

WILLIAM BAIRD

CONTENTS

CONTENTS

I
YESTERDAY AND TODAY

No feature of contemporary life has been more important than the triumph of urban culture. Two sensitive observers of the social scene write:

The rise of modern America is the rise of her cities—the economic and cultural centers of her technological age. Built by countless hands, by the men and women who have come here from all over the earth, the American city towers as the massive symbol of a nation's material achievement and wealth, as an engineering wonder, as an amazing wilderness of the dreams and works of man. Indeed, to understand America, one must understand her cities.[1]

[1] Walter Kloetzli and Arthur Hillman, *Urban Church Planning* (Philadelphia: Muhlenberg Press, 1958), p. 1.

But who can understand this fantastic phenomenon—the "exploding metropolis," the "urban sprawl"? Yet, fathom it or not, the victory of the city is sure. "In brief," writes Gibson Winter, *the United States is now a metropolitan society.*" [2]

I

This triumph, which is heralded by the commuter's horn and the belching smokestack, is well-attested by familiar statistics. Seventy years ago our total population was somewhere around 60 million people, two thirds of whom lived in rural areas. Now the land of amber fields and purple mountains is teeming with some 180 million, and over 105 million of these are urban.[3] Educated guesses suggest that the census takers in A.D. 2000 will list 300 million Americans, and the trend makes it pretty clear that most of these will be city dwellers.

The conquest of urbania has not stopped at the city limits, or even at the edge of the everadvancing suburbs; it has invaded all the frontiers of American life. Tht problem of "keeping them down on the farm" is now complicated by the fact that the farm has become a chief consumer of city culture. Through modern means of communication it is possible that the rural swain has seen "Paree" even before he has viewed the "south forty," and he may have received his introduction to the farm from "Captain Kangaroo" long before he was able to mount a tractor. Radio, television, the newspaper, and the slick-paper magazines come from the city, and they are shaping rural man into the city's image. Martin Marty is right—" 'panurbia' is here." [4]

It doesn't take a sociologist to see that this victory of the city is not without problems; both victors and vanquished are restive. Quite apart from the choked freeways and the crammed classrooms, urban society presents man with serious questions about his own existence. The

[2] Gibson Winter, *The Suburban Captivity of the Churches* (Garden City, N. Y.: Doubleday & Co., 1961), p. 16.

[3] U. S. Bureau of the Census, *Statistical Abstract of the United States: 1960* (Washington, D. C., 1960), p. 4.

[4] Martin E. Marty, *The New Shape of American Religion* (New York: Harper & Row, 1959), p. 91.

move to the city has pulled up fixed roots, and there is no guarantee that they will flourish again by a simple transplant in the suburbs. The fact that in the decade of the 1940's some 70 million people moved at least once may indicate that modern man is looking for a city which has real foundations.[5] Perhaps his silent song is "this world is not my home," but he has forgotten the tune and does not know the meaning of the words.

The move from house to house, from inner city to the suburbs, from row house to ranch house, is not as disturbing as the urban mania to move from lower to higher status. It has been suggested that most people come to the city in order to fulfill the "American ideal of getting ahead." [6] The city simply provides the most efficient ladder to success —so efficient that it appears to the novice like an escalator.

But why shouldn't the urbanite seek for status? Surely his life in the city is devoid of personal meaning. He lives in the midst of a crowd without faces. The people he meets—the policeman on the corner, the bus driver, the elevator girl—are functions, not people; he knows them by their uniforms and not by their faces. They do not know him at all. His life follows a mechanical routine—catching the 7:14, eating at the automat. All sorts of diversions are open to him, of course, but their very multiplicity and familiarity make them only another aspect of the monotony.

Paradoxically, the climb to status which seeks to escape the monotony of the lonely crowd is coupled with a pressure to conform. Once he has mounted a higher rung, the man of upward mobility must make sure he does not slip back. Therefore, he must convince his fellows, and especially himself, that he really "belongs." He becomes what Riesman calls the "outer directed" person, whose thoughts and actions are shaped by his desire to impress others.[7]

The subdivisions which house this "organization man" [8] are a strange

[5] Kenneth D. Miller, *Man and God in the City* (New York: Friendship Press, 1954), p. 36.

[6] *Ibid.*, p. 2.

[7] David Riesman, *et. al.*, *The Lonely Crowd* (Garden City, N. Y.: Doubleday & Co., 1953).

[8] William H. Whyte, Jr., *The Organization Man* (New York: Simon and Schuster, 1956).

13

mixture of friendliness and reclusion. Since he wants to belong, the suburbanite must keep up the appearance of neighborliness. Yet he must not get too involved, since he might be transferred, or perhaps promoted, and so move to a suburb of higher status. And there is always the question, "Do the neighbors really belong?"

Gibson Winter has suggested that these tensions of urban existence are related to two opposing principles operating in metropolitan society: impersonal interdependence and communal insulation.[9] The former is necessitated by the very nature of city life; every individual is dependent on a multitude of people and services for his very livelihood, yet this interdependence is always at a superficial level. The latter evidences an attempt to escape the impersonal to find meaning in a smaller, homogeneous community. The rush to the suburbs is hereby explained, but the problem is not thereby solved. The suburbs do not provide security, but become bastions of a class consciousness whose frantic self-defenses betray a deep and persistent insecurity. The metropolis becomes a house divided; man loses his integrity.[10]

To those of us who love the city, this picture seems all too bleak. The rising towers were portents of greater things—the cultural achievements of man, the opportunities for human community. But as Thucydides observed so long ago, "Men make the city." [11] In our time men have attempted to build towers which reach to heaven, but their language has been confounded, their buildings have no secure foundation, and their houses are furnished with loneliness.

II

What is the church to do in the face of this advancing urbanization and its concomitant problems? For one thing, it is clear that the church has already given considerable ground. In spite of the apparent success of the recent religious revival, there is a question about the

[9] *Suburban Captivity*, pp. 15 ff.
[10] Cf. Maurice R. Stein, *The Eclipse of Community* (Princeton: Princeton University Press, 1960), p. 329.
[11] *The Peloponnesian War*, vii, 77.

depth of American religious commitment. Will Herberg has shown that although a large majority profess religious faith and formal membership in religious institutions, most Americans do not believe that Christianity or Judaism have much to say in shaping their views on economics, business, and politics. Instead of genuine loyalty to the historic faith which he professes, the urbanite is committed to what Herberg calls the "faith embodied in the American Way of Life." [12] The traditional religious faiths are formally followed, but they are actually viewed as irrelevant.

The Protestant tactics in this battle have called for an orderly retreat to a better position; the inner city has been abandoned, and the suburbs have been invaded with vigor and seeming success. Truman Douglas points out, for example, that "during a period when 200,000 people were moving into New York City in the area below Fourteenth Street, 17 Protestant churches moved out." [13] This move to the suburbs has actually been fostered by ecclesiastical strategists, for as Gibson Winter has noted, "Denominational leaders call these 'high potential areas,'— and they do not mean potential for prayer." [14] Of course, some of the old city churches remain downtown, but these citadels of another era have often become commuter churches; the location is urban, the people and the program are suburban.

Yet wasn't the move to the suburbs inevitable? Was it not even commendable? The people had moved from the city. Why not the church? After all, the church's task is to serve the people. But the ecclesiastical planners often forgot that some people were left behind in the blighted areas—their retreat blocked by poverty or racial barriers. Their religious fate was left to the sectarians whose zeal exceeded knowledge, or to the associations of racial minorities whose lower-class exclusiveness left little room for Jew or Greek in the body of Christ. Without adequate funds or leadership, these struggling churches could not offer the sort of program which relevantly ministered to the needs

[12] Will Herberg, *Protestant, Catholic, Jew* (Garden City, N. Y.: Doubleday & Co., 1955), p. 88. Cf. Paul Hutchinson, *The New Ordeal of Christianity* (New York: Association Press, 1957), pp. 109 ff.

[13] "Ecological Changes and the Church," *Annals of the American Academy of Political and Social Science,* November, 1960, p. 86.

[14] *Suburban Captivity,* p. 31.

of the whole man in his community. The sons of the city were left to grow up under the foreboding shadow of the tenement rather than the steeple of the church. Little wonder that many of them preferred the "Egyptian Dragons" to the Christian Endeavor.

Surprising as it may seem, the church in the suburbs had not fared much better. True enough, buildings in neo-gothic, neo-colonial, and neo-modern were springing up like shopping centers; people were joining by the score; activities were being carried on at high pace; but despite the variety of architecture, the church in the suburbs took on the shape of suburban culture. That culture was the culture of the organization—the success-hungry culture, the outer-directed culture, the culture of rigid conformity, the culture of the exclusive middle class. Likewise, the church of the suburbs became an aid to achievement, the thing to do, the temple of insulated fellowship. Suburbia defeated the church without firing a shot. In fact, the church was so busy measuring its success by secular standards that it still thought it was winning.

Thus the sensitive suburban minister, as Paul Musselman observes, has come to see that the "current illusion that church life in suburbia is all gold and a yard wide simply is not true." [15] Indeed, it is a church of serious problems. There is, for instance, a strange mixture of denominational competition and doctrinal indifference. How many a new congregation has been founded within the latest subdivision in the futile attempt to get there before the Southern Baptists? On the other hand, it has been demonstrated by surveys that in selecting a church, parking space is sometimes more important than denominational affiliation. This is part and parcel of the widespread notion that one faith is just as good as another.[16] Yet this quest for a common faith has reduced religion to the least common denominator, and to a faith so shallow as to be almost no faith at all.

Similar is the paradox between passivity and activity in suburban church life. On matters of social concern the suburban church is often immobile. It is a one-class church, and prefers to silently defend the

[15] G. Paul Musselman, *The Church on the Urban Frontier* (Greenwich, Conn.: Seabury Press, 1960), p. 47.

[16] Cf. William Lee Miller, "Religion and the American Way of Life," in *Religion and the Free Society* (New York: The Fund for the Republic, 1958), pp. 5 ff.

interests of that class. Suburban churches, therefore, will rarely participate in programs promoting racial integration, since the suburbs exist in part for the purpose of promoting social segregation. On the other hand, the churches of the suburbs are hotbeds of unceasing activity—committees operating, couples' clubs organizing, cake sales being held. This concern with the practical, but sometimes the irrelevant, has reduced the church to a sort of religious do-it-yourself kit. The directions come wrapped in the package, but there is little concern for the God whose ways are not our ways.

It needs to be observed that some of the currently popular, vitriolic critics of the church, whose wisdom we have been following here, may have overstated their case. These masters of the devastate-by-sarcasm school need to be reminded that their own views of truth have been communicated to them by the church, and that the church provides the platform for voicing their criticism. At any rate, there are people in the suburbs who at 11:00 on Sunday morning prefer the church to the country club, and although the membership dues may be less, the activities are likewise less exciting. Some of these parishioners even engage in serious theological and biblical study; in the free churches some even participate in the administering of the sacraments. Perhaps signs like these, together with the possibility that we may be in the "post-Protestant era"—an era in which the church has past its zenith of success—indicate that the church may again become the church. Perhaps it may even become a pilgrim people, strangers in a foreign land, who look to a city whose builder and maker is God.

In the meantime, however, it must be acknowledged that the church of today often allies itself with forces which are detrimental to metropolitan community. Through abandonment of the inner city it has surrendered the opportunity to redeem the impersonal interdependence of urban society. Through retreat to the suburbs it has supported the demonic forces of communal insulation. In the inner city, which is inhabited by a variety of classes and racial groups, it could have developed into the body of Christ, composed of Jews and Greeks, slaves and free. In the suburbs the church has grown into a maimed form, limping between two sides—loyalty to the Righteous God and obeisance to the baals of contemporary culture.

III

What has the Bible to say to these problems of the church in urban society? At first thought one might suppose that the answer is "nothing." The Bible is a book of another age; it has its setting in an antique, distant culture. Yet for all its differences the civilization of New Testament times was urban. One of the astute observers of Hellenistic culture writes, "It would scarcely be an exaggeration to say that the history of Greco-Roman civilization is the history of the cities." [17] Consequently, the problems of the first century were problems of urban society.

That these problems were not entirely unlike our own can be illustrated by a citation from Seneca, the Stoic philosopher and contemporary of Paul.

But come now, behold this concourse of men, for whom the houses of huge Rome scarcely suffice; most of this throng are now deprived of their country. From their towns and colonies, from the whole world, in fact, hither have they flocked. Some have been brought by ambition, some by the obligation of a public trust, some by an envoy's duty having been laid upon them, some, seeking a convenient and rich field for vice, by luxury, some by a desire for the higher studies, some by the public spectacles; some have been drawn by friendship, some, seeing the ample opportunity for displaying energy, by the chance to work; some have presented their beauty for sale, some their eloquence for sale—every class of person has swarmed into the city that offers high prizes for both virtues and vices.[18]

Ancient urban society was not without its housing shortages, its rootless people, its status seeking, its insecurity.

[17] A. H. M. Jones, *The Greek City from Alexander to Justinian* (Oxford: Clarendon Press, 1940), p. 299. Cf. Carl Kraeling, "The Greek and Roman Orient," in *City Invincible—A Symposium on Urbanization and Cultural Development in the Ancient Near East* (Chicago: University of Chicago Press, 1960), p. 190; Martin P. Nilsson, *Greek Folk Religion* (New York: Harper & Row, 1961), p. 5.

[18] *De consolatione.* Seneca, *Moral Essays,* tr. John W. Basore, "Loeb Classical Library" (Cambridge: Harvard University Press, 1935), II, 429 ff.

Although all roads lead to Rome, nowhere is the urban character of Hellenist society better exemplified than at Corinth. This ancient Greek city had been razed by the Roman troops of Mummius in 146 B.C. It was rebuilt a century later under the command of Julius Caesar, so that for a city of the Greco-Roman period it was, like the urban centers of modern America, relatively new. Although Caesar colonized Corinth with Italians, it was not long before the city was populated with men from all over the Mediterranean Basin—Jews expelled from Rome by the edict of Claudius, Orientals from Egypt and Asia Minor. Soon Latin, the official language, was silenced, and bartering in the noisy market place was carried on in the more universal *koine* Greek. One commentary has aptly observed, "Corinth was the Empire in miniature." [19]

Few cities could boast a more impressive setting.[20] Situated on the narrow isthmus which connected the Greek mainland with the Peloponnesus, Corinth lay nestled beneath the commanding Acrocorinth—a sheer cliff, towering 1,800 feet above the azure sea. The Gulf of Corinth below and to the west of the city reflected the beauty of an inland lake. If one were to dock at this western side of Corinth, he would enter the city by a colonnaded road which led to the market place. Lined with busy shops, temples, and baths, this crowded thoroughfare terminated with a radiant arch crowned with two bronze chariots, one driven by Helius the sun god and the other by his son, Phaethon. Passing through into the agora, the visitor would find himself standing on the pavement of a central square, three hundred feet wide and five hundred long—his view to the south awed by a colossal stoa of seventy-one columns.

The commercial ascendancy of the new city was due to its unique location. The voyage around the Greek peninsula was long and dangerous, as indicated by the ancient proverb: "Let him who sails around Malea first make his will." [21] Rather than risk the hazardous journey, most

[19] Archibald Robertson and Alfred Plummer, *A Critical and Exegetical Commentary on the First Epistle of St. Paul to the Corinthians*, "International Critical Commentary" (2nd ed. Edinburgh: T. and T. Clark, 1911), p. xiii.

[20] For concise descriptions of the setting and ruins of Corinth, cf. American School of Classical Studies, *Ancient Corinth—A Guide to the Excavations* (6th rev. ed. Athens: American School of Classical Studies, 1960), and J. G. O'Neil, *Ancient Corinth*, "John Hopkins University Studies in Archeology, No. 8" (Baltimore: John Hopkins Press, 1930).

[21] Quoted by William Barclay, *The Letters to the Corinthians*, "The Daily Study Bible" (Philadelphia: Westminster Press, 1957), p. 1.

Hellenistic mariners preferred to transport their cargoes across the isthmus at Corinth. Ships which were too large to carry were set on rollers and dragged over the land. The *diolkos,* as this ship road was called, has been unearthed by archaeologists so that the grooves of the ancient trolleys are now visible in the weathered stone.

Also excavated have been the remains of Nero's futile project to cut a canal through the isthmus in A.D. 67. This Roman was not the first ancient ruler to propose such a waterway, and Pliny,[22] who wrote shortly after, concludes that the unsuccessful attempts of Demetrius, Caesar, and Caligula indicate that the plan was a sacrilege. However, Strabo,[23] who had himself visited the site, tells in his *Geography,* written early in the first century A.D., that Demetrius abandoned the effort at the advice of his engineers. They were convinced that the Gulf of Corinth was higher than the Aegean Sea, and that building the canal would result in flooding the Greek islands. Strabo, who knew his Archimedes, considered this an "ignorant opinion," but the Corinthians may have been wise enough to realize that their livelihood was threatened by the proposal. The fact that the modern canal bypasses an unimportant town may be proof of their wisdom.

The commercial virility of Corinth gave birth to a flourishing industry and the consequent accruing of wealth. The old Greek city had been famous for its production of bronze, and there is adequate evidence that the ancient art was revived in the Roman period. Archaeologists have discovered the remains of a bronze factory, while Pausanias, who visited Corinth in the second century A.D., observed that the famous metal was tempered in the water of the Fountain Peirene—the city's primary water supply.[24] That the products of this ancient craft were coveted throughout the empire is well attested by references in Hellenistic authors. Similarly, a potter's quarter has been unearthed, indicating that Corinth afforded a source of excellent white clay as well as manufactured earthenware vessels. A tile factory has also been found, and shipbuilding was an inevitable by-product of the town's commercial activity. It is no wonder that the ancients considered Corinth a great and wealthy city.

[22] *Natural History,* iv, 4.
[23] *Geography,* i, 3, 11.
[24] *Description of Greece,* ii, 3, 3.

The cosmopolitan character of the city has been noted, but the amassing of wealth resulted in rigid social stratification. Most of the Italian colonists had been freedmen, but slavery was assumed as an essential element in the urban economy. Slaves were used extensively in the many construction projects of a new city like Corinth, while the architects who supervised the public works were considered among the highest classes. Slaves were used, too, in the menial tasks of the baths—firing the furnaces to heat the water, massaging the more fortunate clientele.

The baths were the country clubs of the Hellenistic age, and their benefits were not enjoyed by the lower classes. Indeed, the operation of the baths was dependent on the generosity of the more affluent citizens, since they were normally the donors of the all-important olive oil. When Pausanias visited Corinth, he observed baths in many parts of the city;[25] no doubt the foundations of several of the baths had been laid before the time of Paul. Alciphron, the second-century rhetorician, remarked, "Never yet have I been to Corinth, for I know pretty well the beastly kind of life the rich enjoy there and the wretchedness of the poor." [26]

In Corinth, as in most other cities, the rich enjoyed various modes of entertainment. Most famous were the Isthmian games, which were held biennially at Corinth and were second in importance only to the Olympic. As well as the more conventional track events the games included wrestling, boxing, and chariot races. Corinth boasted an out-door theater with a seating capacity of about twenty thousand; it had been remodeled in Roman times to accommodate the popular gladiatorial bouts. Attendance at these events could dispel the gravest gloom, as one of Petronius' characters reveals. "And don't forget there's a big gladiator show coming up the day after tomorrow. Not the same old fighters either; they've got a fresh shipment in and there's not a slave in the batch." [27] Late in the first century A.D. an odeum was erected in Corinth. This was a roofed theater, seating around three thousand, which dispensed the more refined arts of music and drama.

[25] *Ibid.,* ii, 3, 5.
[26] Quoted in Morton Scott Enslin, *Christian Beginnings* (New York: Harper & Bros., 1938), p. 245.
[27] Petronius, *The Satyricon*, tr. William Arrowsmith (New York: New American Library, 1960), p. 53.

21

Apparently there was plenty of time for religion, too. We are told that Paul found the men of Athens to be very religious (Acts 17:22), and the same observation could have been made of the Corinthians. Temples and sacred statuaries were to be found on every corner. Most impressive was the stately temple of Apollo. About 175 by 75 feet in area, the ancient sanctuary was supported by 38 columns. These huge monoliths were about 24 feet high and a little less than 6 feet in diameter; 7 are still standing. Also of interest is the temple to Asclepius, the Hellenistic healing god, which dated back to the fourth century B.C. but was believed important enough to be rebuilt in Roman times. Shrines, altars, and images dedicated to Zeus, Aphrodite, Dionysus, and Tyche were located throughout the city. The chance visitor to Corinth might have been impressed, as was Apuleius' hero Lucius, by an awesome procession of the devotees of Isis—stern white-robed priests carrying the image of their mysterious goddess.[28]

For all this revering of religious forms, Corinth had a reputation for immorality. Perhaps this reputation went back to earlier times when the temple of Aphrodite atop the Acrocorinth featured one thousand sacred prostitutes. Such attractions lent support to the sailors' slogan, "Not for every man is the trip to Corinth," [29] while the implication was, "If you get the chance, don't miss it!" Little had been done in Roman times to dispel this inveterate proverb. The south side of the marketplace was apparently lined with taverns—each equipped with an underground cistern which was probably used for cooling the drinks. At the bottom of these antique liquor lockers fragments of mugs have been found bearing such inscriptions as "cure for hangovers." [30]

But let a firsthand observer describe pagan immorality for himself. "They were filled with all manner of wickedness, evil, covetousness, malice. Full of envy, murder, strife, deceit, malignity, they are gossips, slanderers, haters of God, insolent, haughty, boastful, inventors of evil, disobedient to parents, foolish, faithless, heartless, ruthless." (Rom.

[28] Apuleius, *The Golden Ass*, tr. Robert Graves (New York: Pocket Books, Inc., 1952), pp. 241 ff.
[29] Quoted by Kathleen Freeman, *Greek City-States* (London: MacDonald & Co., 1950), p. 83.
[30] *Ancient Corinth—Guide to Excavations*, p. 52.

1:29-31.) And remember, Paul probably wrote these words to Rome while he was staying at Corinth.

IV

In spite of the pervasive immorality, a Christian church was established in Corinth. Seldom, it seems, had the gospel been planted in more unyielding soil. Yet, a second glance reveals that, unlike the rural character of contemporary Protestantism, the church of the New Testament was urban. The locus of Christian strength was to be found in Jerusalem, Antioch, Ephesus, and Rome. Indeed, Paul felt that after he had evangelized the *cities* from Jerusalem "as far round at Illyricum," his work in the east was done (Rom. 15:19). Sometimes the apostle has been charged with changing the original character of Jesus' simple religion into complex Hellenistic theology. Although this charge has been discredited, one thing is clear: Paul did help to change Christianity from a rural to an urban faith. Jesus saw people as sheep without a shepherd; Paul saw them as athletes ready to run a race.

Those who are interested in the church in the city, then, will be interested in Paul's program in Corinth (cf. Acts 18). No preacher ever had it worse! He arrived in the Achaian metropolis after an unsuccessful mission in Athens. In order to support himself, Paul gained employment in the establishment of Aquila and Priscilla—a Jewish couple who had recently been exiled from Rome. They shared Paul's ancestral trade of tentmaking, and had set up shop perhaps in the agora or along the colonnaded Lechaeum Road.

As usual, Paul began his preaching in the synagogue to which his rabbinic training provided an open door. It is of interest that an inscription, "Synagogue of the Hebrews," [31] has been found not far from that impressive gateway into the marketplace. Archaeologists agree that the writing itself is from a later time, but it may well mark the spot where a Jewish house of worship had stood for generations.

[31] American School of Classical Studies, *Ancient Corinth—A Guide to the Museum* (3rd ed. Athens: American School of Classical Studies, 1956), p. 43.

At any rate, it was not long before the apostle ran into opposition from the Jewish authorities. Turning his attention then to the Gentiles, who were the main goal of his mission anyhow, he moved next door to the house of a God-fearer named Titius Justus. Here the gospel was so effectively proclaimed that Crispus, the ruler of the synagogue, was converted to Christianity. Now having suffered the loss of an important leader, the Jews became even more incensed against the apostate from Tarsus. They brought him before Gallio, brother of the Stoic philosopher Seneca, who had recently arrived as governor of the province. The *bēma*, or judgment seat, before which Paul was tried has been unearthed at the center of the agora—a high platform, decorated in Paul's time with ornately carved marble. From this vantage point, however, it was evident to Gallio that the charge was a matter of religion, so that he refused to render an official judgment. A riot ensued which the noble Roman viewed with complete disinterest. Apparently the populace took the side of Paul, for Sosthenes, the new ruler of the synagogue, was beaten by the mob.

In face of all this opposition a strong church was founded. Paul speaks of the "saints who are in the whole of Achaia" (II Cor. 1:1), as if there were congregations throughout the province as well as the one which met in the house of Titius. We know for sure that there was a suburban church in Cenchreae, Corinth's eastern seaport (Rom. 16:1). Within the whole community there seems to have been a variety of people and classes. Aquila and Priscilla, as we have observed, were Jewish artisans, while Crispus must have been a man of means. The appearance of names like Titius Justus and Fortunatus gives evidence that converts had been made among the descendants of the Italian colonists. I Cor. 7:21 indicates that there were slaves among the congregation. In fact most of the members must have been from society's lower ranks. For,

> not many of you were wise . . .
> not many were powerful,
> not many were of noble birth (I Cor. 1:26).

There were, however, people like Chloe, whose household, or whose slaves, were able to travel to Ephesus in order to discuss ecclesiastical problems with Paul (I Cor. 1:11). In Rom. 16, which was almost certainly written from Corinth, there is included a greeting from Erastus, the city treasurer. This could be the same Corinthian official whose memory is preserved by an inscription found near the theater: "Erastus, the commissioner of public works, laid this pavement at his own expense." [32] If this is the case, it is clear that the Corinthian church included very wealthy officials as well as the "low and despised"—Greeks and barbarians, wise and foolish, slaves and free.

It is not surprising that a church composed of such variety, and opposed with such vigor, would have difficulties. No sooner had Paul left town than trouble broke out. This trouble led to a series of exchanges between the apostle and the church; the written residue of this encounter comprises some of the most important material of the New Testament—the Corinthian correspondence. This correspondence, in turn, confronts the biblical scholar with some of his most complex critical problems,[33] and the attempt to solve them is simply beyond the scope of our interest. For instance, it is usually held that Paul wrote not just two but at least four epistles to the troubled Corinthians. It is also widely agreed that Paul made a hurried visit to Corinth sometime between the writing of the First and Second Corinthians of our canon. The unity of Second Corinthians is a complex and hotly debated issue.

Rather than enter into these discussions, we will focus primarily on the canonical First Corinthians. Although there is some competent scholarly opinion against the conclusion,[34] we shall agree with the majority of commentators that the first epistle is a unity written pretty much in the order in which it now stands.[35] It is obvious, of course, that our First Corinthians was not Paul's first letter to the church at Corinth. In I Cor. 5:9 he reminds them of his previous letter which had not been correctly understood. Apparently this letter dealt with the proper relation of Christians to immorality, and it is possible that II Cor. 6:14–7:1 preserves an actual fragment of that earlier epistle.

[32] *Ancient Corinth—Guide to Excavations*, p. 74.

[33] For a brief summary of the critical problems of the Corinthian correspondence, cf. A. H. McNeile, *An Introduction to the Study of the New Testament*, ed. by C. S. Williams (2nd rev. ed. Oxford: Clarendon Press, 1952), pp. 132 ff.

[34] Cf. E. Dinkler, "Korintherbriefe," *Die Religion in Geschichte und Gegenwart* (3rd ed., 1960), IV, 18.

[35] For a recent statement of this opinion, cf. Robert M. Grant, *A Historical Introduction to the New Testament* (New York: Harper & Row, 1963), p. 181.

In any event, the occasion for writing a second letter, our First Corinthians, is relatively clear. Paul was in the midst of his arduous ministry in Ephesus. Word came to him of the difficulties within the Corinthian church. This word was communicated through two or three media. For example, information was brought to him by "Chloe's people" (1:11), perhaps her slaves or, as some suppose, the traveling agents of her business firm. Also, a letter had been delivered to Paul raising specific questions about particular ecclesiastical problems (cf. 7:1). This letter was apparently carried to Paul by three members of the Corinthian community: Stephanas, Fortunatus, and Achaicus (16:17). It goes without saying that these couriers filled Paul's ears with news and gossip from the church back home. First Corinthians, therefore, was written to answer these particular problems.

It is assumed here that Paul is dealing with a variety of difficulties in this epistle. There has been a tendency among critics to homogenize the opponents of the apostle in Corinth and elsewhere. The older scholars, for instance, were inclined to identify Paul's foes universally as Judaizers, while in more recent times the New Testament has been subject to a "pan-gnostic" mode of interpretation whereby the opponents of apostolic Christianity are generally identified as loosely defined adherents of Hellenistic gnosticism.[36]

The complexities of this important debate are beyond the concern of our study, yet some things seem clear to the less studious reader of the Corinthian correspondence. For one, First Corinthians deals with a variety of subjects—factionalism in the church, sexual immorality among Christians, legal disputes between church members, marriage and divorce, food offered to idols, hair styles for worshipers, spiritual gifts, the Lord's Supper, death and resurrection. Just why these many problems must be blamed on one particular brand of opponent is somewhat baffling. Also, why, in a church composed of such a variety of people, Paul is supposed to have suffered most of his opposition from one quarter is similarly a mystery. Even in the more homogeneous middle-class churches of today, a minister is fortunate indeed if he has to deal with only one contentious group, or if his problems can all be reduced to one. In short,

[36] Cf. Walter Schmithals, *Die Gnosis in Korinth* (Göttingen: Vandenhoeck & Ruprecht, 1956), pp. 34 ff.

the content of First Corinthians and the situation of the Corinthian church argue for a variety of opposition and a variety of problems.

It is the purpose of this book, therefore, to investigate various problems of the Corinthian church with the hope that insight may be given into the understanding of the difficulties of the urban church of our own time. An underlying conviction will soon be apparent that Paul's answers as found in First Corinthians are still relevant. This epistle, which deals with such mundane matters as legal disputes and marriages, hair styles and matters of diet, is among the most practical books of the Bible. Its importance rests on the relevance of its application.

However, the intention here is not to offer the ancient and the modern material in a one to one ratio. It is obvious that in spite of some of the similarities of the two urban cultures, the difficulties of the Corinthian church are not identical with contemporary problems. For instance, few modern Christians are bothered with deciding whether or not to eat meat offered to idols, and feminine members of the congregation today seldom wear veils to church because of the angels (11:10). Underlying these external expressions are fundamental ethical issues—the problems of man in the world, the problems of man before God. The organization of our material, then, is not intended to modernize the Corinthian epistle in order to force it into contemporary molds, but is a serious attempt to order the material so that a penetrating analysis of the basic moral problems may be facilitated.

Of course, if Paul's solutions to these problems are no more than specific directions on antique issues, this whole study would be defeated at the outset. For instance, if the whole meaning of First Corinthians rests on the necessity of wearing veils to worship, or literal belief in the imminent end of the world, then the ethical instructions of Paul may well be relegated to the museum of antiquated morality. Fortunately, however, the ethic of Paul is a protest against that very kind of literalistic and legalistic teaching. His concern with the practical should not be construed as a banal particularism. Rather, the concern with particulars rests on the conviction that basic ethical concerns are relevant to every aspect of human conduct.

It is apparent, therefore, that practicality must not be equated with

27

simplicity. Although the apostle deals with mundane matters, his analysis and his answers rise to theological heights. Again and again throughout First Corinthians Paul begins with an everyday concern, probes it to the depth of theological understanding, and then applies his theological principles to the practical experience of the Christian. The epistle which deals with pagan revelling also describes the table of the Lord; the epistle which discusses emotional babbling also announces the word of the Cross; the epistle which decries intellectual cynicism also proclaims the hope of resurrection.

The attempt here, then, is to offer an essay in biblical ethics. The treatment of contemporary social and cultural issues will be at best amateurish. It is hoped, on the other hand, that the exposition of New Testament material will be more adequate. The experts, if they should happen to read this book, may decide that concern for relevance has led to popularization, although the notes are intended to indicate that conclusions have not been reached apart from exegetical endeavor. It is firmly believed that only in the investigation of the details of application and their relevance can the profoundly theological ethic of Paul be adequately understood. First Corinthians is consequently the elemental source for this investigation. Here, as in no other place, is the tension between the practical and theological so consistently maintained. Here is the clearest and most concrete expression of the thoroughly Christocentric character of Paul's thought. Indeed, for all the variety of problems yesterday and today, Paul's various answers rest on the same rock; and the rock is Christ, in whom all the questions of man hear the "yes" of God.

II
THE PROBLEM OF DIVISION

In discussing the difficulties of the Corinthian church Paul begins with the problem of division. The fact that he puts this problem first and continues its discussion for four chapters indicates the significance of the issues. The serious situation at Corinth is described in vss. 11 and 12 of Paul's first chapter. "For it has been reported to me by Chloe's people that there is quarreling among you, my brethren. What I mean is that each one of you says, 'I belong to Paul,' or 'I belong to Apollos,' or 'I belong to Cephas,' or 'I belong to Christ.' "

I

Considerable debate has revolved around the interpretation of this passage. The older view is that real factions existed within the

29

Corinthian church—factions which could be classified as three or four ecclesiastical parties, each with a definite set of beliefs and practices. Recently, however, Johannes Munck has described Corinth as the "church without factions";[1] he views the attempt to identify the parties or any one of them as Judaizers to be part of the mistaken effort of the Tübingen school to find a Jewish-Hellenistic antithesis throughout the early church. It is certainly true that nothing like modern denominationalism existed in Corinth, for as Kümmel observes, Paul was able to address one letter to the whole church, and the various factions were presumably able to listen.[2]

Nevertheless, there were actual divisions *within* the Corinthian church. This is seen in Paul's terminology throughout the passage. The word he uses for "quarreling" is *eris*—a term employed by Homer to mean "battle-strife" in the *Iliad,* and "contention" or "rivalry" in the *Odyssey*. The Greeks personified the concept in Eris, the goddess of war, while later writers like Herodotus used the term to describe political and domestic strife. The fact that Paul lists *eris* as one of the works of the flesh (Gal. 5:20), and that those who do such things are said not to inherit the kingdom, gives evidence that the apostle is speaking of a serious matter which has disrupted the essential character of the Christian community.

In vs. 10 Paul insists that there be no *schismata* among the members of the church. Since he uses the verb *eimi* ("to be") and not *ginomai* ("to become") it is apparent that the *schismata* are actually present. The word *schisma* itself means "cleft" or "division." It is the term which Mark 2:21 and Matt. 9:16 use to depict a tear in an old garment; it is the word used in John 7:43 to describe the division which occurred among the masses in regard to Jesus. Paul employs the word elsewhere for divisions at the Lord's table (I Cor. 11:18), and for discord which cannot exist within the physical body (I Cor. 12:25). Therefore, it no doubt refers here to actual divisions within the body of Christ.

The presence of divisive cliques within the Corinthian church is also attested by Paul's question, "Is Christ divided?" As a matter of fact, this

[1] *Paul and the Salvation of Mankind,* tr. Frank Clarke (Richmond: John Knox Press, 1959), pp. 135 ff.
[2] Werner Georg Kümmel, in Hans Lietzmann, *An die Korinther I-II,* "Handbuch zum Neuen Testament" (Tübingen: J.C.B. Mohr, 1949), p. 167.

sentence is open to a variety of interpretations. It may not be a question at all, but a simple declarative sentence: "Christ is divided; your party strife actually divides what by essence cannot be divided." Yet if the sentence is a question, as it may very well be even though our earliest Greek manuscripts are without marks of punctuation, it could expect either a negative or an affirmative answer. "Is Christ divided? No, he is not, and your efforts to divide the church are in danger of destroying the body of Christ!" "Is Christ divided? Yes, he is divided by your party strife—a sinful effort which threatens the essential life of the church."

The problem of interpretation is also complicated by Paul's use of *merizo*—the verb which we have been translating "to divide." It can, however, carry the idea "to distribute" or "to assign," so that the resulting question could read, "Has Christ been apportioned out to some and not to others?" But regardless of the variety of interpretations, one thing seems certain. There were warring factions within the church at Corinth. In a sense divisions already existed among the members. These cliques had not yet established separate schismatic groups, but such an eventuality was a present threat.

The attempt to identify the Corinthian factions has generated considerable scholarly disagreement. The traditional identification, which seems obvious to many, has had a persistent influence on popular commentators. The party of Paul consists of the church's "charter members." These were proud of their priority in the community and their conversion at the hands of the great apostle to the Gentiles. In point of view they maintained loyalty to the liberal, antilegalistic faith of their leader.

The party of Apollos was composed of personal devotees of the powerful Alexandrian preacher. According to the account in Acts 18 Apollos was "an eloquent man, well versed in the scriptures" (vs. 24). His rhetorical flare may have entranced some of the Corinthians who remained unimpressed by the homiletical ineptitude of Paul (cf. II Cor. 10:10). Perhaps they said, "Never have we heard a 'pulpit-man' like Apollos!"

"Cephas" is the Aramaic word for Peter. Some have supposed that the faction flying his banner resulted from an actual missionary effort in the city of Corinth by this member of the original twelve. Apart from our text, however, such a visit is without historical support. It is more likely that the Cephas party was composed of Christian converts who had moved to Achaia from Palestine. These are supposed to have advocated the superiority of the Jerusalem leadership, and to have supported a faith more sympathetic to the Jewish heritage than that of either Paul or Apollos.

Those who shouted, "I belong to Christ," however, have created the greatest problem of identification.[3] Some have suggested that the whole sentence is a gloss, perhaps inserted into the text by a copyist who wanted to oppose all factionalism in the name of Christ. Others believe "I belong to Christ" was the cry of all the parties; each was claiming that his party—the faction of Paul or of Cephas—was *the* Christian party. Some commentators, on the other hand, suggest that the phrase was original with Paul and was germane to his argument against factionalism. "You may belong to Paul, Apollos, or Cephas; but as for me, I belong to Christ. That confession you all should make, for when you do you will recognize that inordinate loyalty to any leader is contrary to your basic commitment to Jesus Christ."

In the main, however, scholars have identified the Christ party as a fourth faction within the Corinthian church. Indeed, the members of this party have usually been viewed as the apostle's most ardent foes in Corinth. Precise identification has followed three main lines: (1) The Christ party was a Judaizing faction. Its adherents may have been converts of James, the brother of the Lord, and thereby could have laid special claim to the name of Christ. In faith they were extreme legalists, bitterly opposed to Paul's devotion to liberty.

(2) The Christ party was a libertine faction. Its members were advocates of complete religious and ethical freedom. They opposed apostolic authority in any form. They claimed to have received, on their own, special revelation from the Spirit. While the former view had the support of Baur and the Tübingen school, and has had a persistent influence on Corinthian studies, this idea of Lütgert that the Christ faction was composed of "spirituals" has not commanded great academic enthusiasm.

In recent times, however, the followers of Rudolf Bultmann have

---

[3] Cf. Mary E. Andrews, "The Party of Christ in Corinth," *Anglican Theological Review*, XIX (1937), 17 ff.; Frank Hamilton Marshall, *The Judaizing Faction at Corinth* (Leipzig: W. Druglin, 1927).

vigorously supported a similar identification: (3) The Christ party was a faction of Gnostics. This is revealed in their love of knowledge, their demand for liberty, their concern with the spirit to the neglect of the body.

What are we to say about the identification of the Corinthian factions? How are we to explain this variety of different and even conflicting conclusions? For one thing it is assumed by some interpreters that problems encountered throughout the Corinthian correspondence are somehow related to the church's factions. Thus when they read, "Let each man take care how he builds upon" the foundation which has been laid (I Cor. 3:10), certain scholars suppose that Paul had Apollos in mind. That same opponent is thought to be the foil of Paul's thrusts against rhetorical and Hellenistic wisdom in I Cor. 1 and 2. Similarly, reference to the Christ party is often presumed in II Cor. 10:7: "If any one is confident that he is Christ's [Christou], let him remind himself that as he is Christ's [Christou], so are we." On the basis of this interpretation, it is easy to conclude that all of chapters 10 to 13 of Second Corinthians is a refutation of those who cry, "I belong to Christ" (egō de Christou).

It is also apparent that certain efforts to identify the Corinthian parties result from prior conclusions about the nature of Paul's opponents in Corinth and elsewhere. The Tübingen school, for instance, was intent on reconstructing early Christian history after the Hegelian triad. It was necessary, then, to see Hellenistic Christianity as the antithesis to a Judaistic thesis, to understand all of Paul's struggles as conflict with Judaizers. This theory is openly exposed by Baur's notion that there were not four but only two parties at Corinth—the Gentile faction, made up of the followers of Paul and Apollos, and a Jewish faction, composed of the parties of Cephas and Christ.

It is difficult to avoid the conclusion that the recent attempt to identify the Christ party as a Gnostic group rests on similar presuppositions. Quite apart from the fact that the existence of a "pre-Christian gnosticism" is a hotly debated issue it is evident that the universal identification of Paul's opponents as Gnostics rests in part on a certain theology of history. This view of history, not unlike Hegel's, is dialectical; it sees Christianity as standing in sharp focus against the dark backdrop of the Hellenistic age. Although Christianity employs some of the terms

33

of this mythological environment, it is in no way to be equated with the symbols or cosmology of first-century man. Gnosticism with its rejection of history and its cosmological concern, therefore, affords the sharpest contrast to the existential faith of the early church—a faith which stands on no mythological or cosmological ground. When Schmithals suggests that there are really only two factions in Corinth—the apostolic party (those who claim to belong to Paul, Apollos, and Cephas) and the Gnostics (those who claim to belong to Christ) [4]—the effect of such presuppositions is in evidence.

Since the identification of the Corinthian parties seems to rest on such varying exegetical and theological presuppositions, is there any possibility of solving the problem? At the outset let us acknowledge that the exact identity of these factions will continue to elude us. The paucity of information, together with the profusion of theories based upon it, indicates that certainty is an impossibility. Kümmel has said, "Concerning the viewpoint of the Christ party, we know nothing at all," [5] and this might be said of the other factions as well. Nevertheless, some conclusions can be drawn which will be useful to our purposes.

First, the argument of I Cor. 1:12 ff. is not primarily directed against any *one* of the factions of the Corinthian church; it is directed against *all* the parties. Just as it can be demonstrated that the one epistle is heard by all and that there are therefore no separate schisms in Corinth, so it can be argued that the entire exhortation of chapters 1-4 is addressed to the whole church. Thus when Paul says, "I appeal to you, brethren . . . that all of you agree" (1:10), he no doubt has in mind all the factions. Moreover, if Paul had wanted to refute the theological position or practice of any one of the parties, he would probably have supported the position of the Paul party, which presumably shared his doctrinal perspective. Instead, his questions, "Was Paul crucified for you? Or were you baptized in the name of Paul?" are aimed against the very party which is supposed to have been loyal to his gospel. The fact that Apollos is used to support Paul's argument (3:6), rather than as a representative of an opposing view, also serves to show that no one party is being

[4] Schmithals, *Die Gnosis in Korinth*, pp. 164 ff.
[5] "Handbuch zum Neuen Testament," p. 167.

selected for censure, but that all the factions have fallen under the wrath of the apostle.

Second, the argument of I Cor. 1:12 ff. is not primarily directed against Paul's major foes at Corinth. Bitter opposition to the apostle has not yet crystallized, and although that will happen before the writing of II Cor. 10-13 the relationship of the opponents faced there to the factions of I Cor. 1 cannot be ascertained. It is apparent, however, that those opponents observed certain beliefs and practices which the apostle attacks in that section of the "second" epistle; the probability that the precise theological and ecclesiastical character of the parties of First Corinthians is not yet clear to Paul himself is indicated by his remark about factionalism at the Lord's Supper: "I hear that there are divisions among you; and I partly believe it" (I Cor. 11:18).

Finally, if it is true that the argument is not directed against any *one* of the factions, but against *all* of them, and if it is agreed that the exhortation is not aimed directly at the ominous foes faced in Second Corinthians, then it is obvious that I Cor. 1:12 ff. is concerned with one major problem—the problem of factionalism.[6] Paul is not primarily occupied here with the beliefs and practices of any or all of the various factions; he is concerned with a schismatic spirit pervading the church and threatening the unity of the body of Christ. As Moffatt says, "Paul does not analyze the opinions of the various parties. He was concerned not so much with them in whole or in part as with the quarrelsome spirit which they bred."[7] The first and fundamental question of the whole passage is found in vs. 13: "Is Christ divided?"

II

What is Paul's reaction to the threat of division within the Corinthian church? For one thing he obviously considers the situation to be serious. We have already noticed that the apostle takes up this

[6] Cf. Ulrich Wilckens, *Weisheit und Torheit—Eine exegetisch-religionsgeschichtliche Untersuchung zu 1. Kor. 1 und 2* (Tübingen: J.C.B. Mohr, 1959), p. 5.

[7] *Moffatt New Testament Commentary* (New York: Harper & Bros., 1935), p. 9.

problem first and spends four chapters on it. We have also seen that he begins his refutation of factionalism immediately with the ambiguous sentence: "Is Christ divided?" (vs. 13.) Even though the exact meaning of this question or statement cannot be determined, it is clear that the possibility of schism is a live option which Paul wants to reject at once. The tone of his whole appeal reveals a mood of anxious concern.

The seriousness of his judgment on factionalism is also reflected in Paul's characterization of the Corinthians as "fleshly" (3:1-3). In vs. 1 he states that he could not address them as "spiritual men, but as men of the flesh," while in vs. 3 he insists that as long as there is jealousy and strife among them they are "fleshly," acting like ordinary men. Actually, the apostle uses two words in the passage to describe this fleshly character of the Corinthians: *sarkinos* and *sarkikos;* but recent scholarship agrees that the two are synonymous in the Hellenistic period. Although these terms can be used in either a material or a metaphorical sense, it is clear that Paul takes up the latter. Fleshly men are those who live *kata sarka*—those who live under the power of sin (cf. Rom. 8:12; II Cor. 10:2).

Thus those who have created factionalism in the church are guilty of sinning. Although they should have received the Spirit of God, they act as though they have accepted only the spirit of the world (2:12). Although they should have produced the fruit of the spirit, they display instead the works of the flesh (Gal. 5:19 ff.). Although they should be new creatures in Christ (II Cor. 5:17), they are behaving like ordinary descendants of Adam. As the New English Bible puts it, "You are living on the purely human level of your lower nature," so that Paul can go on to ask, "Are you not all too human?"

The apostle analyzes three major causes of factionalism within the Corinthian church. The first of these is *false wisdom.* This sort of wisdom is decried in I Cor. 1:17 ff., where Paul insists that the gospel he preaches could in no way contribute to the disunity of the church; rather, it prohibits that eventuality. It must, then, be the false wisdom of the world—the wisdom which cannot accept the proclamation of the Cross —which is causing dissension among the Christians.

Paul finds reference to the futility of this wisdom in the Old Testament where God says:

> I will destroy the wisdom of the wise,
> and the cleverness of the clever I will set aside. (WB)*

In quoting this passage (Isa. 29:14) Paul follows as usual the Septuagint (LXX) version. The LXX is salutary to his purpose here since the Hebrew of the first phrase reads, "The wisdom of their wise shall perish"; the Greek translation, on the other hand, presents God as more active: "I will destroy the wisdom of the wise." In the second phrase Paul even strengthens the LXX. There God is said simply *to conceal* (*kruptō*) the cleverness of the clever, while Paul makes the divine act more decisive: "The cleverness of the clever I will *set aside*" (*atheteō*).

Although Isaiah predicted this divine activity long ago, Paul believes that the prophecy has now been fulfilled. God has so acted that the wisdom of the world is brought to naught. This can be supported by empirical evidence, or lack of it. Let the world produce some wisdom if it has any!

> Where is the wise man?
> Where is the scribe?
> Where is the debater of this age?

These sarcastic questions show that the world's wise men have wandered in ways which do not lead to truth. "Claiming to be wise, they became fools." (Rom. 1:22.) Thus when Paul raises the important questions, no Hellenistic intellectual raises his hand.

These rhetorical questions also give us some insight into Paul's understanding of the character of the false, worldly wisdom. It is sometimes supposed that when the apostle says, "In the wisdom of God, the world did not know God through wisdom" (I Cor. 1:21), he has in mind some sort of cosmological or natural revelation, as perhaps in Rom. 1:18 ff. Others imagine that Paul's assault on worldly wisdom is directed against his main foes at Corinth—that his attack displays disapproval of the Christology of his opponents since his own wisdom is grounded in an idea of Christ (1:23 ff.).

The appellation of men addressed in the questions—the wise man, the scribe, and the debater of this age—indicates that a precise definition

---

* Passages marked WB indicate translations by the author.

of the wisdom of the world is not Paul's main concern here. The *sophos*, or wise man, is the Greek sophist who was searching for truth by philosophical means. Paul is not his only critic in the Hellenistic age, as the epitaph of Trimalchio shows:

> Let it be said to his eternal credit
> That he never listened to philosophers.[8]

The *grammateus,* or scribe, on the other hand, is the professional Jewish rabbi, whose straining out the Scriptures to find one gnat of truth was well known to Paul. The word *suzētēs ("debater")* can be translated "searcher," or even "researcher," so that we are reminded of the men of Athens who "spent their time in nothing except telling or hearing something new" (Acts 17:21). But, in any case, the fact that both Jewish and Greek intellectuals are listed indicates that Paul has no specific set of beliefs in mind. The wisdom of the world is human wisdom *per se,* be it philosophical or biblical; it is false wisdom which does not know God; it is folly before God (I Cor. 3:19).

Moreover, the difficulty of this pseudowisdom is not so much its content as its effect—an effect manifest in Corinthian factionalism. Although the Christians there were not really wise, they thought they were. This gave rise to the second and more serious cause of division within the church—*pride*. The pride of the Corinthians is revealed immediately in their party slogans. In the cry, "I belong to Paul," or "I belong to Apollos," the first person pronoun (*egō*) is emphatic. The implication of the Greek construction here is: "*I* belong to Paul and you don't! *I* belong to Paul, and I'm proud of it!"

The pride of the Corinthians is manifest throughout these four chapters of the first epistle. For instance when Paul declares in 1:29 that "no human being might boast in the presence of God," it is apparent that the Corinthians have been attempting just that. When he goes on to quote scripture, "Let him who boasts, boast of the Lord," it is clear that they have been boasting of themselves. Similarly, his word in 3:18 indicates that the Corinthians have entertained a false estimate of their

---

[8] Petronius, *The Satyricon,* p. 72.

wisdom. "If any one among you thinks that he is wise in this age, let him become a fool that he may become wise."

A still more scathing denunciation of Corinthian pride is found in 4:6 ff. There the apostle describes the Christians as "puffed up in favor of one against another" (vs. 6). As members of particular factions they are proud of the religious benefits which have accrued to them. They even suppose that all the promised blessings of the eschaton are theirs now.

> Already you are filled!
> Already you have become rich!
> Without us you have become kings!

Paul, of course, insists that the glories of the end time are yet to be consummated, and even those benefits which the Christians now possess have been granted by the grace of God. "What have you that you did not receive? If then you received it, why do you boast as if it were not a gift?" (vs. 7.) Paul's summary statement is well interpreted by Moffatt: "Who in the wide world sees anything special in you?"

It may be argued, of course, that Paul's concern here is theological or even christological. The fact that the Corinthians hold an erroneous eschatology is apparent. It is also obvious that Paul's answer includes a denial of their notion of the end. However, the argument indicates that the theological question is secondary; the problem is not so much the error of Corinthian eschatology as it is the failure of Corinthian ethics. They have used an incorrect view of the end to foster a false idea of themselves—an idea which has engendered sinful pride. That pride manifests itself in party strife, as the context of the passage shows: "I have applied all this to myself and Apollos for your benefit, brethren, that you may learn by us to live according to scripture, that none of you may be puffed up in favor of one against another" (vs. 6).

A third cause of factionalism in the church is *false loyalty to religious leaders*. Such loyalty should not be surprising when it appears among recent converts from certain of the Hellenistic cults. In the mystery religions, for example, the neophyte often felt a particular devotion to the

39

officiant who administered to him the rites of initiation.[9] Thus Apuleius' hero Lucius maintained a special loyalty to the priest who had initiated him into the cult of Isis at this very city of Corinth.[10] Apparently a similar loyalty was felt in the church by those who declared, "I belong to Paul; I belong to Apollos." Evidence of this loyalty is ascertained in the apostle's question, "Were you baptized in the name of Paul?" (1:13.)

This question indicates that Paul would allow no such loyalty to himself. The significance of baptism is not that it brings the convert into a special relationship with the baptizer, but that it brings him into a unique relationship with Christ. Not Paul, but Christ, had been crucified for the Corinthians, so that baptism in his name meant union with his death (Rom. 6:3)—a death which challenged any proud loyalty to those who baptized in his name.

Few members of the Corinthian church could validly boast such loyalty to Paul. "I baptized none of you except Crispus and Gaius; lest any one should say that you were baptized in my name," he says (1:15). But then the apostle, whose records were apparently not as accurate as the modern evangelist's, remembers a few others: "I did baptize also the household of Stephanas. Beyond that I do not know whether I baptized any one else" (1:16). It is fallacious to suppose that Paul is here opposing baptism *per se,* since in 1:13 it is used as an argument for the church's unity. The problem is not baptism; the problem is false fidelity to baptizers.

This inordinate loyalty to leaders involved more than the baptismal relationship.[11] Although the argument seems to suggest that only those baptized by Paul could claim special loyalty to him, it is obvious that others boasted membership in the Pauline party. Crispus, Gaius, and Stephanas might constitute a committee, but hardly a faction! What Paul appears to be arguing is that even those who might seem to have some claim to special loyalty because of their baptism at his hands have

[9] Cf. Richard Reitzenstein, *Die Hellenistischen Mysterienreligionen* (3rd ed. Stuttgart: B. G. Teubner, 1956), pp. 40 ff.

[10] *The Golden Ass,* p. 255.

[11] Oscar Cullmann, "The Early Church and the Ecumenical Problem," *Anglican Theological Review,* XL (1958), p. 187, suggests that a "cult of personality" had developed in Corinth.

no claim at all. Christ did not send him to baptize (1:17). But if these have no grounds for personal loyalty to the apostle, how much less the other members of the party of Paul. Moreover, since neither Cephas nor Christ had ever baptized converts in Corinth, it is obvious that baptism is not the main issue under discussion. I Cor. 1 is not primarily concerned with baptism; it is concerned with a serious mislocation of loyalty.

It is also evident that major responsibility for this inordinate loyalty must rest with the people and not with the leaders themselves. Although Paul does warn that ministers must be careful how they build on his foundation, and that their work will undergo a testing (3:10 ff), he enlists the support of Apollos in the building of his own argument. This indicates that just as Paul himself is in no way responsible for factionalism, neither is his colleague Apollos. The use of the latter in the argument presupposes that he would be in agreement with Paul—that he also would oppose immoderate loyalty to himself. The main problem is with the party members. Thus Paul says, "I have applied all this to myself and Apollos *for your benefit*, brethren" (4:6).

The causes of factionalism in Corinth, therefore, are false wisdom, pride, and loyalty to leaders. These factors have led to a situation which seriously disturbs the apostle. Although he is probably distressed by the Christology or eschatology of the members of the various factions, Paul's central concern is with the nascent division within the church. He views the party strife in Corinth as sin, and admonishes its perpetrators "not to go beyond what is written" (4:6, Moffatt).

This latter statement has engendered considerable exegetical debate. Some suppose that Paul is referring to what he himself has just written in this epistle, but normally "what is written" is a technical Pauline term for the Scriptures of the Old Testament. Just what text the apostle may have in mind here is not clear, although it is often assumed that he means the particular references which he has just cited to support his argument. It is also supposed that he is positing the nonscriptural character of the Corinthian theology or their antinomian ethic. However, it is better to conclude that Paul is using "scripture" in a general sense, and that his argument, as the context shows, is aimed at factionalism. What he intends to say is that division in the church is against Scripture; it is against the will of God; it threatens the body of Christ.

III

In attempting to solve the problem of division Paul deals with the causes of Corinthian factionalism. He advocates instead of the wisdom of the world, the *wisdom of God*. Indeed, that latter wisdom is revealed through the gospel which he proclaims. His act of proclamation stems from a divine commission and gives no ground for petty quarreling. It may be that baptism can be distorted into some basis for misplaced loyalty, but not the message of the apostle. "For Christ did not send me to baptize but to preach the gospel" (1:17)—a gospel which stands in judgment on all the strife of men.

Care must be employed in the method of preaching this gospel, since its proclaimer actually has to do with the powerful action of God. Paul, therefore, insists that he does not proclaim the message "with eloquent wisdom" (1:17). The Greek here is literally "in the wisdom of speech or rhetoric," and the New English Bible says that he preaches the gospel "without relying on the language of worldly wisdom." This caution is necessary since the proclamation, or as he calls it here the "word of the cross," may "be emptied of its power" by an artificial concern with homiletical style. Paul here sounds much like the satirists who complained of the "claptrap," the "sham heroics," and the "petty drivel" of the rhetoricians who poured out on their listeners "great sticky honey-balls of phrases." [12]

The apostle's concern, however, is much more serious. Quite apart from the fact that the word of the Cross is incongruous with fancy rhetorical flourishes, Paul insists that preaching in the ways of worldly wisdom actually nullifies the significance of the crucifixion. If proclaiming the word of the Cross by improper method can empty the message of its essential power, it is clear that the way by which the event of the Cross becomes a powerful event for man removed from the historical happening is by proper proclamation of the gospel. The preaching of the Word of God, then, is itself a dynamic event. The wisdom of God

[12] Petronius, *Satyricon*, p. 3.

42

which redeems the divisive wisdom of men does not result from human intellectual endeavor; it is revealed by an act of God in the cross of Christ—an act which is powerfully reenacted in the *kerygma* of Paul.

This divine power is not perceived by all auditors of the apostolic preaching. To some the message is the power of God; to others, presumably sitting in the same audience, it is pure folly. What makes the difference? Paul tells us that those who receive the gospel as power of God are men who are being saved; that is, they are those who respond to the proclamation with faith (1:21). On the other hand, those who consider the word of the Cross to be sheer foolishness are people who are perishing. The latter do not have faith, for they seek some showy wisdom of the world—some wisdom which can be demonstrated by empirical evidence or defended by philosophical reasoning. To these the gospel of a crucified Christ is a stumbling block and foolishness (1:23).

What Paul seems to be saying in the context of his discussion of the problem of division is that participation in party strife at Corinth gives evidence that the Corinthian Christians have returned to the worldly quest for wisdom. Although they had responded to the testimony to Christ so as to be enriched with every spiritual gift (1:5 ff.), the Corinthians are now acting like the sophists, the scribes, and debaters of this age. Evidence of this is seen in the egocentric cries of their factions, "I belong to Paul"; "I belong to Apollos." Such trust in their own ability to find truth and to hoard it in their own cliques displays signs of abandonment of faith in God. Their party strife, like the concern for rhetorical display, reveals a preoccupation with the self-deceptive wisdom of the world. This wisdom denies the saving power of the Cross.

Yet the proclamation stands in judgment on this wisdom which knows not faith. "We preach Christ crucified," says Paul, "a stumbling-block to Jews and folly to Gentiles, but to those who are called, both Jews and Greeks, Christ the power of God and the wisdom of God" (1:23-24). This is the wisdom which denies Corinthian factionalism. This is the wisdom which judges the false wisdom of the world. This is a wisdom which can be reduced to no set of intellectual propositions; it is a wisdom which is personally revealed in a divine act in the midst of history. This is not a wisdom which can be captured by intellectual striving; it is a

43

wisdom which can only be received by the self-resigning act of faith. This wisdom does not primarily give new ideas; it gives new life. But the fact that the Corinthians can be addressed as "men of the flesh" is evidence that they do not bear fruits of life in the spirit. Rather, their roots are still implanted in the noxious soil of this age.

Paul concludes this section of his epistle with a striking statement in parallelism:

> For the foolishness of God is wiser than men,
> and the weakness of God is stronger than men.

It is often supposed that these phrases should be given a comparative interpretation: God's wisdom even at its most foolish is still wiser than the greatest wisdom of men; God's power even at its weakest is still stronger than the power of man at its highest. Others have interpreted the verse as an expression of the reversal of values in the eschaton: Now God seems foolish, then he will be acknowledged as wise; now God appears weak, then his power will be confessed as almighty.

Both of these interpretations miss the mark. Can we conclude that God's revelation in the Cross is to be understood in any sense as God at his worst? Can we suppose that the act of God in crucifixion of Christ has its value only in this age and is to be transcended by some greater wisdom and power in the eschaton? No! The action of God in the cross of Christ is a revelation of how God always acts—at the beginning, in the midst, and at the end of history. The crucifixion is not God at his weakest, but God at his best. The power of God—so scandalous to human wisdom—achieves its purposes in weakness. The Cross is the symbol of how God works. As Wendland says, "The foolishness of God is indeed the true wisdom. . . ; the weakness of God is indeed the true power of God." [13]

This is why factionalism in Corinth is so dangerous. In magnifying the divisive works of men it denies the work of God. It threatens the very life of the church, the temple of God, for that structure is built on the one foundation which is Jesus Christ. The remedy for factionalism is for

[13] Heinz-Dietrich Wendland, *Die Briefe an die Korinther*, "Neue Testament Deutsch" (Göttingen: Vandenhoeck and Ruprecht, 1954), p. 19.

the Corinthians to receive the gospel anew as the Thessalonians had done at first, for they "accepted it not as the word of men but as what it really is, the word of God, which is at work in you believers" (I Thess. 2:13).

Now it is sometimes supposed that I Cor. 1:17 ff. advocates a certain anti-intellectualism. If Paul denies the validity of human wisdom and offers instead religious knowledge based purely on faith, he seems only a short step from Tertullian's dictum: "It is by all means to be believed, because it is absurd." [14] Paul's decision "to know nothing . . . except Jesus Christ and him crucified" is not intended to ground religious knowledge in absurdity nor to reduce theological learning to a bare minimum. Rather, it intends to present the basis for the comprehension of true knowledge—the wisdom of God whose judgments are unsearchable and whose ways are inscrutable (Rom. 11:33). To know nothing but Christ and him crucified is to know everything significant.

Paul discusses these fuller implications of the divine wisdom in I Cor. 2:6 ff., where he says, "Yet among the mature we do impart wisdom." This passage has created considerable debate.[15] Some believe that the apostle is describing here a special, esoteric knowledge which he conveys to a spiritual elite. It is true that in this passage Paul employs terms and concepts not unlike those popular in the mystery cults. For instance, the word *teleios* (mature), which Paul uses for those who can perceive this "special" wisdom, is a technical term in the Oriental societies for the full initiate within the cult. Also, the apostle does sound as if he is depicting secret doctrine when he suggests that the wisdom of God is a mysterious and hidden wisdom (2:7).

Nevertheless, thorough study of the passage indicates that Paul is not discussing some superior knowledge reserved for a spiritual inner circle within the church, but is simply describing the fuller implications of the one wisdom which he knows and proclaims—Jesus Christ and him crucified. This conclusion is supported by the apostle's declaration that if the rulers of this age had understood the wisdom of God, they would not have crucified the Lord of glory (2:8). That is, Christ, the Lord

[14] *De Carne Christi*, v.
[15] Cf. William Baird, "Among the Mature—The Idea of Wisdom in I Corinthians 2:6," *Interpretation*, XIII (1959), 425 ff.

of glory, is the one through whom the wisdom of God is revealed. That wisdom involves the understanding of the whole divine drama of redemption, for it was "decreed before the ages for our glorification" (2:7). Thus the wisdom described in I Cor. 2:6 ff. is nothing else but the wider implications of that wisdom discussed in I Cor. 1:17 ff.—Jesus Christ, the crucified one, through whom God has revealed his creative and redemptive purposes for mankind.

This interpretation is also supported by the context of Paul's discussion of the problem of division. If he had suggested in I Cor. 2 that he actually parceled out esoteric doctrine for a special elite within the Christian community, then his whole argument against factionalism would have been defeated. What could have added more fuel to the glowing pride of the Corinthian parties than the apostle's admission that there actually was a superior group of spirituals within the church. Indeed, that is apparently what some of them were claiming and what Paul is ardently denying. His point is rather than factionalism has no basis at all. Truly mature Christians would know that Christ is the key to understanding all divine wisdom, but the infantile Corinthians in their attempt to go beyond Christ in a passion for the egocentric wisdom of the world have forfeited the basic elements of the faith. The truly spiritual man can understand the Cross as revelation of the divine history of redemption, but the Corinthians are not spiritual but fleshly, not mature but babes. Nowhere is their spiritual immaturity so apparent as in their cries, "I belong to Paul; I belong to Apollos."

As a second solution to the problem of division Paul offers, instead of pride, *humility*. In I Cor. 1:17 ff. he has been arguing that his gospel gives no ground for factionalism; in I Cor. 1:26 ff. he goes on to insist that the Corinthians' condition at the time of response to that gospel gives no such ground either. Paul begins this section of the epistle with a description of the Corinthians as they were on their own:

> Not many of you were wise . . .
> not many were powerful,
> not many were of noble birth.

The word for "wise" is *sophos*, which he used in vs. 20 to describe the Hellenistic sophist. The word rendered "powerful" (*dunatos*) is often employed by Greek authors in speaking of prominent people. The phrase "noble birth" represents the term *eugenēs,* and is used in Luke 19:12 for the "nobleman" of Jesus' parable of the pounds. All three of these terms are modified by the phrase *kata sarka* ("according to the flesh"), which suggests that "according to worldly standards" not many of the Corinthians were wise, powerful, or noble. Yet just these standards of the world are assumed in their party pride. But if by those same standards they are nobodies (vs. 28), what ground have they for proud boasting?

Against the background of this situation of the Corinthians Paul portrays the redemptive activity of God.

> God chose what is foolish in the world
> to shame the wise,
> God chose what is weak in the world
> to shame the strong,
> God chose what is low and despised in the world,
> even the things that are not,
> to bring to nothing things that are. (1:27-29.)

This portrayal of the divine action further clarifies the condition of the Christians at the time of God's act. They were foolish, weak, low, and despised—so insignificant that Paul describes them with neuter terms; they were "nothings." It is only by the act of God which ignores all human standards that they have become something.

However, the description of the divine activity in this passage may make a dissonant sound on modern ears. Although it may be admitted that God chooses what is not worthy of choice, it is difficult to agree that God actually chooses some men for the purpose of shaming others. Of course, it is grammatically possible to construe the clause as "consecutive" rather than "purpose," so that the passage might be translated: "God chose the foolish, with the inevitable result that he shamed the wise." Paul, on the other hand, would not be so squeamish about such terminology. The results of God's actions are always congruent with his purposes, and the judgment of God continually falls on men of pride. At any rate the meaning in the context is clear. Even if the Corinthians actually were wise, powerful, "somebodies" in the eyes of the world they would be "nobodies" in the presence of God. Indeed, only by renouncing these claims to worldly pride and prestige can men receive the redemptive deed of God. Lowliness is the way of God's work; his power is the weakness of the Cross.

This powerful action of God has resulted in a new situation for the Corinthian Christians. They have a new life in Christ. "If any one is in Christ, he is a new creation" (II Cor. 5:17), or as Paul puts it in vs. 30, "From him [God] you are in Christ," (WB) or as the Revised Standard Version translates it, "He is the source of your life in Christ Jesus." This new life in Christ is characterized as the true wisdom from God—"our righteousness and sanctification and redemption." It is again obvious that the wisdom which Christ imparts is not primarily new ideas but new life. Through Christ, God has declared unrighteous man to be righteous (Rom. 3:21 ff.), moved him to holiness (Rom. 6:19), and redeemed him to sonship (Gal. 4:4 ff.). The way to receive this wisdom is not in pride but in the humility of faith.

But once this saving wisdom of God has been received, a new situation results. The Corinthians who were foolish, weak, lowborn have become wise, powerful, newborn. In the eyes of the world they are still foolish, indeed, more foolish. Yet in the presence of God they are "heirs of God and fellow heirs with Christ" (Rom. 8:17). This new situation is the result of God's doing. As Paul says in II Cor. 5:18, "All this is from God." How then can the Corinthians boast? How can they revel in party pride? As the scripture says, "Let him who boasts, boast of the Lord" (I Cor. 1:30). The proper attitude before God is not pride but utter humility.

Genuine humility as a remedy for Corinthian pride is also advocated in I Cor. 4:8 ff. There Paul depicts the apostles' suffering as judgment upon the pretensions of the Christians. In answer to their deluded claim of experiencing already the eschatological benefits Paul sarcastically declares, "And would that you did reign, so that we might share the rule with you!" (vs. 8.) In other words, Paul wishes that the eschaton had actually come, since its blessings would certainly be shared by the apostles. But the fact that the end has not yet arrived is proved by the present situation of these heralds of God; they are "ill-clad and buffeted and homeless" (vs. 11), "reviled," "persecuted," "slandered" (vss. 12-13).

Paul's description of the apostolic situation here is particularly graphic. He says, "I think that God has exhibited us apostles as last of all, like men sentenced to death; because we have become a spectacle to the world, to angels and to men" (vs. 9). Some interpreters suggest that the phrase "last of all" implies that in contrast to the Corinthians, who suppose that they are first in everything, the apostles are always last. It is possible, too, that Paul has the Roman triumphal procession in mind, so that the apostles would be viewed as the last of the captives led in humiliating public display. But the context indicates that his figure of speech is taken from the arena. He says that the apostles are a "spectacle," using the word *theatron*—a term which could be employed for the events of the amphi-theater. When he says that they are "last of all," he implies that the apostles are the "last act of the show"—a place reserved for the lowliest criminals with no chance of escape.

This lowliness of the apostles is in sharp contrast to the Corinthian pretensions.

> We are fools for Christ's sake,
> but you are wise in Christ.
> We are weak,
> but you are strong.
> You are held in honor,
> but we in disrepute. (4:10.)

That is, those who most accurately represent the Christian faith—those in whom the proud loyalty of the Corinthians is placed—are totally without status according to the standards of the world. They willingly exemplify in themselves the evaluation which Paul has made against the reluctant Corinthians (1:27 ff.). The latter still suppose that they are wise, strong, honored, while the apostles readily admit that they are fools, weak, without repute. For them pride is no possibility.

Paul concludes this description of apostolic humility with a final statement of self-debasement: "We have become, and are now, as the refuse of the world, the offscouring of all things" (4:13). The words which are rendered "refuse" and "offscouring"—*perikatharma* and *peripsēma*—are open to a variety of interpretations. For instance, they can refer to debris which is scraped or swept away. They also can be used as terms of derogation to describe men of disrepute. However, they may refer to the scapegoats of certain Greek cities—criminals or deformed men who were executed or banished from the town to bear away the city's guilt.[16] The probability that Paul has referred to the arena earlier in the passage gives support to a similar figurative interpretation here, particularly in view of the fact that the means of execution was often public stoning or burning.

Regardless of the precise exegesis of this statement the essential meaning of the passage is clear. As judgment on Corinthian pride Paul depicts apostolic humility. This solution offers more than a mere raising of the ethical sights—a simple suggestion that it's nicer to be humble than proud. Paul believes that human pride is against the will of God. It is in human weakness, in radical humility, that God can work. Paul had learned this the hard way himself in the suffering service of his entire ministry and under the persistent pain of the thorn in the flesh. For although he earnestly prayed for deliverance from this satanic harassment, God continued to answer, "My grace is sufficient for you, for my power is made perfect in weakness" (II Cor. 12:7 ff.).

Finally, as solution to the problem of division, Paul urges instead of loyalty to leaders *loyalty to God*. Indeed, he insists that the apostles are not worthy of special loyalty. After arguing that neither his gospel nor the situation of the Corinthians gives ground for partisan pride, Paul goes on in I Cor. 2:1 ff. to maintain that his own activity at Corinth defies factional loyalty. His whole intent in the Achaian capital was to focus attention on his message of the crucified Christ. Consequently his proclamation was "without display of fine words of wisdom" (vs. 1, NEB). Rather than call attention to his own method he displayed instead weakness and "much fear and trembling" (vs. 3).

This idea of "fear and trembling" reflects Old Testament motifs and stresses the concept of man standing in awe in the presence of God.[17] Paul uses the same terminology to describe the "fear and trembling" of man responsive to the saving power of God at work in him (Phil. 2:12). Some suppose that Paul's external display of weakness was distinctively

---

[16] Cf. H. J. Rose, *Ancient Greek Religion* (London: Hutchinson's University Library, 1948), pp. 86 ff.; Erwin Rohde, *Psyche*, tr. W. B. Willis (London: Routledge & Kegan Paul, 1925), pp. 296, 321.

[17] Cf. Job 4:14; Ps. 2:11.

Corinthian; since powerful argument had failed in Athens (Acts 17:16 ff.), he tried another tack in Corinth. More likely weakness was typical of his ministerial method. He was a fragile earthen vessel in which the transcendent power of God was conveyed (II Cor. 4:7). His message was not in plausible words of human wisdom, but a demonstration of spirit and power. The reason for this personal weakness is clear: "That your faith might not rest in the wisdom of men but in the power of God" (I Cor. 2:5).

To further disarm inordinate loyalty to leaders Paul presents in chapter three his understanding of the apostolic office. He begins the discussion in vs. 5 by raising the pertinent questions: "What then is Apollos? What is Paul?" His answer is unequivocal: They are servants through whom you had faith, each performing a service which God has assigned to him. The word which Paul uses for "servant" here is *diakonos* —a term which basically means servant of some master and which could be used for such menial tasks as waiting tables.[18] The work of the apostles, then, is ultimately the work of God. As his lowly servants they deserve no singular loyalty.

Paul goes on to describe the apostolic function by two figures of speech. The first of these is agricultural. He says,

> I planted,
> Apollos watered,
> but God gave the growth (I Cor. 3:6).

The "planting," of course, refers to Paul's original mission in Corinth (Acts 18:1 ff.), just as "irrigation" symbolizes the later work of Apollos in that place (Acts 18:24 ff.). By saying that God gave the growth Paul is asserting that regardless of apostolic activity it is God who adds to the church (cf. Acts 2:47). This is borne out by the tenses of the verbs employed. The words for "planting" and "watering" are used in aorist tense, while the term *ēuxane* ("to give growth") is imperfect; aorist is used for single action completed in the past, while imperfect describes

---

[18] Cf. W. A. Beardslee, *Human Achievement and Divine Vocation in the Message of Paul*, "Studies in Biblical Theology, No. 31" (Naperville, Ill.: Alec. R. Allenson, 1961), p. 101.

continuous past action. Thus, at one time Paul labored in Corinth, and later Apollos ministered there; but God was working all along.

Paul proceeds to draw certain implications. For one thing he concludes that "neither he who plants nor he who waters is everything, but only God who gives the growth" (3:8). Actually the Greek construction is still more explicit. In the last clause the use of *alla* (the strong adversative conjunction) suggests the following translation:

> He who plants is nothing,
> he who waters is nothing,
> but [*alla*] God who gives the growth *is everything*.

As Hans Lietzmann says, "We are nothing, God accomplishes everything." [19] How then can one boast of belonging to Paul or to Apollos?

Another implication is stated in vs. 8: "He who plants and he who waters are one." This means that no one of the apostles is superior to the others. Thus partisan loyalty to any is senseless. As the Revised Standard Version translates it, "He who plants and he who waters are equal." They are equal, too, in that they are doing the same work—a work which is nothing unless it is ultimately the work of God. It is true that there are varying degrees of apostolic responsibility, and that "each shall receive his wages according to his labor" (vs. 8), but the height of achievement is to attain transparency to the work of God (cf. I Cor. 9:18). Such transparency demands selfless loyalty to the one divine mission. On the basis of this sort of loyalty the apostles may become worthy to be called "fellow workers in the service of God" (vs. 9, WB).[20]

The second figure which Paul employs to describe the nature of the apostolic ministry is architectural. The transition is clear in 3:9. "You are God's field, God's building." Paul goes on to say, "According to the commission of God given to me, like a skilled master builder I laid a foundation, and another man is building upon it." Again it is obvious that the laying of the foundation refers to Paul's original work in Corinth and that the building upon that foundation describes the mission of Apollos

---

[19] "Handbuch zum Neuen Testament," p. 15.

[20] Victor Paul Furnish, "Fellow Workers in God's Service," *Journal of Biblical Literature*, LXXX (1961), 364 ff., argues convincingly for this translation rather than "we are God's fellow workers."

and his successors. Paul insists that his own activity is responsive to the commission of God, who had set him apart for the gospel before he was born (Gal. 1:15).

All subsequent work must be solidly based on the foundation, "for no other foundation can anyone lay than that which is laid, which is Jesus Christ" (3:11). This means that Christ, the crucified one, is the touchstone by which all ministerial activity is to be tested. Since that activity demands the radical humility of the Cross, no apostolic function which arouses inordinate loyalty to human leaders is allowed.

It is possible, continues Paul, to utilize a variety of materials in constructing a building—"gold, silver, precious stones, wood, hay, stubble" —all probably symbolic of ministerial methods of varying value. This implies, as we have seen, that some of Corinth's leaders might have been partially responsible for the church's divisions. Such irresponsibility, if it does exist, will be condemned, although the erring minister will be finally saved, "but only as through fire" (vs. 15). Thus even divinely commissioned apostles are unworthy of men's allegiance if they should in any way modify the blueprint so as to weaken the structural unity of the temple of God.

A final discussion of the nature of ministerial function is found in I Cor. 4:1-5. There Paul says that "one should regard us, as servants of Christ and stewards of the mysteries of God." The terms used imply a paradoxical understanding. *Hupēretēs* (here translated "servant") can be used for the oarsmen in the lowest level of the trireme, so that a lowly, slavish service is suggested. *Oikonomos* ("overseer"), on the other hand, is employed elsewhere for a slave who supervises other slaves or even for the manager of an estate. The ministry has both aspects. As a mere man Paul has no claim to human loyalty; as a faithful servant of God he is respected as a leader who points men's loyalty to his master. As he is to write later to the Corinthians, "Not that we are sufficient of ourselves to claim anything as coming from us; our sufficiency is from God" (II Cor. 3:5).

The real responsibility of such stewards is "that they be found trustworthy" (I Cor. 4:2). Indeed, all apostles shall stand before the eschatological judgment of God. Paul himself believes that his own ministerial conduct is without malice, but he is "not thereby acquitted" (vs. 4). The

53

problem of the Corinthians is that they have pronounced eschatological judgment already; their partisan loyalty reveals condemnation of some and commendation of other servants of God. Instead of usurping the divine prerogative now they should wait until the Lord comes. "Then every man will receive his commendation from God" (vs. 5). As Paul has already shown, inordinate loyalty to particular leaders not only creates an idolatrous personality cult which denies allegiance to God, it also robs the church of the full benefit of his servants' ministries. "So let no one boast of men. For all things are yours, whether Paul or Apollos or Cephas or the world or life or death or the present or the future, all are yours; and you are Christ's; and Christ is God's." (3:21-23.)

IV

Paul's hope of solving the problem of division has never been realized. Indeed, the factionalism of the early church has been replaced by actual schism. The most recent issue of the *Yearbook of American Churches* lists 258 different denominations of which 228 are Protestant.[21] Most of these claim to be the true, or at least the truest, church, while many purport to have restored precisely the church of the New Testament. The New Testament church which American Protestantism seems to have best restored, however, is the church at Corinth, where Christians were shouting partisan loyalty to Paul, Apollos, and Cephas. Actually, the problem is more serious in the contemporary church than it was at Corinth. Whereas Paul could address one letter to the whole Christian community, now meaningful communication does not always occur between the separated segments of the body of Christ.

Nevertheless, one must be wary of magnifying our ecclesiastical disunity. Although over 250 denominations exist, some 50 of these claim the loyalty of over 90 per cent of American Protestants. Seventy-five per cent of our church members are affiliated with one of the five major de-

[21] Benson Y. Landis, ed., *Yearbook of American Churches* (New York: National Council of Churches, 1963), p. 248.

nominational families. Some thirty-four denominations, representing an aggregate membership of about forty million Christians, participate in the activities of the National Council of Churches. In the past fifty years no less than fifteen church mergers have been consummated, and some of these have united denominations of differing thought and polity. These signs of ecumenicity serve to show that a spirit of oneness is moving within the people of God.

What has been the role of urban culture in relation to this problem of the division and union of the church? The earlier view, classically expressed in H. Richard Niebuhr's *The Social Sources of Denominationalism,*[22] is that social and economic factors—factors of race, class, and national origin—have been decisive in the shaping of the divisions of American Protestantism. However, as we have observed, the recent period of urban growth has been a time of ecumenical achievement. Could it be that the triumph of urban culture has contributed to the unity of the church? Robert Lee would answer in the affirmative. "In short," he writes, "ecumenicity of the American scene is favored by the increased cultural unity of American society."[23]

The same socio-cultural factors which have succored the development of mass culture have contributed to the growth of a common faith. Social mobility, for instance, has dulled sectional interests; it has also blurred creedal distinctions.[24] Rootless people seeking a secure fellowship are more interested in the church as a social organization than in the people of God proclaiming the gospel of Christ. Thus it may be that the apparent success of the ecumenical movement lies at a superficial level. It may be that the movement for the unity of the church, though itself theologically sensitive, has been fostered by social and cultural developments which are antithetical to the church's essential life.

But social and cultural forces have not only contributed to superficial unity, they have also promoted a type of division which is less obvious and more ominous than traditional denominationalism. We have observed

---

[22] (New York: Henry Holt and Co., 1929). Cf. Elmer T. Clark, "Non-Theological Factors in Religious Diversity," *Ecumenical Review,* III (1951), pp. 347 ff.

[23] *The Social Sources of Church Unity* (Nashville: Abingdon Press, 1960), p. 18.

[24] Cf. Yoshio Fukuyama, "The Theological Implications of Mobility," in J. Robert Nelson, ed., *Christian Unity in North America* (St. Louis: Bethany Press, 1958), pp. 197 ff.

that recent urban developments have created a sharp cleavage in American culture—a cleavage between downtown, impersonal interdependence and suburban, communal insulation. The church's retreat from the city to its fringes has given religious sanction to this division. As Gibson Winter observes:

The metropolis is a religiously broken, fragmented cluster of insular pockets estranged from one another. Its religious life is split through the middle by a schism—a truly satanic division—and its religious organization upholds social class identities rather than the universal identity of those who are interdependent in Christ.[25]

In the inner city, where cooperation is most needed, there is, with notable exceptions, the sharpest division. In the suburbs, where variation might be the sign of some vigor, there is considerable cooperation at a superficial level.

Yet even where unity has been most successful, the church is still far short of the goal of organic union. Christians are not entirely free to move from one church to another without some creedal or liturgical tokens. Although trained in interdenominational seminaries pastors cannot migrate from flock to flock simply at will; psychological as well as ecclesiastical fences suggest that it is better to tend the sheep of their own folds. The demonic character of our divisions is well attested to by the fact that some delegates to ecumenical meetings, who obviously display serious concern for the unity of the church, find it impossible to sit together at the table of the Lord. Moreover, those who consider mere attendance at certain ecumenical gatherings to be anathema are suggesting that the old fundamentalist-modernist controversy be renewed [26]— a controversy which more optimistic churchmen believed settled once and for all by the liberal saints. Social and cultural unity has not erased serious, even bitter, theological differences.

What reaction has the contemporary church expressed to the division in its midst? Of course, there are those who are happy with the situa-

[25] *Suburban Captivity of the Churches*, p. 172.
[26] Cf. the editorials "Dare We Renew the Controversy," *Christianity Today*, I (1957), Nos. 18-21.

tion as it is, spouting the values of healthy competition and the importance of individual differences. These seem to suppose that the real business of the church is to promote a sort of religious free enterprise system and to satisfy the various whims of men. Others masquerade under the guise of a concern for unity, but underneath betray a persistent passion for sectarianism. They submit that oneness can be attained if all Christians will simply adopt the program that God has revealed exclusively to them. This, of course, is sectarianism pure and simple. Perhaps one of the main lessons to be learned from the Christ party is that sectarianism is bad even when it calls itself by good names.

Most sensitive Christians, however, would agree with Paul that factionalism within the church is an evil force. As Daniel Jenkins has said, "All who participate in the World Council believe that disunity is a sin for which all churches, in varying degrees, are responsible." [27] The major thrust of our analysis of I Cor. 1-4 is to indicate that the early church's most incisive theologian viewed incipient division as a threat to the church's life. Paul was not primarily occupied with the theology or ecclesiology of the various Corinthian parties; his central concern in these chapters was with the problem of division. When modern Christians shout exclusive loyalty to Luther, Calvin, or Christ, they demonstrate that they too are "men of the flesh."

Many would agree that Paul's analysis of the causes of division is still relevant. Surely false wisdom contributes to the disunity of the church. Whenever a segment of the church supposes that it has the true plan and program for the body of Christ, the wisdom of the world has been presupposed. The content of that plan and program may be indefensible on theological and biblical grounds, but even where its advocates can cite chapter and verse, human interpretation is involved. Interpretation of the divine wisdom is necessary, but the factor which turns this wisdom into folly is the notion that one particular understanding is true —that man's wisdom is God's. It is also true that wherever socio-cultural factors determine either the division or the unity of God's people,

[27] *The Strangeness of the Church* (Garden City, N. Y.: Doubleday & Co., 1955), p. 143.

there the wisdom of the world has replaced the wisdom of God. But, as Paul says, "The wisdom of this world is folly with God" (3:19).

Pride is another persistent cause of division. Although it may appear in the guise of honor to a "great tradition" or loyalty to a "distinctive witness," pride is still detrimental to the life of the church. It often advertises itself in the columns of our denominational weeklies. We like to boast of our activities and achievements—the number of souls saved and budgets raised. These facts and figures are all the more impressive when they stand in good comparison to those of another denomination or to those of the church across the street. Martin Marty writes of the church which is anxious to "build a tower higher than St. Babel's down the block." [28] But not only in local and denominational loyalties is pride to be seen; it also raises its pretty head in the movements seeking some unity at a superficial level. The disorder of the churches may be corrected by man's design—some grandiose plan devised by a theological elite. "But consider your call, brethren; not many of you were wise" (1:26).

Inordinate loyalty to leaders still divides the church. In some circles it is more important to ask what Luther had to say about a matter than it is to ask whether the principle is true. Denominational groups are inclined to honor their heroes disproportionately—to write books which attempt to present some simple frontier preacher as a theologian handling subtleties too complex to be comprehended by the contemporary debate. Some Christians, like the Corinthians, encircle their minister with a personality cult, supposing that no one else can do the work of God so effectively as he. And within the ecumenical movement a little of the superficial unity results from this sort of loyalty. A man (who would prefer to remain anonymous) spoke of a friend who had gone to the higher echelons in Geneva and now spoke only to Visser t' Hooft, and supposed (wrongly, of course) that Visser t' Hooft spoke only to God. But "neither he who plants nor he who waters is anything" (3:7).

Paul's suggested solutions to the problem of division will also prove useful in our time. Surely the wisdom of God can heal the broken body of Christ. But one must be wary here of trying to offer some divine pro-

[28] *The New Shape of American Religion*, p. 127.

gram. The wisdom of God is never to be confused with the wisdom of men, so that all our plans and projects stand under the divine judgment. This suggests that ultimately unity is God's concern and our efforts must humbly strive to conform to his purposes. As long as we are mere men what unity we achieve will be a unity with diversity. The unity which we seek, of course, will be God's—a unity so intimate that the church can be called one body, one person. The wisdom of God which moves us toward such oneness is revealed in the cross of Christ, so that unity must always be Christocentric.[29] The Cross judges all our feeble efforts at oneness, even our Christologies. Yet the Cross also loves us and shows us that oneness is essential to the church's life and that this one living doctrine is more important than all the dogmas we may devise.

Humility, too, is a prerequisite for unity. Whenever the church becomes another rung in the ladder of social success, whenever the church becomes a patron of prestige, then it needs to take a long look at the apostles—"the refuse of the world, the offscouring of all things" (4:13), or at the Suffering Servant of God—"despised and rejected by men" (Isa. 53:3). The church needs to be on its knees confessing its sin and acknowledging the grace of God. Indeed, it is by his grace, not by our doing, that we have been called to be the people of God. He has made us nobodies to be his children, and "it does not yet appear what we shall be" (I John 3:20). We are a new creation, and God can ever make us new. He can even unite us in a oneness so personal and so compelling that "if one member suffers, all suffer together; if one member is honored, all rejoice together" (12:26).

However, one must avoid giving too much of the wrong kind of honor to the right people; the inordinate loyalty to leaders must be replaced with a loyalty to God. Naturally our leaders seem to deserve some honor; the minister may very well be the first citizen of the community. The kind of loyalty that goes wrong is that which divides—which honors some heroes to the exclusion of others, which forgets that "all things are yours" (3:21). Of course, in offering loyalty to particular leaders we honor our own, and this is just another form of pride. Inordinate loyalty also re-

[29] Cf. Robert L. Calhoun, "Christ and the Church," in Paul Minear, ed., *The Nature of the Unity We Seek* (St. Louis: Bethany Press, 1958), p. 60.

sults in a focus on man and a blurring of God. The job of Christian leadership, on the other hand, is loyalty to the Almighty—a kind of loyalty wherein leaders become transparent to the work of God. This is why Jesus Christ is the "pioneer and perfecter of our faith" (Heb. 12:2); he always pointed away from himself to God (cf. Mark 10:18); "All are yours; and you are Christ's; and Christ is God's" (3:22-23).

III
THE PROBLEM OF MORALITY

Cities have been proverbial centers of iniquity. According to the Genesis account, mankind's first city was founded by a descendant of Cain, and ever since, men have been lured to places like Sodom. Modern students of urban society assert that the "mere presence of extremes makes it inevitable that the city will be the site of deviant behavior of every imaginable variety." [1] So it was in Corinth. To its citizens Paul declared that the unrighteous—the immoral, the idolaters, the adulterers, the homosexuals, the greedy, the drunkards, the revilers, the robbers—would not inherit the kingdom of God. Then he charged,

[1] T. Lynn Smith and C. A. McMahan, *The Sociology of Urban Life* (New York: Dryden Press, 1951), p. 669.

"And such were some of you" (I Cor. 6:9-11).[2] What ethical advice could the apostle offer to Christians who had come out of a culture like that?

It is clear that Paul does not shrink from giving moral advice, that he even talks about such taboo topics as sex. The question is, does he offer anything worth listening to? Many thoughtful Christians find Paul's view, formulated out of a bachelor experience, inadequate. When the apostle declares that "it is well for a man not to touch a woman" (7:1), it must be admitted that he sounds a bit ascetic. Many exegetes believe his view of women and marriage to be the weakest link in Paul's entire theological system. He is sometimes described in anomalous fashion as the "father" of celibacy. But before one reaches this conclusion too readily, he needs to be reminded that on occasion Paul could refer to the church as the bride of Christ (II Cor. 11:2).

I

Paul discusses the problem of morality in I Cor. 5 through 7. The situation at Corinth involved a variety of ethical issues. Most blatant was a case of incest within the church. Paul describes the circumstances in 5:1: "It is actually reported that there is immorality among you, and of a kind that is not found even among pagans; for a man is living with his father's wife." The precise character of the situation is not clear, although it is evident that an illicit relationship exists between a church member and the wife of his father. Since no mention of the mother is made, the woman is probably the violator's stepmother. It may be that she is divorced from the father or is perhaps his widow, since no continuing relationship with the father is implied.

Regardless of the exact details, Paul considers this a case of gross immorality. The Hebrew law clearly prohibited such conduct, as seen

[2] It is not necessary to conclude that all these misdemeanors were actually represented by members of the Corinthian church. Paul is simply employing one of the typical "vice-lists" which were a stereotyped form used by Hellenistic authors to criticize the general immorality of the times. Cf. Adolf Deissmann, *Light from the Ancient East*, tr. Lionel R. M. Strachan (New York: Harper & Bros., 1927), pp. 315 ff.

in Moffatt's translation of Lev. 18:8: "You shall not have intercourse with any wife of your father." As Paul says, this sort of thing is not even found among the pagans. Cicero supports the apostle's contention when he denounces a Roman matron's passion for her son-in-law as an "unbelievable crime, unheard of except for this case." [3] Sex ethics seem to have reached a nadir with Hellenistic society, but this deviation is still lower.

Paul places the blame firmly at the feet of both the man and the church. The fact that this man can be numbered with the immoral, the greedy, the robbers, the idolaters, indicates that the woman involved was probably a pagan. Had she been a member of the congregation, Paul would no doubt have censured her as well. But the surprising thing to his readers is that he so severely reproaches the church. "And you are arrogant!" he charges. "Ought you not rather to mourn?" (5:2.) Their arrogance, or being puffed up, as the more literal translation would suggest, is probably not *because* of this sexual aberration but *in spite* of it. Pride or arrogance was the typical attitude of the Corinthian Christians, as their factionalism indicates. Nevertheless, Paul has addressed them with an emphatic expression. *You* are arrogant! "But why blame us?" they object. "What have we done? Why is the responsibility for taking drastic action foisted upon us?"

Besides the case of incest, Corinth was also bothered by a variety of questions about marriage. Whereas the incestuous situation was probably related to Paul by well-founded rumor, the questions of marriage were raised by an actual letter from the church to the apostle. Thus in 7:1 he says, "Now concerning the matters about which you wrote." They must have written at some length, since Paul takes up several specific problems.

These questions also reveal that the Corinthian church was composed of men from many moral backgrounds. Some were Jews who maintained strict notions of marriage and divorce but honored a history which had tolerated polygamy. Among the Greek members of the church some may have advocated asceticism while others promoted sexual license. It is a strange feature of Hellenistic dualism that either ethical conclusion could be drawn: Only the spirit is good, so that the lusts of the body must

[3] *Pro Cluentio*, vi.

63

be rejected; only the spirit is important, so that what one does with his body is of no moment. This latter notion was given impetus within the church, where men were freed from legalism and where all things were lawful, while the advocates of the former thought they had an ally in Paul, who unlike Cephas and the brothers of the Lord, was never accompanied by a wife (I Cor. 9:5).

In view of this variegated background and in light of Paul's answers, a hypothetical reconstruction of the Corinthian questions may be postulated. Some of the Christians, perhaps, were wondering if any kind of sexual relations were to be allowed and whether it was proper for them to marry at all. Within the marriage bond what sort of sexual activity was in harmony with the gospel's demand of holiness? Was any amount of extramarital sex to be tolerated? Some of these questions reflect an ascetic interest, but in the main they represent the notorious sexual laxity of the Hellenistic age. Martial, for instance, writes of the Roman lady who was "now marrying her tenth husband," and goes on to comment that "by a more straightforward prostitute I am offended less." [4]

It is not surprising either that Corinthians were concerned about divorce, for as Jerome Carcopino observes, Rome after the days of the Republic suffered from an "epidemic of divorces." [5] Within the Hebrew-Christian tradition Moses had allowed divorce on certain conditions, while Jesus had opposed any breaking of the marriage bond (Mark 10:4 ff.). Would divorce be permitted in the church, and if so, what strictures would be placed on the divorcee? In particular, did a "mixed marriage"—a marriage between a Christian and a pagan—constitute grounds for separation?

The Corinthians were also asking about the advisability of marriage for particular groups. For instance, should widows or widowers be permitted to remarry? Should young men and women of the congregation be encouraged to marry? Some of these individuals are difficult to identify, for when Paul addresses the man who is not behaving properly toward his "virgin" (7:36, KJV), it is not clear whether the question concerns a father and the marriage of his daughter, a man and the marriage of his

---

[4] *Epigrammata*, vi, 4.

[5] *Daily Life in Ancient Rome*, ed. Henry T. Rowell, tr. E. O. Lorimer (New Haven: Yale University Press, 1940), p. 97.

betrothed, or a couple whose "spiritual marriage" of abstention is to be consummated by sexual fulfillment.[6]

At any rate, it is apparent that Paul deals frankly with a variety of questions about sex and marriage. It is apparent, too, that underlying the queries of the Corinthians was a more basic question. Are the responsibilities of intimate personal relationships in conflict with Christian commitment? Paul makes this question explicit. Positively he suggests that loyalty to Christ involves all our ethical action. It is for this reason that Paul's answers to the Corinthians are relevant for our own time.

II

In regard to the case of incest Paul recommends drastic action. First, he insists that instead of being arrogant, the church ought to mourn (5:2). The term which he uses (*pentheō*) is often employed to describe mourning for the dead. It suggests here that the church must take seriously this sin in its midst. This case of gross immorality is really the responsibility of the people of God. When they are assembled in the power of the Lord, they must act. This is an action of the whole church, for though Paul is across the Aegean in Ephesus, his spirit is present.

Of course, the church must do more than be sorry about this member's sin; it must throw him out of the fellowship. In vs. 2 Paul says, "Let him who has done this be removed from among you," and later in chapter 5 he concludes, "Drive out the wicked person from among you" (vs. 13). For the latter demand he has scriptural support; it is a quotation from Deut. 13:5. Yet what does Paul mean in vs. 5 when he recommends that "you are to deliver this man to Satan for the destruction of the flesh, that his spirit may be saved in the day of the Lord Jesus"?

It is sometimes argued that the "destruction of the flesh" means the death of the physical body. Indeed, the New English Bible supports this interpretation by its translation: "This man is to be consigned to Satan for the destruction of the body." But what action could or should the

---

[6] Cf. Roland H. A. Seboldt, "Spiritual Marriage in the Early Church," *Concordia Theological Monthly*, XXX (1959), 103 ff., 176 ff.

church take which precipitates the physical death of one of its members? The possible suggestion that death of the flesh is a means whereby man atones for sins committed in it is quite without Pauline support. If true, it would suggest that Paul should have been preaching salvation by death rather than justification by faith.

Still more difficult is the declaration that, though the sinner's body is now destroyed, his spirit will be saved on the eschatological day of the Lord. Such an interpretation suggests a dualistic view of man—that although the body is corruptible, the spirit is immortal, destined for fellowship with God. Paul here is forced into either advocating this Hellenistic dualism or supporting a sacramental notion that the grace of God experienced within the church has a continuing, irresistible effect on an excommunicate. Elsewhere the apostle gives little evidence of holding either.

Althought the text is admittedly difficult, surely some more satisfactory exegesis is possible. The point of departure is the meaning of "flesh." The word *sarx*, of course, can refer to the physical aspect of man's nature. But in the epistles it is often a moral term. To live "according to the flesh" (*kata sarka*) is to live under the power of sin (Rom. 8:4, 5, 12), and the works of the flesh include such "nonfleshly" sins as "strife, jealousy, anger, selfishness" (Gal. 5:20). Sin holds sway in this world, and the ruler of this world is Satan (II Cor. 4:4).

Thus "to deliver this man to Satan" is the same as driving the "wicked person from among you." When a man is thrown out of the church, he is cast into the world where Satan rules. The purpose of this drastic action is disciplinary—the destruction of the flesh and the salvation of the spirit. But since "flesh" here is probably not to be taken literally, the destruction of the flesh may mean the annihilation of the power of sin. That is, the man who has experienced the protecting benefits of the Christian community is now driven out into the realm of Satan. There his sin is seen to be sin, and the necessity of repentance is made imperative. On the ground of this experience the sinner can turn to the Lord, who abundantly pardons.

To suppose that this penitent actually returns to participation in the body of Christ requires some romanticizing, although it remains a possibility. At any event, the salvation of his spirit—the essential man—is ultimately dependent on faith and the overt expression of that faith in ethical obedience. That Satan can play a disciplinary role is evidenced in the ancient story of Job, as well as in Paul's own recognition of his thorn in the flesh as a messenger of Satan, sent to keep him from being too elated (II Cor. 12:7).

Regardless of the interpretation of this verse, it is clear that Paul demands excommunication; to the tolerant ears of modern man this sounds like a dissonant chord echoing from the days of the Gregorian chant. What right has anyone, even Paul, to put someone out of the church? Well, for one thing, it is important to remember that incest was a serious crime. This man was not guilty of some small sin like attending the races or supporting Sunday baseball; he had actually violated civil and religious law. Paul is saying that serious sin calls for drastic action. We need to remember, too, that Paul, in spite of our difficulty in understanding him, believes this drastic remedy will benefit the patient. The action will eventuate in the saving of his spirit on the eschatological day of judgment.

Still more important, excommunication will benefit the church. Paul charges, "Your boasting is not good," indicating that their attitude in the face of this sin is detrimental to the life of the whole community. To make his point the apostle borrows an analogy from the Jewish feast of Passover—an analogy perhaps suggested by the imminence of *pascha* season (16:8).

Cleanse out the old leaven that you may be fresh dough, as you really are unleavened. For Christ, our paschal lamb, has been sacrificed. Let us, therefore, celebrate the festival, not with the old leaven, the leaven of malice and evil, but with the unleavened bread of sincerity and truth. (5:7-8.)

The point of the analogy is that Passover is a time for putting all impurity out of the household of faith (Exod. 12:15, 19; 13:7). For the Christian the new "Passover" is now being celebrated, since the lamb, Christ, has already been offered. Just as the elimination of the fermenting leaven symbolized the purification of the covenant people, so it suggests the eradication of gross evil from the church of Jesus Christ.

This analogy seems to offer two significant implications. First, sin is contagious. Paul asks, "Do you not know that a little leaven ferments

67

the whole lump of dough?" (vs. 6.) The Greek form of the question requires a "yes" answer, but any cook knows that, without having studied Attic grammar. The point of the question is, of course, that sin spreads like yeast. Changing the analogy Paul might ask, "Do you not know that one sinner infects the whole church?" This sinful member must be amputated before the fatal disease spreads over the whole body of Christ.

The second implication is that the church is a corporate unity. Sin is highly infectious in the Christian community because the church is the very opposite of the isolation ward. As Paul says later in this epistle, "If one member suffers, all suffer together" (12:26). Here, however, he employs the figure of bread instead of body—the church is compared to a lump of dough. The two metaphors are linked in chapter 10, where Paul says, "Because there is one loaf, we who are many are one body" (vs. 17). Therefore, the sin of one member is the sin of the whole body; the trespass of one man is the responsibility of the entire church. Since the wages of sin is death (Rom. 6:23), eradication of sin is necessary to the life of the body. This is much more than saying sin is contagious in a society where individuals are in close proximity; it means that the church is a corporate unity in which the sin of one is the sin of all—the sin of one is the responsibility of all.

Although Paul urged drastic action in this case of gross immorality, it must not be imagined that the church was a society of pure saints. We have noted that its members displayed immaturity and sinfulness in their factionalism, but Paul does not insist that these "fleshly" men be put out of the church. Moreover, in 5:9 ff. he insists that the people of God must have dealings with the children of darkness, since the church is in the world. Paul himself had worked in the shop of Priscilla and Aquila in the Corinthian market place, and he, too, had learned to make friends by the mammon of unrighteousness. In such a world some of the dealings of the Christian are no doubt dimmed by the evil clouds of this age; the bright light of the kingdom of God does not yet glow with all its radiance even within the church.

Some of the Corinthians, however, seemed to feel that Paul viewed the church as a holy island in the midst of a pagan sea—an island whose shores were never eroded by the forces which beat against them. Thus these Corinthians had misunderstood his previous epistle. "I wrote to you in my letter not to associate with immoral men," he reminds them, "not at all meaning the immoral of this world . . . since then you would need to go out of the world" (5:9-10). Instead, the church must stay in the world; its essential purpose is to witness in the world to what God has done in Jesus Christ. As L. H. Marshall comments, "Paul does *not* advise flight from this wicked world; on the contrary, the Christian is to play his part right manfully in it." [7]

What, then, did the previous letter advise? Paul goes on to say, "I wrote to you not to associate with any one who bears the name of brother if he is guilty of immorality or greed, or is an idolater, reviler, drunkard, or robber—not even to eat with such a one" (vs. 11). Thus his original intention was to warn them against association with evil men within the church. It may be that the earlier epistle had the incestuous man in mind, but, at any rate, we now see that other serious sins could be ground for excommunication too. Thus the Christian is allowed, even forced, to have dealings with the greedy, the robbers, the idolaters in the world, but not in church. This is because the fellowship of the church is too intimate. The word translated "to associate" here is *sunanamig-numi*—a verb which literally means "to be mixed up together with." Such close association is prohibited by the apostle's command not to eat with gross sinners. Although this may refer only to social occasions, it is possible that Paul here is alluding to the most intimate expression of the church's *koinonia*—the celebration of the Supper of the Lord.

It is obvious that the apostle is here involved in a discussion of ethical relativity. Certain sinners are expelled from the church, while others who have fallen short of the glory of God are allowed to remain. Church members are to have no dealings with Christians who are guilty of gross immorality, but may have association with pagans who have committed serious sins. The advice seems to be varied in relation to the magnitude of the sin and the character of the association. A gross transgression such as incest threatens the life of the body of Christ; the intimate fellowship of the church provides an opportunity for infectious sin to destroy the corporate community. The real issue is the distinction between the church and the world. The church is in the world, but not of the world. Any

[7] *The Challenge of New Testament Ethics* (London: The Macmillan Company, 1947), p. 223.

sin or association which would confuse this distinction demands drastic denial. This is why "those who deal with the world" should be "as though they had no dealings with it" (I Cor. 7:31). In insisting on severe treatment of gross immorality Paul is not demanding that the church go out of the world, but that the world go out of the church.

III

In answering the various questions about marriage Paul enunciates his principles of sexual morality. For one thing, he betrays a preference for *celibacy*.[8] In 7:1 he writes, "It is well for a man not to touch a woman," and later in the chapter he urges the unmarried to remain as they are. This advice is meted out to various groups within the church. The widows and widowers (vs. 8) and the divorcees (vs. 11) should "remain single"; those who have not known marriage should not seek it (vs. 27). Paul ends this section of the epistle by admitting that a woman whose husband has died is free to remarry. "But," he warns, "in my judgment she is happier if she remains as she is" (vs. 40).

This last quotation indicates that celibacy is not an absolute demand. Although the unmarried state is preferable, marriage is allowed. Some things are worse than matrimony. For instance, "It is better to marry than to be aflame with passion" (vs. 9). Actually, celibacy is a demand too stern for some mortals, and men maintain it only by the grace of God. As Paul says, "I wish that all were as I myself am. But each has his own special gift from God" (vs. 7).[9] It certainly would have taken a sizable gift to have maintained celibacy within a "spiritual marriage"—a marriage of cohabitation and sexual abstention which may actually have

[8] For a complete discussion of Paul's negative view toward marriage and sex, cf. Gerhard Delling, *Paulus' Stellung zu Frau und Ehe* (Stuttgart: W. Kohlhammer, 1931), pp. 57 ff. For a more positive interpretation, cf. Else Kähler, *Die Frau in den paulinischen Briefen* (Zürich & Frankfurt: Gotthelf, 1960).

[9] Arthur Carl Peikorn, "St. Paul on Social Relationships," *Concordia Theological Monthly*, XI (1940), 739: "Ultimately . . . the matter is entirely one of vocation."

Piepkorn.

been practiced in Corinth (7:36 ff.).[10] Yet Paul concludes, "Thus he who marries his partner does well, and he who does not will do better" (vs. 38, NEB).

In displaying this preference for celibacy, Paul admits that he merely gives his own opinion, yet he says, "I think that I have the Spirit of God" (vs. 40). But how has Paul come to such a negative conclusion about marriage? The answer is found in part in 7:29 ff. Paul points out that the "appointed time has grown very short" (vs. 29), and that the "form of this world is passing away" (vs. 31). In other words, because of the nearness of the eschaton, marriage should be avoided. The ancient command "to multiply and replenish the earth" is hardly to be heeded when the form of the world is passing away. Moreover, those who spawn a family in times like these simply breed trouble for themselves and their offspring. As the ancient apocalyptic tradition says, "Alas for those who are with child . . . in those days" (Mark 13:17). It is this same sort of apocalyptic which perhaps leads Paul to say, "Every one should remain in the state in which he was called" (7:20)—a notion supporting a social conservatism which has plagued the church ever since.

Besides this apocalyptic reason, Paul has other ground for advocating celibacy—the demand of undivided devotion to the Lord. He says:

I want you to be free from all anxieties. The unmarried man is anxious about the affairs of the Lord, how to please the Lord; but the married man is anxious about worldly affairs, how to please his wife, and his interests are divided. And the unmarried woman or girl is anxious about the affairs of the Lord, how to be holy in body and spirit; but the married women is anxious about worldly affairs, how to please her husband (7:32-34).

Some wag has suggested that this text is proof enough that Paul had never been married—the idyllic picture of the wife scurrying about with no other interest than waiting on her spouse has little relation to reality.

Actually Paul is simply mirroring views common in his own time and always—that marriage and family bring trouble and woe. Menander, whom Paul may have quoted on occasion, had said, "To have a wife

---

[10] Cf. Seboldt, "Spiritual Marriage in the Early Church," and Delling, *Paulus' Stellung zu Frau und Ehe,* pp. 86 ff.

and to be father of children . . . brings many cares to life." [11] It seems, however, that Paul had never entertained the notion that "undivided devotion to the Lord" might have been better expressed within the marriage relationship than outside it. One wonders why he had not learned this from Priscilla and Aquila, his "fellow workers in Christ Jesus," to whom both Paul and the churches were in debt (Rom. 16:3 ff.).

At any rate we may conclude that Paul's preference for celibacy displays deficiency of insight. Not only did he lack the experience of a Christian marriage himself, he adopted an apocalyptic timetable of the eschaton which ensuing history has simply abrogated. The appointed time had not grown short, and the form of the world is still with us. Yet, when Paul's eschatology is shorn of its apocalyptic elements, his views of marriage have continuing value. The important feature is not the nearness of the end but its certainty. The eschaton has started to come in Christ, and it will be consummated in the future. In the meantime man is confronted with an eschatological decision in the proclamation of Christ. This decision is an ultimate one; it involves all man's ethical action. Therefore, in the time of crisis between the beginning of the end and its consummation, marriage must be responsive to the ultimate decision, it must give expression to the Christian's undivided devotion to the Lord.

A second principle from Paul's sex ethic is his insistence on *monogamy*. Although the apostle allows marriage as a concession to human weakness, he demands strict morality within the marriage bond. He says, "Because of the temptation to immorality, each man should have his own wife and each woman her own husband" (7:2). Some Jewish sages were perhaps still advocating polygamy,[12] but Paul was probably more concerned with the prevalent adultery of the Hellenistic age. In a similar vein, Juvenal writes of the woman who

is lord of her spouse. But soon she abandons this kingdom, occupies house after house, and her bridal veil gets pretty ragged. Then she comes flying back to the bed she scorned and abandoned, leaving behind her the doors

---

[11] Unidentified Minor Fragments (649 Kock).

[12] The *Talmud* continued to tolerate polygamy. *Yebamoth*, 65a: "A man may marry wives in addition to his first wife; provided only that he possesses the means to maintain them."

in festal array, and the garlands new on the walls, and the branches still green over the lintel. So her conquests grow: eight husbands in five Octobers —O illustrious feat, worth being carved on her tombstone! [13]

Paul's advice, therefore, addresses a serious need of his own time. That "each man should have his own wife and each woman her own husband" clearly forbids extramarital sex relations and is in harmony with Paul's forceful opposition to adultery throughout the epistles.

In spite of his preference for celibacy and his prohibition of adultery, Paul is not opposed to sex *per se*. Within the marriage relationship there is to be mutual satisfaction of sexual desires. The apostle says: "The husband should give to his wife her conjugal rights, and likewise the wife to her husband. For the wife does not rule over her own body, but the husband does; likewise the husband does not rule over his own body, but the wife does (7:3-4). As Phillips translates vs. 5, "Do not cheat each other of normal sexual intercourse." It is significant to note that Paul considers sexual relations to have value beyond mere procreation, and that he attributes to woman here a position equal to men.

Of course, by mutual consent couples may refrain from sexual activity for religious purposes, as he says, "for a season, that you may devote yourselves to prayer" (vs. 5). Here Paul reflects the ancient view that participation in worship requires sexual abstention. For example, the temple of Athena at Pergamon prescribed the following rules for its worshipers: "Whoever wishes to visit the temple of the goddess . . . must refrain from intercourse with his wife (or husband) that day, from intercourse with another than his wife (or husband) for the preceding two days, and must complete the required lustrations." [14] The ethic here is obviously sub-Pauline, but it does suggest a certain tension between devotion to deity and sexual activity. Paul may display some of this, but his Hebrew concept of the creator God demands a more positive view toward sex. Probably his notion of mutual abstention stems from his ideal of undivided devotion, since one must admit, sex can be a distracting

[13] *The Satires of Juvenal,* tr. Rolfe Humphries (Bloomington, Ind.: Indiana University Press, 1958), p. 71.
[14] Quoted in Frederick C. Grant, ed., *Hellenistic Religions—The Age of Syncretism* (New York: Liberal Arts Press, 1953), p. 6. Cf. Joel 2:16 for sexual abstention in Jewish cultic practice.

factor. Paul does remind his readers that they should come together again before too long a vigil, "lest Satan tempt you through lack of self-control" (7:5).

A third principle of Paul's sex ethic is his disallowance of *divorce*. Although his disapproval of marriage rests on his own opinion, here he has a word from the Lord. "To the married I give charge, not I but the Lord, that the wife should not separate from her husband." (7:10.) By a word from the Lord he probably does not imply that he has received some special revelation about the matter; more likely he knows a traditional word from the historical Jesus like that preserved in Mark 10:9: "What therefore God has joined together, let not man put asunder." Incidentally, this word from Paul also supports the contention of many scholars that the exception clause in Matt. 5:32 is a later interpolation; the fact that Paul uses the word of Jesus without equivocation indicates that he did not know about exceptions "on the ground of unchastity." Paul simply repeats the absolute command of his Lord: There must be no divorce at all!

The exact situation in Corinth is not clear. Paul does mention the wife first, and only as an afterthought adds, "that the husband should not divorce his wife" (vs. 11). It may be that the wives of the Corinthians were more active in instigating divorce proceedings than the husbands, and there is evidence elsewhere, as we shall see, of a feminist party in the church. Movements for the rights of women were not uncommon in Paul's day, and one of the attractions of some of the Hellenistic cults was their view of the equality of the sexes. Rights of divorce were evidence of feminist achievement. Whereas in much earlier times women had almost no such prerogatives, in the imperial period they were given rights of divorce practically equal to men. The Augustan law which protected the women's dowry in event of divorce gave considerable power to the feminists in both the making and breaking of marriages.[15] Paul had been reared on the much stricter practices of the Jewish community.[16] His opposition to divorce, however, is not due simply to a traditional antipathy toward women's rights, as his inclusion of the husband indi-

[15] Cf. Carcopino, *Daily Life*, pp. 95 ff.; William Graham Cole, *Sex and Love in the Bible* (New York: Association Press, 1959), p. 207.

[16] George Foot Moore, *Judaism in the First Centuries of the Christian Era* (Cambridge: Harvard University Press, 1927), II, 122 ff.

cates. His opposition to divorce, whether instigated by husband or wife, rests on the belief that a union ordained by the creative purposes of God should not be broken.

On occasion it can and perhaps should be broken. After insisting that a wife should not separate from her husband, Paul adds, "but if she does. . . ." In other words, the Lord's demand for no divorce is an absolute which cannot always be obeyed. This, no doubt, is the reason for the exception clause in Matthew—the church found adherence to the absolute impossible and perhaps unchristian. The application of the demand requires a relativity. There are cases in which some alternatives are worse than divorce; there are cases in which separation is preferable to maintenance of marriage. This admission of ethical relativity, however, should not be understood as a defeat of the moral demand. The acceptance of the relative does not cancel the absolute. Although divorce may in some circumstances be tolerated, it is still against the demand of God, and those who disobey this demand stand under divine judgment.

Moreover, the person who has committed the sin of divorce is placed under special obligation. Paul says of the divorcee that if she does separate from her husband, "Let her remain single or else be reconciled to her husband." As well as indicating further Paul's aversion to divorce, this text reflects again his inadequate view of marriage. Surely, if an irreconcilable marital relationship has been terminated by divorce, a penitent party should not be denied the joy of a genuinely Christian marriage. It is still possible that a union may be accomplished which will allow expression of undivided devotion to the Lord. In any event, the Christian who has experienced divorce and the consequent judgment of God will certainly agree with Paul that marriage is a serious business.

In presenting a situation in which divorce is to be allowed Paul states a fourth ethical principle—marriage involves a *physical-spiritual solidarity*. This principle is implied in a discussion of mixed marriages. Probably some of the church members were married to pagan partners. Such marriages were no doubt consummated before the individual entered the church, since Paul seems to approve only marriages "in the Lord" (7:39). But now one party has accepted the gospel while the other has remained a nonbeliever. Can such a marriage be maintained? Should the Christian seek a divorce?

75

Paul's answer is that the Christian should not seek such a separation, but a divorce is to be permitted if the pagan partner desires it. This again emphasizes Paul's distaste for divorce; if it must be done, let the pagans do it! His reasons for allowing divorce in this instance have a certain ring of modernity.

> Wife, how do you know whether you will save your
> husband?
> Husband, how do you know whether you will save
> your wife? (7:16.)

Apparently the Corinthian church, like many of ours, was populated with those persistent souls who continue to suppose that somehow their spouses are eventually going to flock into the fold. This may be a vain hope. Paul also suggests that "God has called us to peace" (vs. 15), and therefore the kind of squabbling that goes on between Christians and pagans within the home deserves to be silenced.[17]

However, in giving the reasons for maintaining a mixed marriage Paul states principles much more profound. He says:

> the unbelieving husband is consecrated through his wife,
> and the unbelieving wife is consecrated through her husband.

Hagiazō, the word which is translated "consecrated" here, normally means "to be sanctified"; it is used by Paul to describe the Christians as "those sanctified in Christ Jesus" (I Cor. 1:2). He has just told them in 6:11 that "you were washed, you were sanctified (*hagiazō*), you were justified in the name of the Lord Jesus Christ and in the Spirit of our God." In other words Paul is using a word which usually is employed for the sanctifying activity of the Spirit in the life of the baptized believer in order to describe the religious function of the marriage relationship. The very spiritual benefits which one member receives through the ministration of the church are communicated to the other through

---

[17] Some commentators (*Moffatt New Testament Commentary*, pp. 84-85) do not interpret vs. 16 as a question and understand Paul here as advocating (as in vs. 13) the preservation of a mixed marriage; the counsel of "peace" (vs. 15), in this view, opposes separation rather than opposing strife within the marital relationship. The majority take the line followed above.

the intimacy of wedlock. The sexual relationship is an important link in this union, for Paul asks, "Do you not know that he who joins himself to a prostitute becomes one body with her?" (6:16.) How much more the purity of marital intercourse witnesses to an interpersonal oneness, "for, as it is written, 'The two shall become one'" (6:16). Thus, through this union God can work for the sanctification of his people, and Paul might even be attributed a "sacramental" view of sex.[18]

In defending this concept of marriage solidarity Paul also posits the solidarity of the family. He argues that if the marriage cannot sanctify, then "your children would be unclean, but as it is they are holy" (7:14). The word for holy, *hagios,* is the cognate of *hagiazō,* so that the sanctifying effect of the marriage is conveyed also to the children. Paul's argument, of course, rests on the presumption that the Corinthians actually acknowledged the children of a mixed marriage as holy; that they must have done. Such acknowledgment, according to Paul, recognizes the spiritual oneness of the family; the faith of one parent affects the life of the whole household.

This text has sometimes been used to support a doctrine of infant baptism;[19] if the Corinthians really recognized the children as holy, some sign of this recognition might have been made. Perhaps the children had been washed as well as sanctified (6:11). Unfortunately the evidence is too sparse to guarantee such a conclusion, but churches who pretend that children have no membership in the Christian community until they reach the "age of accountability" need to be reminded that when the parents are a part of the church the grace of God functions in the whole family.

It is now evident that Paul's view of sex and marriage is not as negative as his preference for celibacy would imply. When he advocates monogamy and opposes adultery and divorce, the apostle again seems to

[18] Cf. Otto A. Piper, *The Biblical View of Sex and Marriage* (New York: Charles Scribner's Sons, 1960), pp. 129 ff.

[19] Oscar Cullmann, *Baptism in the New Testament,* tr. J. K. S. Reid, "Studies in Biblical Theology, No. 1," (Chicago: Henry Regnery Co., 1950), p. 44, says that the "passage proves neither child nor adult Baptism," but that "from the idea of holiness represented here there is a direct line to infant Baptism." Cf. Joachim Jeremias, *Infant Baptism in the First Four Centuries,* tr., David Cairns (London: SCM Press, 1960), pp. 44 ff. Against these arguments, cf. G. R. Beasley-Murray, *Baptism in the New Testament* (London: Macmillan & Company, 1962), pp. 192 ff.

display a hostility toward sexual activity. This, however, was probably due in part to the prevailing immorality of his time, just as his commendation of celibacy was mainly dependent on a mistaken notion of the end. Within the marriage bond, on the other hand, sex is to be allowed for more than procreative reasons. It provides communication at the deepest level of interpersonal relationship; it offers a medium for the sanctifying grace of God.

IV

On what basic ethical concepts are Paul's instructions on marriage based? We have observed that he suggests a principle of the absolute and the relative. On some ethical matters, as the case of incest, Paul is unequivocal. Put the evildoer out of the church! On other issues, such as divorce, Paul allows some compromise under certain circumstances. A pagan, for instance, has a right to separate from his Christian partner if he so chooses. If a woman finds a marital difficulty insoluble and perpetrates divorce, then she must conform to certain requirements. The important thing, however, is that a responsible decision be made. The fact that an ethical decision is difficult is no ground for retreating from moral responsibility. One of the major lessons to be learned from Paul here is that all aspects of human life fall under the demand of the Christian ethic, and even where no clear-cut right or wrong decision is possible, the Christian is required to act responsibly. On many of the matters discussed in chapter 7 Paul has no word from the Lord, yet he feels impelled to give his own opinion, hoping that it is in harmony with the Spirit of God.

We have also noted that the principle of relativity does not destroy the absolute demand; the relative and the absolute must be held in tension. The person who acquires a divorce still stands under the judgment of God; divorce is always wrong even when necessary. Just as the enforcement of the absolute would reduce religion to a legalism which Paul deplores, so a relaxing of the absolute would distort the essential righteousness of God's demands. The tension must be maintained.

A further illustration of this tension between the absolute and the relative is offered in 6:1 ff.[20] There Paul describes a situation in which the Corinthians had become involved in legal disputes. This is not surprising since the Romans had a genius for the judicial arts and a certain "passion for litigation." Paul, however, seems to have been opposed to Christians carrying their civil disputes before pagan judges. "When one of you has a grievance against a brother," he asks, "does he dare go to law before the unrighteous instead of the saints?" (6:1.) His advice is that such legal disputes should be put to the church. "Are you incompetent to try trivial cases?" (vs. 2.) "Can it be that there is no man among you wise enough to decide between members of the brotherhood?" (vs. 5.)

Paul's reason for advocating judgment by the church seems to be twofold. For one thing, he takes up the Jewish notion that in the eschatological day the "saints will judge the world." If they can participate in such an ultimate litigation, how much more they are able to try the trivial disputes among their own people. The second aspect of his reasoning is present only by implication; exposing strife among the brethren defeats the basic witness of the church. "Brother goes to law against brother and that before unbelievers." How, then, are unbelievers even to know that Christians are brothers?

But suddenly at vs. 7 Paul declares a radically new principle: "To have law suits at all . . . is defeat for you. Why not rather suffer wrong? Why not rather be defrauded? But you yourselves wrong and defraud, and that even your own brethren." In short, Paul is here announcing the absolute. Have no legal disputes at all! Rather than demand your rights, suffer wrongs. In place of illegal conduct give your brother no ground for litigation. Such a command, of course, is too hard for them, and Paul knows full well that legal disputes are bound to arise within the church. When they do, the principle of relativity operates. They should be heard by the Christian community. But this relativity does not compromise the absolute: "To have law suits at all . . . is defeat for you." The tension must be maintained.[21]

---

[20] For the complexities and varieties of interpretation of this text, cf. Lukas Vischer, *Die Auslegungsgeschichte von I. Kor. 6, 1-11—Rechtsverzicht und Schlichtung* (Tübingen: J. C. B. Mohr, 1955).

[21] The problem of tension in this passage is clearly pointed out by Erich Dinkler, "Zum Problem der Ethik bei Paulus—Rechtsnahme und Rechtsverzicht (I. Kor. 6, 1-11)," *Zeitschrift für Theologie und Kirche*, XLIX (1952), 167 ff.

Another illustration of this tension is found in Paul's discussion of freedom and responsibility (6:12 ff.). The principles are clearly stated in vs. 12:

> All things are lawful for me,
> but not all things are helpful.
> All things are lawful for me,
> but I will not be enslaved by anything.

The first phrase, which is announced twice, is the absolute. The Christian is absolutely free. As Paul has said, "All things are yours" (3:21). This absolute, however, must be held in tension with two principles of relativity. Some things which are lawful are not helpful for the life of the Christian community; some things which are lawful can so enslave the Christian that his basic freedom is lost. The relative must be responsible to the essential character of the church; the relative must not itself be absolutized so as to invalidate the ultimate. The tension must be maintained; the Christian is both free and responsible. These two texts also show that the principles of the absolute and the relative apply to ethical matters beyond sexual morality; the ethical principles being discussed here are relevant for the Christian's entire moral existence.

But what is the nature of the absolute, and in what light can the Christian be guided to make decisions which are relatively right? The basic principle underlying all of Paul's ethical advice is this: Respond in faith to the revelation of God's righteousness in Jesus Christ. This is the ground for the serious denial of gross immorality; the despicable sinner must be put out of the corporate fellowship, since "Christ, our paschal lamb, has been sacrificed" (5:7). The stark figure on the Cross stands in stern judgment on all the immorality of men.

On this basis, too, Paul attempted to make all his relative judgments about sex and marriage. Only those relationships could be allowed which were commensurate with fellowship in Christ. "Do you not know," he says, "that your bodies are members of Christ?" (6:15.) Only those actions which give glory to God are to be encouraged. "Do you not know," he asks, "that your body is a temple of the Holy Spirit?" (6:19.) Although they are free, the Christians are not their own. Just as they had seen the manumission of slaves purchased in the pagan temples,[22] so they had experienced freedom in the church. But theirs was a freedom to serve another master. "You are not your own; you were bought with a price." (6:20.) Of course, when one attempts to make all his decisions in light of that service of the one whose face reflects the glory of God, he is never fully assured that his relative judgments are absolutely correct. Yet he may be able to say with Paul, "I think that I have the Spirit of God" (7:40).

V

The problem of morality plagues modern America. Whereas major crime has increased rapidly in recent years, crimes of sexual violence have increased even more.[23] Recent studies, like the much heralded Kinsey reports, indicate that sexual activity of various sorts has been greatly augmented in our era; the incidence of premarital and extramarital sexual relations is surprisingly high.[24] If we are to believe novels like John Keats' *Crack in the Picture Window*,[25] or John McPartland's *No Down Payment*,[26] we might suppose that adultery and rape are as common in the suburbs as split-level houses and high mortgages. This view is no doubt exaggerated, and genuine evidence confirming the existence of "key clubs" and other forms of "wife swapping" is difficult to find.

Nevertheless, preoccupation with sex is one aspect of contemporary urban culture. Seward Hiltner, for example, suggests that the general

[22] Cf. C. K. Barrett, ed., *The New Testament Background: Selected Documents* (New York: The Macmillan Company, 1957), pp. 52 ff.

[23] Bureau of the Census, *Statistical Abstract of the United States: 1960*, p. 136. Cf. Mabel A. Elliott, *Crime in Modern Society* (New York: Harper & Bros., 1952), pp. 50 ff.

[24] Alfred C. Kinsey, *et. al.*, *Sexual Behavior in the Human Male* (Philadelphia: W. B. Saunders Co., 1948); *Sexual Behavior in the Human Female* (Saunders, 1953). Kinsey and his associates have been criticized both for their method and results; cf. Erdman Palmore, "Published Reactions to the Kinsey Report," *Social Forces*, XXXI (1952), 165 ff.; Herbert Hyman and Paul Sheatsley, "The Scientific Method," in Donald Porter Geddes, ed., *An Analysis of the Kinsey Reports on Sexual Behavior in the Human Male and Female* (New York: E. P. Dutton & Co., 1954), pp. 93 ff.

[25] (Boston: Houghton, Mifflin, 1957).

[26] (New York: Simon and Schuster, 1957).

movement of urban population is one of the factors contributing to increased sexual activity.[27] The same mobility which has uprooted countless people has pulled up ancient mores. Freed from these antique inhibitions, and protected by urban anonymity, the new city or suburban dweller finds opportunity for sexual experience which simply was not available down on the farm. The notion that people are objects to be manipulated may contribute to the supposition that sexual powers are to be exploited, and that the mastery of sexual mechanics offers a blueprint for marital bliss. The pain of urban monotony is to be remedied by the elixir of sexual excitement.

Regardless of the causes it is evident that Eros is one of the major deities of the urban pantheon. Pitirim Sorokin writes of *The American Sex Revolution* and goes so far as to say: "During the last two centuries, and particularly the last few decades, every phase of our culture has become invaded by sex. Our civilization has become so preoccupied with sex that it now oozes from all pores of American life." [28] Sorokin proceeds to argue that this preoccupation has had a debilitating effect on both the individual and society; it has undermined physical and mental health; it has disrupted our finest social institutions. When so eminent a social philosopher displays such concern with the problem of sexual morality, it is time for the church, like Paul, to speak clearly too.

When Christians talk about sex, if they ever do, they usually express one of two or three common views. The first is ascetic; the less said about sex the better. This view, which has been popular in the church ever since the virgin daughters of Philip were recognized as prophetesses (Acts 21:9), assumes that sex has a purely reproductive function; it has no value of its own. But Paul, as we have seen, sees sex as a positive force within the marriage bond. The sharing of conjugal rights is a duty of both wife and husband (7:3). Moreover, through the practice of this right, the purposes of God are fulfilled; a pagan marriage partner is made holy and children of the union are sanctified (7:14).

The second view of the church is unabashed frankness. Sex is good; let's talk about it! The advocates of this notion deem any premarital

---

[27] *Sex Ethics and The Kinsey Reports* (New York: Association Press, 1953), p. 118.
[28] Pitirim A. Sorokin, *The American Sex Revolution* (Boston: Porter Sargent, 1957), p. 19.

interview doomed to failure if it does not discuss in detail the mechanics of sexual relations—matters which most candidates for marriage have learned in a high-school course in hygiene or from the more competent family physician. To object to this approach is not intended to suggest that discussion of sex has no place in ministerial marriage counseling. Rather, it implies that the minister should address himself primarily to the ethical and religious problems of sex. This is why Paul took up such matters as temporary abstention in order to "devote yourselves to prayer" (7:5); this is why he hoped for a word from the Lord (7:10); this is why his ruling principle was the securing of "undivided devotion to the Lord" (7:35).

A third view may be characterized by what has been dubbed the "three monkey" theory of ethics;[29] see no sex, hear no sex, speak no sex. Sex is not the sort of thing that nice people talk about in public, and the church is composed of nice people. These fastidious church members blushingly propose that sex education is to be provided by the school or the YMCA, or perhaps the home. Such a view suggests that the Christian ethic is irrelevant to one of the serious problems of our time. It leaves the field open to the sensualists whose propaganda crowds the newsstands and movie screens, whose theme is "Love Is a Many Splendored Thing," and love for them is *eros*, not *agape*. The counsel of silence also fails to recognize the fact that Paul discussed such "embarrassing" matters as homosexuality (Rom. 1:26 ff.), sexual intercourse (I Cor. 7:3 ff.), and adultery (I Cor. 6:9), with utter candor. If Holy Scripture displays such frankness, the church "must speak clearly and firmly about the subject." [30]

When the church turns to the writings of Paul, it will find much help in regard to some of the specific moral problems which plague it. No doubt his preference for celibacy reflects a mistaken apocalyptic and even a distorted ethic, yet his insistence on monogamy and his stress

[29] Oliver Read Whitley, *Trumpet Call of Reformation* (St. Louis: Bethany Press, 1959), p. 224.

[30] Otto A. Piper, *The Christian Interpretation of Sex* (New York: Charles Scribner's Sons, 1955), p. ix. A good sign that such clear and frank discussion is going on is such books as W. Norman Pittenger, *The Christian View of Sexual Behavior* (Greenwich, Conn.: Seabury Press, 1954); Helmut Thielicke, *The Ethics of Sex*, tr. John W. Doberstein (New York: Harper & Row, 1964).

on the seriousness of divorce demand the church's attention. However, the relevance of Paul's ethic rests primarily on its underlying principles. The apostle insists that all sexual practices must conform to the confession of loyalty to Christ. This loyalty points man to the creator God, for he "has shone in our hearts to give the light of the knowledge of the glory of God in the face of Christ" (II Cor. 4:6). Thus man sees his whole self—body and spirit—created in the image of the Author of Light for the fulfilling of His purposes. These purposes the Christian man has come to know through the experience of the new creation. He confesses:

For us there is one God, the Father,
   from whom are all things and for whom we exist,
and one Lord, Jesus Christ,
   through whom are all things, and through whom we exist (I Cor. 8:6).

Therefore, the Christian views himself as a new being with a new relationship to the Creator, for "if any one is in Christ, he is a new creation; the old has passed away, behold, the new has come" (II Cor. 5:17).

Not only is the Christian man a new being in a new relationship to God, he is a member of a new society in a new relationship to man. As a member of the new society he participates in a new humanity—the corporate personality of the church. The church has a oneness wherein sin—all that separates from God—spreads rapidly; indeed, it has a oneness where the sin of one member is the sin of the whole body. Participation in this body demands serious moral responsibility since it is the body of Christ—the means whereby the redemptive work of God begun in Christ is carried on in the world. The nature of that work is clearly revealed in Christ, for "God shows his love for us in that while we were yet sinners Christ died for us" (Rom. 5:8). All of man's dealings with his fellows must be characterized by this *agape* of God.

Since sex is a part of man's nature, its function must be harmonious with this new relationship to God and the church. Sex, since it is a creation of God, cannot be viewed as evil *per se*; yet, like other elements of the divine creation, it can be perverted to evil purposes. Thus Paul points out that sexual union may provide a channel for the operation of

God's grace, or it may be the link which chains man in unity with a prostitute. The latter union is in revolt against Paul's basic theological principles. He asks, "Shall I therefore take the members of Christ and make them members of a prostitute? Never!" (6:15.)

This latter illustration also indicates that the principle of commitment must be applied to specific situations. Since sex is not right or wrong in itself, the question is: How is sex to be used in response to the revelation of God? No easy answers are forthcoming. Paul's principle of the absolute and relative, however, may be employed. On issues of gross immorality, like the case of incest, a firm answer of "no" is possible. But on matters like divorce, although a "no" is preferable, the situation may suggest a "maybe" or qualified "yes." The answer is determined by a second question. What in this situation makes possible the relatively highest degree of commitment to Christ?

It must not be supposed, however, that this principle of the absolute and relative is simply an easy device to solve difficult questions. Actually it rests on a profound understanding of Christian theology. By way of contrast, the attempt to reduce sex ethics to a precise moral code is antithetic to the biblical faith. Either a code is so stringent that man cannot keep it and is driven to a guilt for which there is no absolution, or the code is so reduced that man may keep it at the expense of God's righteous will and with the delusion of his own self-righteousness. The absolute-relative principle, on the other hand, never attempts to evade the righteousness of God's demands. It also recognizes man as a free moral agent who can decide, and whose decisions—right, wrong, or mixed—stand under the judgment of God. Rather than making ethical decisions easy, it makes them real. Fortunately, the God before whom the deciding man stands in judgment is the Father of Jesus Christ, who loves us and gave himself for us.

How would these theological principles apply to specific moral issues of our time? For instance, what would Paul's ethic say to the question of premarital sex and extramarital sex relations? His prohibition of these practices is clearly revealed in I Cor. 7, and his reasons are apparent. These activities pervert sex, since they deviate from the will of God; they are practiced out of egocentric and idolatrous motives. Sex and its symbols are worshiped with a wanton abandon. The man who pays homage at this shrine becomes its cultic slave; the Christian whose freedom has been purchased by Christ falls back into bondage. These activities also pervert sex since they violate man's proper relation with his fellows. Sex becomes a means whereby the individual is shorn of personal meaning, becoming an object to be manipulated. He is no longer respected as the "brother for whom Christ died" (8:11), and love for neighbor which is the fulfilling of the divine law has been distorted into *eros,* the overt expression of the egocentric self.

Yet even the denial of adultery is not to be crystallized into an absolute code. Particularly in our time of increasing sexual aberration, it is important that the church avoid a stance which belies forgiveness. It similarly must shun a position which appears to affirm asceticism. Extramarital sex is no doubt wrong, but sexual activity within the marriage bond is a means of deepest interpersonal communion. When that sort of communion is withheld, personal meaning is again denied, and the channel of God's grace is diverted. Frigidity, which is sometimes abetted by a distortion of the Christian ethic, can be an aberration as serious as adultery.

Paul, however, is not satisfied with mere teaching about sex; he demands drastic action by the church. Is there an occasion when sexual sin calls for excommunication? Who in the church has this right, and how in light of the foibles of all its members can any presuppose to judge the others? Answers to these questions must be left to the polities of the various segments of the body of Christ, yet some implications are important for us all. For one thing, it is evident that the morality of the members is a responsibility of the whole church. The body of Christ must be conscious of disease in its midst and take remedial action. This action may not precipitate excommunication, but it should address the violator with his sin in terms of the church's ethical demands. Along with its infinitude of committees, perhaps the church ought to have one on discipline.

This advice of Paul also confirms our view that church unity transcends organizational structure. Sin in the church is dangerous because the church is a corporate unity. But in the modern church people are so isolated that they scarcely can catch chicken pox, let alone sin. Paul suggests that any member's sin is every member's responsibility.

But although it may be obvious that the church should make moral demands, it is also clear that the church must remain in the world. It is not a community of pristine purity; many of its saints wear tarnished halos. Although it stands under an absolute demand, its achievement is always relative. Although its relative achievement stands under judgment, its confession is always open to the mercy of God. Its relativity of ethical response is due in no small measure to its limited life in the world. With the world and its sinful society the Christian must have dealings. How may those who have dealings with the world live as if they have no dealings with the world?

IV

THE PROBLEM OF SECULARISM

A. Roy Eckardt has written, "The real problem of the current religious situation is the secularism of a religious people." [1] This may sound like a contradiction in terms, since secularism is traditionally defined as the rejection of religion. In modern parlance, however, secularism refers to the basic orientation of one's life—an orientation which may reveal little loyalty to the faith professed. The problem is created by the conviction that the church must remain in the world; the church, for all its aspiration to holiness, is in a sense a secular institution. But how can Christians live in the world without becoming one with the world? How can the church maintain its secular status and still remain the church of God?

[1] *The Surge of Piety in America* (New York: Association Press, 1958), p. 33 ff.

I

Secularism, the temptation to conform to the patterns of the world, was an acute problem for the Christians of Corinth. The church there was like a tiny boat tossed about in a vast sea of paganism. Its members had until recently flourished in that ocean, and its happy waves continued to beckon them. Did fellowship in the Christian community mean that old ways had to be forsaken? Was the Christian to be different from his fellow townsmen? If so, how different should he be, and what should be the character of his distinctiveness? Could the church provide the habitat where that new kind of personality might be developed?

Secularism in the Hellenistic age can be practically identified with paganism, and the symbol of that worldly worship is seen in idolatry. As we have noted, the streets and squares of Corinth were crowded with idols. Statues of Zeus, Aphrodite, Dionysus, and a host of others decorated the town. At Athens Paul found an altar dedicated to the "Unknown God"—an image which has been discovered elsewhere and which is symbolic of the Hellenistic concern to omit none.

The Christians, of course, had been accustomed to stopping at these shrines and paying their homage. They still passed by the alluring images on their way to work or to the marketplace. Should they stop now? Surely a small pinch of incense to Asclepius would not hurt. Perhaps it would help; he is the healing god, and sick men need every prayer. Many men of the Hellenistic age, like Apuleius' hero Lucius, felt insecure in their faith unless they belonged to two or three cults.[2] Now that the Christians had joined the church, an additional kind of insurance had been appropriated, but to give up the old securities would seem to place undue confidence in the new faith. In short, the problem of secularism expressed itself in a question: Could one worship the God of the Christians and continue to supplicate the pagan idols?

Before we score the practice of idolatry too readily, let us remember that the pagans were not as naïve as we sometimes suppose. For in-

[2] *The Golden Ass,* pp. 255 ff.

stance, the Epicureans considered the worship of idols to be nonsense. One Hellenistic author says of the gods that they "are far away, or they have no ears, or they do not exist, or they pay not the least attention to us." [3] The Stoics, too, abandoned pagan polytheism for a kind of monotheism, or better, pantheism, while the Cynics and Skeptics were highly critical of the ancient cults in general.

Yet even the commoner who found faith in the ancestral deities salutary did not suppose he really worshiped the idol. It was the god behind the image whom he revered—a supernatural being not confined to lifeless stone. Thus Cicero could write, "Since the gods exist it follows that they are animate beings with a joint control over the one world." [4] However, the image itself had an aesthetic value which was worthy of veneration. What ancient Greek (or modern man) could ascend the acropolis at Athens—through the columned propylaea, the gem-like Nike temple to the right, the pure-lined Erechtheum to the left—and stand before the Parthenon uninspired? Here the transcendent was enshrined; here the eternal was captured in timeworn marble.

But after it has been appraised at highest value, idolatry remains a problem. For one thing, it presupposes a plurality of deities. The problem of polytheism is simple—too many gods. Of course, a variety of deities has always been attractive. Just as man can explain the vicissitudes of war by the notion that certain gods are on the side of Troy and others on the side of the Greeks, so also he can venerate one deity in his business affairs and another in his association with his friends. Not only does this result in a kind of religious schizophrenia in man, it also blurs the reality of God. Although it offers many gods made in the image of man, it fails to acknowledge the transcendent Lord.

Shaping the gods in human image also indicates another difficulty of idolatry. Its gods are manageable. Although the idol only symbolizes the object of adoration, it is itself an object with human characteristics. Not only does the statue of the god look like a man, the very character of the god is thoroughly human. The god loves and hates, laughs and weeps, consorts with women and is jealous of men. Idolatry gives an-

[3] Quoted by A. M. J. Festugière, *Epicurus and His Gods,* tr. C. W. Chilton (Cambridge: Harvard University Press, 1956), p. 51.

[4] *De Natura Deorum,* ii, 31.

thropomorphism concrete expression. Moreover, these gods who are shaped in the image of man are created to do his bidding. Idolatry is utilitarian religion unashamed. The gods fight man's wars, run his errands, heal his ills. As the author of Isa. 44 points out, man cuts down a tree, builds a fire, cooks his food, and from the remains of the wood carves an image—a god, we presume, who will help him fell another tree. But the God who created all things and who judges all man's doings is forgotten.

Nevertheless, idolatry has always had a deceptive attraction. Man needs something outside himself to worship; only as he finds some object of loyalty beyond himself can he escape the persistent sin of egocentricity. Any god, even an idol, offers such an object. Yet the deceptive element is this: The object of adoration is a creation of the hand of man. Thus he escapes himself in worship, but the object of his worship is ultimately himself. Overt egocentricity has been replaced by a devotion to self more subtle and beguiling. This is why idolatry has been such a persistent sin. For although temples to Aphrodite are confined to antiquity, temples enshrining the splendid creations of man's hand and mind are erected on every corner of the modern metropolis.

As well as actual idolatrous worship, the Corinthians were also faced with the opportunity of eating meat which had been offered to idols at a pagan shrine. Apparently this issue was raised by the Christians themselves in their letter to the apostle, for he begins his discussion with the phrase, "Now concerning food offered to idols" (8:1). To the modern mind this seems like a trivial matter; why should a Christian be concerned with pagan sacrifices?

To the ancient, however, this was an issue which could not be avoided. Nilsson reminds us that animal sacrifice was the "best known and most prominent of all the rites of Greek religion." [5] The Greeks were also prudent enough to realize that what was not consumed by the deities was fit for human consumption. In fact, what was offered to the gods was not. To them were dedicated the entrails or perhaps the forelock of the animal's hair. The choice cuts were devoured by the priests or participants in the cultic meal. What remained was sent off

[5] Martin P. Nilsson, *Greek Folk Religion,* p. 74.

to the shops. Thus, out back of most every Hellenistic shrine was a meat market.

In Corinth an inscription has been unearthed marking the location of such a shop in the probable vicinity of the temple of Apollo.[6] The well of one of the shops along the south stoa has yielded a stone fragment reading, "Lucius, the butcher." [7] In Pompeii archaeologists have found a configuration of buildings including both a chapel of the imperial cult and a counter for the selling of sacrificial meat.[8] In the ancient world it was almost impossible to secure meat which had not been offered to an idol.

Moreover, some of the pagan temples appear to have provided auxiliary "clubrooms" which offered social dining as well as the more religious cultic meals. The latter were held in recognition of a host of public occasions—marriage, victory in battle, honor to a hero. The prominence of such dining customs made it difficult for the Corinthian citizen to avoid sacrificial meat. When he was invited out to dinner, it was inevitably served as the main course. For instance, if his host were a devotee of Artemis, a successful hunt would be consummated by an elaborate banquet after the animal had been sacrificed to the patron deity. Could a Christian attend such a party? If he attended should he eat the sacrificial meat?

Hellenistic banquets were fabulous affairs, as one of Petronius' characters indicates:

Let's see, first off we had some roast pork garnished with loops of sausage and flanked with more sausages and some giblets done to a turn. And there were pickled beets and some wholewheat bread made without bleach. . . . Then came a course of cold tart with a mixture of some wonderful Spanish wine and hot honey. . . . Then there were chickpeas and lupins, no end of filberts, and an apple apiece. . . . The main course was a roast of bear meat.

[6] *Corinth—Results of Excavations Conducted by the American School of Classical Studies*, ed. Allen Brown West (Cambridge, Mass.: Harvard University Press, 1931), VII, ii, 102; Henry J. Cadbury, "The Macellum of Corinth," *Journal of Biblical Literature*, LXX (1934), 134 ff.

[7] William A. McDonald, "Archeology and St. Paul's Journeys in Greek Lands," *Biblical Archeologist*, V (1942), 44.

[8] The plan of this group of buildings is presented in Lietzmann's commentary, "Handbuch zum Neuen Testament," p. 52.

. . . It reminds me of roast boar, so I put down about a pound of it. Beside, I'd like to know, if bears eat men, why shouldn't men eat bears? To wind up, we had some soft cheese steeped in fresh wine, a snail apiece, some tripe hash, liver in pastry boats and eggs topped with more pastry and turnips and mustard and beans boiled in the pod and—but enough's enough.[9]

Allowing for some exaggeration and certain differences of taste, it is obvious that a pagan banquet was not to be missed.

The Christians at Corinth, however, did not indulge without some qualms of conscience. Perhaps their judgment had been shaped by the Jews in their midst; these devotees of ancient monotheism considered the idolatrous food anathema. Not only was it not kosher, it was truly tainted by pagan polytheism. Apparently some of the Jerusalem Christians shared this view (cf. Acts 15:29). Paul had evidently said some strong things about paganism on his first visit to Corinth, for the question of the Corinthians reveals a certain sensitivity to the threat of secularism. The word which he uses here for meat sacrificed to idols (*eidōlothuta*) is of Jewish and not pagan origin.[10] Some had even misconstrued his previous letter to recommend a stringent asceticism (5:9 ff.). But, as we have seen, Paul suggests that the church is not to retreat from the world; it must maintain its distinctive witness within this transitory age. The line between the church and the world—the line between Christianity and secular culture—must be clearly drawn. How is this line to be maintained in the face of two practical questions: Can a Christian engage in pagan worship? Can a Christian eat food which has been offered in pagan sacrifice?

II

Paul's answer to the first question is a decisive "no!" The Christian can make no compromise with idolatry. His answer is grounded in profound theological principles.

[9] *The Satyricon,* pp. 64 ff.
[10] Cf. IV Macc. 5:2.

We know that "an idol has no real existence," and that "there is no God but one." For although there may be so-called gods in heaven or on earth—as indeed there are many "gods" and many "lords"—yet for us there is one God, the Father, from whom are all things and for whom we exist, and one Lord, Jesus Christ, through whom are all things and through whom we exist. (8:4-6.)

The basic principle stated here is monotheism. This Paul had learned from his Jewish heritage. In their morning and evening worship the Jews continually repeated the ancient Shema: "Hear, O Israel: The Lord our God is One Lord" (Deut. 6:4). If there is only one God, it is clear that "an idol has no real existence." Therefore, the worship of idols is sheer folly; it is the worship of nothing.

Yet in the minds of some of his readers, the images do represent something. There are many so-called gods and lords in heaven and on earth (vs. 5a). Thus the distorted thoughts of the pagans have turned into gods what in reality are no gods. But once these false forces are recognized as gods, they become a real power over the lives of their devotees. This power, however, is not divine but demonic. As Paul says in chapter 10, "What pagans sacrifice they offer to demons."

Is Paul guilty of inconsistency? In 8:4 he insists that an "idol has no real existence," while in 10:20 he asserts that pagan sacrifice is offered to demons. That Paul shared the common belief in the existence of angelic and demonic powers is evident from passages like Rom. 8:38. Yet in our text he goes so far as to write, "Indeed there are many 'gods' and many 'lords' " (I Cor. 8:5b). The answer to this apparent contradiction is perhaps twofold. On the one hand, Paul's argument may be existential; pagan gods exist for those who acknowledge them to be a reality; for the Christian ("for us," vs. 6) they have no existence at all. On the other, his distinction between gods and demons is clearly drawn. What the pagans suppose to be gods are really demons; only in poetic expression can a demon be construed as a god. The song of Moses supports this.

> They sacrificed to demons which were no gods,
>> to gods they had never known,
> to new gods who had come in of late,
>> whom your fathers had never dreaded (Deut. 32:17).

Paul's positive expression of the monotheistic faith may reflect an early Christian confessional formula.

> There is one God, the Father,
>   from whom are all things and for whom we exist,
> and one Lord, Jesus Christ,
>   through whom are all things and for whom we exist. (8:6.)

J. N. D. Kelley insists that the "formulary character of this is unmistakable," [11] while Oscar Cullmann refers to I Cor. 8:6 as the "most ancient bipartite formula." [12] Thus, this confession was made at the Christian's baptism or at the height of liturgical expression. As we have seen, the apostle prefaces this creedal statement with the phrase "for us." That is, his belief in God and Christ is not grounded in objective observation or rational argument; it is based on existential faith. He knows God as creator through his own experience of the new creation. But if God is acknowledged as creator of all things, it is evident that worship of an idol—some part of God's creation—is absurd. Indeed, it is the root of sin—the confusion of God and his creation. As Paul describes the basic sin of men he says, "They exchanged the truth about God for a lie and worshiped and served the creature rather than the Creator" (Rom. 1:25).

Not only is the object of true worship the Creator of all, he is also Father. This further indicates that Paul is speaking here out of personal experience. God is known intimately as Father. This view the apostle must have gained from his Christian experience, since the Jews of his day stressed the remoteness of the deity. Thus in a time when the Jews considered God too holy to call by name, Paul referred to him as "Abba" (Rom. 8:15; Gal. 4:6)—a term which an Aramaic-speaking child would use exclusively for direct address to his own father, a term which Jesus used in the intimate prayer of Gethsemane (Mark 14:36).[13] If one had such a close and exclusive commitment to the One God, how could he divide that loyalty among false gods or demons?

[11] *Early Christian Creeds* (London: Longmans, Green & Co., 1950), p. 19.

[12] *The Earliest Christian Confessions,* tr. J. K. S. Reid (Naperville, Ill.: Alec R. Allenson, 1949), p. 32.

[13] According to Joachim Jeremias, "The Present Position in the Controversy Concerning the Problem of the Historical Jesus," *Expository Times* LX (1957-58), 337, the term "Abba" as address to God is found in no Jewish prayer prior to the time of Jesus. Jeremias concludes that Jesus invented the usage.

As well as exclusive loyalty to the One God, Paul confesses his obedience to one Lord. The term *kyrios* (lord) has engendered considerable scholarly debate. Wilhelm Bousset's view that the title had its roots in Hellenistic soil,[14] though still maintained by the Bultmann school, has been abandoned by a variety of scholars. Oscar Cullmann has attempted to show that the phrase *marana tha* (our Lord, come! I Cor. 16:22) proves a Palestinian origin of the early confession of Christ as *Kyrios*.[15] Some who favor a Jewish background readily conclude that this word, which could stand for the divine name in the Old Testament, indicates deity when applied to Christ. Thus Cerfaux can write that "God the Father and the Lord are on the same level in Paul's thought." [16]

Although this latter conclusion deserves consideration, the question of the origin of the title "Lord" need not detain us. It is clear that Paul's usage in First Corinthians is determined by Hellenistic backgrounds. He is writing to a Hellenistic audience, and the immediate context of his confession includes reference to the "many gods" and "many lords" of the pagan pantheon. Moreover, he does not use the Aramaic form here, but the Greek *kyrios*. We can agree with Bousset that in I Cor. 8:6 Paul is contrasting the one Lord with the principalities and powers of the pagan cults.[17] The meaning of the former may be determined by reference to the latter.

The lords of the gnostic cults represent cosmic powers. In origin they may have descended from the astral deities—gods of the heavens who controlled the destiny of the earth.[18] The gnostics looked upon these powers as evil; the structure of the cosmos was supported by demonic forces. For Paul, of course, no principality or power can separate one from the love of God (Rom. 8:38), so that gnostic dualism

[14] *Kyrios Christos* (3rd ed. Göttingen: Vandenhoeck & Ruprecht, 1926), pp. 77 ff.

[15] *The Christology of the New Testament,* tr. Shirley C. Guthrie and Charles A. M. Hall (Philadelphia: Westminster Press, 1959), pp. 199 ff. Cf. A. E. J. Rawlinson, *The New Testament Doctrine of the Christ* (London: Longmans, Green, & Co., 1926), pp. 231 ff.; Elias Andrews, *The Meaning of Christ for Paul* (New York and Nashville: Abingdon-Cokesbury Press, 1949), pp. 137 ff.

[16] L. Cerfaux, *Christ in the Theology of St. Paul,* tr. Geoffrey Webb and Adrian Walker (New York: Herder and Herder, 1959), p. 474.

[17] *Kyrios Christos,* p. 99.

[18] Cf. G. H. C. Macgregor, "Principalities and Powers: The Cosmic Background of Paul's Thought," *New Testament Studies,* I (1954-55), 17 ff.

is essentially denied. The apostle lists the powers along with the things of God's creation (Rom. 8:39). They have lost their essential nature, however, and have become what Schlier calls "autonomous self-centeredness."[19] They must be redeemed (Rom. 8:21). In the Christian confession, therefore, Paul affirms the reality of the cosmic order. There is one God, the creator of all things, and one Lord, "through whom are all things." Rather than many lords, Jesus Christ is the ruler of the cosmic order.

The lords of the Hellenistic cults also assert their authority over men. Demonic possession and a host of diseases may be blamed on these evil dominions. More than this, they hold man in a death grip which hurtles him fatefully toward destruction. For Paul the death and resurrection of Christ—a deed perpetrated by these demonic forces themselves (I Cor. 2:8)—has broken this fatal stranglehold on mankind. This is what has led some commentators to refer to Christ's saving accomplishment as a "cosmic redemption."[20] But what can this mean to man? Surely, the apostle is using mythological terminology to suggest that man's being is under the control of powers not his own; that he is captive of forces which deceive his essential nature.[21] This is why he speaks as confession, why his words are set in the context of "for us." Indeed, for the man of faith, there is one God, the Father "for whom we exist," and one Lord, Jesus Christ "through whom we exist." Rather than the bondage to evil, man has the freedom of a new being in Christ.

All the implications that this may have for Pauline Christology cannot be investigated here. Suffice it to say that the apostle's idea of Christ rests on the resurrection faith; it is the risen and triumphant Christ who is called Lord (Phil. 2:9 ff.). The fact that the term *kyrios* translates the divine name in the Old Testament need not force us to the conclusion that Paul is stressing the deity and preexistence of a supernatural being. Certainly the prepositions of our text suggest a sub-

[19] Heinrich Schlier, *Principalities and Powers in the New Testament* (New York: Herder and Herder, 1961), p. 38.

[20] Macgregor, "Principalities and Powers," p. 23.

[21] Cf. Rudolf Bultmann, *Theology of the New Testament,* tr. Kendrick Grobel (New York: Charles Scribner's Sons, 1951), I, 257 ff.

ordination of the Son, since all things are said to be *from* God but only *through* Jesus Christ, the Lord.[22] Questions about the metaphysical nature of the Christ, which so occupied the Nicaean fathers, simply did not occur to the apostle.[23] It is difficult to imagine that Paul, steeped in Jewish monotheism, could entertain the notion of two heavenly persons sitting on the cosmic committee for creation.

Perhaps the reconciliation of Paul's monotheistic heritage with his confession of Christ as Lord may be found in Cullmann's concept of a functional Christology.[24] He insists that the later christological controversies must be disregarded in order to comprehend correctly the biblical idea of Christ.[25] The New Testament is, in this view, not primarily concerned with the nature of the Son, but with his work. Thus, Christ must be viewed as the means of the revelatory and redemptive action of God. He is not to be observed as a person of the same essence with God or as some subordinate half-deity; he is the one through whom God's exclusive claim upon man is made. In just this exclusiveness of God's call is the genius of Jewish monotheism.[26] Consequently, the lordship of Christ is not understood as different from God's; it is the same. To confess Christ as Lord is to acknowledge God as creator of heaven and earth, ruler of men. This confession does not test monotheism, it confirms it.

In context, this confessional standpoint is demanded. The point of the passage is the recognition of the lordship of Christ in contrast with all the pagan lords. The monotheism demanded is not primarily concerned with the existence of the gods apart from their existential reality in the lives of the pagans, but with the absolute character of God's demand. In the muffled tones of the mystery cults one could hear the cry, "Serapis is Lord"; in the measured cadence of the imperial troops, one could hear the shout, "Caesar is *Kyrios*"; but in the church there is an exclusive confession: "Jesus Christ is Lord." Yes, it is in the com-

[22] Cf. I Cor. 15:28.
[23] Cf. Bultmann, *Theology of the New Testament*, I, 191.
[24] *Christology of the New Testament*. Cf., for example, p. 326: "Functional Christology is the only kind which exists."
[25] *Ibid.*, p. 3.
[26] Cf. Werner Foerster and Gottfried Quell, "Lord," *Bible Key Words from Gerhard Kittel's Theologisches Wörterbuch zum Neuen Testament*, tr. J. R. Coates and H. P. Kingdom (New York: Harper & Bros., 1958), II, 78 ff.

munity of faith that Christ is acknowledged as present Lord—this Christ who has triumphed over the last enemy, this Christ who will come at the end to defeat every power—it is in the church that Christ is known now as ruler of heaven and earth. So the Christian can confess no other lord; he can make no compromise with idolatry.

After stating his argument against idolatry on the basis of the Christian confession, Paul goes on to support it with scripture (10:1-13). His is no simple proof-texting, but "existential interpretation." He insists that these things were "written down for our instruction" (vs. 11). Moreover, his concern is not merely with words but with events. Paul is giving the lessons of history—a history of God's deeds for man's salvation, the story of the people of God of whom the Corinthian Christians are now a part. They are the eschatological community, the men of the messianic time "upon whom the end of the ages has come." [27]

The events of the history of God's people, then, become types for the understanding of their role in the present. "I want you to know, brethren, that our fathers were all under the cloud, and all passed through the sea, and all were baptized into Moses in the cloud and in the sea." (10:1-2.) The use of the word baptizō (to baptize) makes it evident that Paul views the Exodus as somehow involving a typological baptism.[28] Apparently passing through the sea and under the cloud are understood as symbolizing this Christian rite. The account in Exodus presents the cloud as leading the Israelites, but the idea that it hovered over them is not lacking (cf. Num. 10:34; Ps. 105:39). The fact that no water actually touched the people has given some commentators pause, but probably Paul sees the complete envelopment in sea and cloud as typifying immersion. Thus, the people of God at the

---

[27] In spite of the fact that Paul usually does not refer to the end by the plural of the term telos (telē), an eschatological meaning of the end of the ages or the point where the two ages intersect is probable. Cf. Jean Héring, The First Epistle of Saint Paul to the Corinthians, tr. A. W. Heathcote and P. J. Allcock (London: Epworth Press, 1962). The view of M. M. Bogle, "ta telē tōn aionōn I Corinthians x. 11—A Suggestion," Expository Times, LXVII (1956), 246 ff., that telos here should be translated "mystery" is not convincing.

[28] G. Gander, "I Cor. 10:2 parle-t-il du baptême?" Revue d' Histoire et de Philosophie Religieuses, XXXVII (1957), 97 ff., argues that no idea of baptism is intended in the passage; baptizō here is a mistranslation of an Aramaic term meaning "to pass." This argument is hardly worth serious attention.

moment of their salvation were baptized. Just as Christians are baptized into Christ, so their fathers had been baptized into Moses—the prophet who prefigured him.

Besides, the ancients had partaken of a kind of eucharist, for

> all ate the same spiritual food
> and all drank the same spiritual drink (vss. 3-4, WB).

The food, of course, is to be identified as the miraculous manna, that "fine, flake-like thing, fine as hoarfrost on the ground" (Exod. 16:14). That this food could typify the bread of the Lord's Supper is seen in the Greek version of Ps. 78:24 (77:24, LXX) where manna is called the "bread of heaven."

The cup of the Eucharist, however, is symbolized by the supernatural water which sustained Israel in her wilderness wanderings. Paul speaks of the "spiritual Rock which followed them" (vs. 4, KJV), and thereby refers to the stone which Moses struck to secure water for the thirsting pilgrims (Num. 20:7 ff.). But when he states that the rock followed them, he seems to refer to a rabbinic legend in which the rock was a sort of ambulatory well which accompanied the children of Israel throughout the entire wilderness period, providing a perpetual water supply.[29] Perhaps the rabbis identified the water of Meribah (Num. 20:13) with the water of the well at Beer (Num. 21:16) which supplied Israel at a later time.

Some scholars find it difficult to imagine that Paul could have employed a legend so puerile,[30] but they seem to forget that Paul had been to school where just such absurdity was taught, and that his idea of baptism in the sea and cloud, not to mention his interpretation of muzzling the ox (9:9 ff.) and the baptism of the dead (15:29), is about as farfetched.

However, the next step in his exegesis is still more startling—"the

[29] Cf. Hermann L. Strack and Paul Billerbeck, *Kommentar zum Neuen Testament aus Talmud und Midrasch* (München: Beck, 1926), III, 406 ff.; Louis Ginzberg, *The Legends of the Jews,* tr. Henrietta S. Zeld (Philadelphia: Jewish Publication Society, 1911), III, 50 ff.

[30] Cf. E. Earle Ellis, "A Note on First Corinthians 10:4," *Journal of Biblical Literature,* LXXVI (1957), 53 ff. The weakness of Ellis' argument is his failure to deal with Paul's statement that the rock "followed them."

Rock was Christ." Some interpreters have understood this as a profound christological statement; the identification of the rock and Christ argues for the latter's preexistence.[31] That theological point can be supported better elsewhere (e.g., Phil. 2:6 ff.), for surely Paul does not intend an absolute identification of Christ and this ancient stone. His view that Israel was baptized "into Moses" (vs. 2) does not mean to suggest that Moses and Christ are one and the same. Rather, the rock, like Moses, stands for the gift of life which came to the Israelites by the act of God. Since this action provided a spiritual drink, it was not unlike the gift of life in Christ—a gift remembered and present in the church's Eucharist. Perhaps, in view of his confessional statement, this text does say something about Paul's idea of "preexistence": the gift of life, like creation, comes from God *through* the one Lord who embodies God's redemptive activity.[32]

But the point of all this is that just as the church has received the spiritual benefits of God's redemption, so Israel had received "baptism" and the "Lord's Supper." Neither, however, could presuppose upon these blessings. Of the Israelites it can be said, "With most of them God was not pleased; for they were overthrown in the wilderness" (vs. 5). The cause of their overthrow was idolatry, and this same thing could happen at Corinth. "Now these things are warnings for us, not to desire evil as they did. Do not be idolaters as some of them were." (vss. 6-7.)

Then follows a recital of Israel's apostasy and a record of God's wrath. First, Paul warns that the church should not "desire evil as they did" (vs. 6). He probably has in mind passages like Num. 11:4 ff., where the Israelites are depicted as craving the fleshpots of Egypt even though God had given them manna from heaven; the Christians at Corinth are thereby reminded of their longing for the plenitude of pagan meals in spite of their participation in the chaste service of the Lord's Supper.

When the apostle proceeds to criticize Israelite idolatry and says that "the people sat down to eat and drink and rose up to dance," he has in mind the golden calf incident of Exod. 32. The word translated

[31] For example, Héring, *The First Epistle of Saint Paul to the Corinthians.*
[32] Cf. Cullmann, *Christology of the New Testament,* pp. 235 ff.

"dance" here can be rendered "to play" or "sport"; the licentiousness of pagan ritual is suggested, and the close connection of idolatry and immorality is implied (cf. Rom. 1:18 ff.).

Paul's warning, "We must not indulge in immorality as some of them did" (vs. 8), refers to Israel's consorting with the daughters of Moab (Num. 25:1 ff.), where false worship is again involved. The plague which God sent in punishment claimed the lives of 24,000 men in a day (Num. 25:9); Paul's record of 23,000 is perhaps a slip of memory involving a confusion with the 3,000 of Exod. 32:28.[33] His mention of Israel's grumbling reminds the Christians of the continual dissatisfaction of Israel (Num. 14:36; 16:11) with the ways of God—a murmuring which tempted God to further miraculous deeds and tested his patience. Just this sort of grumbling led the Lord to send pestilence upon his people—fiery serpents whose sting brought death to many of Israel (Num. 21:6 ff.). The grumbling mentioned in 10:10 perhaps refers to the revolt of Korah, Dathan, and Abiram (Num. 16), where the violators were swallowed up by the earth; the passage makes no mention of the Destroyer, but Paul's usage rests, no doubt, on later Jewish legends of the angel of destruction (I Chr. 21:15).

The relevance of all this is clear. Just as Israel received the spiritual benefits of God but resisted his will, so the church may reject God in spite of his spiritual blessings. The temptations which continually face the people of God are summed up in idolatry—the worship of that which is not God, revolt against the Almighty. The point of danger is seen in the problem of eating; the Corinthians are attracted to the table of the demons. False worship, particularly of this sort, leads readily to immorality. The answer of the righteous God to this kind of conduct is judgment, and its end is destruction and death.

In I Cor. 10:14 ff. Paul applies his principles on idolatry to the specific problem at Corinth. His admonition is that the Corinthians should not engage in pagan ceremonies. The situation he is describing here is not the ordinary social meal in a pagan house (10:27), or even the luncheon of some civic club in the auxiliary room of a pagan temple. Paul is talking about actual idolatrous worship. Apparently some people

---

[33] Or perhaps the mistake results from a scribal misreading of the abbreviation for "four" (*trs*) as representing "three," as Héring suggests.

of Corinth believed membership could be maintained in the cult as well as in the church; reverence could be offered to the one God along with the many. Paul's stern advice is clear: "Shun the worship of idols" (vs. 14).

The basis for this flight from idolatry is found in the central act of Christian worship—the Lord's Supper.

> The cup of blessing which we bless,
>   is it not a participation in the blood of Christ?
> The bread which we break,
>   is it not a participation in the body of Christ? (10:16.)

A full discussion of this rite must be postponed until the next chapter, but already it is apparent that partaking of the Supper puts the worshiper into a particular relationship to the present Lord. The background to this view can be found in contemporary cultic beliefs. "The sacrificial feast," writes Nilsson, "was in a way a communion, a shared meal, which united gods and men in a bond whose inviolable sanctity is an outstanding feature of all older culture." [34]

But in this context of Old Testament reminiscences Paul points out that the same thing is true for Judaism. "Consider the practice of Israel; are not those who eat the sacrifices partners in the altar?" (vs. 18.) The use of "altar" here seems surprising; is it not with *God* that the worshiper finds communion? Perhaps Paul is employing a typical Jewish circumlocution wherein the altar stands for the deity, but more likely he wants to stress the parallel points of contact—the table of the Lord and the table of the pagan cult-meal. It is interesting that an early Hellenistic inscription has been found which refers to the piece of temple furniture on which meats of pagan sacrifice were placed for distribution to the devotees as the "table of the gods." [35] Paul, however, will not grant this sort of respect to the pagan altar. Worship there brings one into fellowship not with gods but with demons. Thus his conclusion is clear:

[34] Martin P. Nilsson, *Greek Piety*, tr. Herbert Jennings Rose (Oxford: Clarendon Press, 1948), pp. 11 ff.

[35] Quoted by Royden Keith Yerkes, *Sacrifice in Greek and Roman Religions and Early Judaism* (New York: Charles Scribner's Sons, 1952), p. 108.

You cannot drink of the cup of the Lord and the cup of demons.
You cannot partake of the table of the Lord and the table of demons (vs. 21).

The implication of these principles is obvious; the Corinthians must not engage in idolatry. Paul had reminded the Thessalonians that they had "turned to God from idols, to serve a living and true God" (I Thess. 1:9), and his implication was that they should not turn back. The Christian can be content to worship nothing else than the one God—creator of heaven and earth and Lord of all men. Should they scale the lofty Acrocorinth to view the beauty of the snowcapped Parnassus, the Corinthian Christians dare not pause at the summit to do homage at the shrine of Aphrodite.

III

Although Paul's answer to idolatry is unequivocal, his instruction in regard to food offered to idols is not so clear. On occasion he can say, "I will never eat meat" (8:13), and at other times he remarks, "Eat whatever is set before you without raising any question" (10:27). It is obvious that the apostle is again involved in relativity, but what decides the difference? On what principles can the Christian say "yes" or "no" when the tempting platter is passed?

First, Paul enunciates the principle of *knowledge*. Some in the church seem to be saying, "All of us possess knowledge" (8:1). These may be intellectuals who would agree with Paul's view that an "idol has no real existence" (8:4), but probably they are gnostic Christians who suppose that the acquisition of divine knowledge frees one from any qualms about participating in any of the expressions of pagan culture. They, too, agree that an idol stands for nothing, and if the image is nothing, how can it possibly taint the sacrificial food? Paul agrees with this conclusion when he says, "Eat whatever is sold in the meat market without raising any question" (10:25).

Although Paul agrees with the conclusion which this knowledge attains, he is not content with its character. This sort of knowledge, he says, "puffs up" (*phusioō*, vs. 1). That is, this kind of knowing, correct though it may be, falsely inflates the ego. If Paul is scolding the intellectuals here, he may be suggesting that their knowledge comes by the wrong method; it supposes that absolute truth is to be found by human effort, so that it inevitably engenders human pride. The Gnostics, with their notion of a superior gift of wisdom, are even more susceptible to this sort of sin. Paul punctures their pride: "If any one imagines that he knows something, he does not yet know as he ought to know" (8:2). Moreover, this egocentric kind of knowledge has the wrong object. It supposes that truth is to be equated with the data which man's mind can produce or the gnostic secrets which man can receive—puny details about idols and gods. Its devotees fancy that they know *something*.

The "object" of true knowledge, on the other hand, is not a thing to be possessed by man's mind; it is God himself, the Almighty One who possesses us. God cannot be reduced to fact or doctrines; with the mind's eye, no one has seen God at any time (John 1:18). When God passes by, man remains hidden in the cleft of the rock; he sees God's back but never his face (Exod. 33:23). The way to know God, then, is not by the exercise of intellectual effort, since that can result in a sort of mental idolatry. The true method of knowing is *agape*—spontaneous personal commitment which forfeits all selfish striving. "If one loves God, he is known by him." (8:3.) Paul's doctrine of knowledge rests on a view of divine revelation wherein God's knowledge of man has priority.

But how can man love God unless he has previously known God? The idea of man's love for God is rarely found in the Pauline writings; as Nygren reminds us, the normal response of man to God is said to be "faith." [36] Perhaps Paul is here stressing the personal character of God's revelation, since it is evident that man comes to know God in response to God's self-manifestation. As Paul implies, first "one is known by him"; or as he writes to the Galatians, "Now that you have come to know God," and then corrects himself, "or rather to be known by God" (4:9). Man comes to know God only as God first knows him.

This grounding of the idea of knowledge in a concept of revelation seems to play into the hand of the Gnostics. They too stressed the

[36] Anders Nygren, *Agape and Eros,* tr. Philip S. Watson (rev. ed. Philadelphia: Westminster Press, 1953), pp. 123 ff.

priority of the divine *gnōsis* and the necessity of enlightenment by divine disclosure. However, Paul's use of gnostic categories is consciously and radically different. For him, knowledge is neither theoretical nor mystical, it is practical and ethical. Its content is not secret data but divine love. Its possession is not human achievement but is grounded in the God who acts. This knowledge, for all its external similarities, has no community with Hellenistic *gnōsis;* rather, it reflects the Old Testament concepts of confession and commitment.[37] On the basis of gnostic inspiration the question of meat offered to idols is of no moment; on the ground of God's *agape* it is of great importance.

On this same ground is based Paul's second principle—the *love of the brother.* Apparently the enlightened members of the community considered eating sacrificial food a badge of their liberty. They may have even held that those who had scruples about such things ought to be shocked into maturity. The Gnostics, therefore, found that their freedom to eat was a positive value to be exploited. Although Paul agrees with their conclusion about the character of sacrificial meat, he does not agree with their view that eating affords some special Christian grace. "Food will not commend us to God," he says. "We are no worse off if we do not eat, and no better off if we do." (8:8.) Since there is no special benefit in eating, those who are free to eat or to abstain need to govern their action by other concerns.

Just such a concern is presented in the weaker brethren of the church. The "weak" are those who do not possess the knowledge that idols cannot taint food, and thus are weak of conscience (vs. 7).[38] That is, their conscience is defective, so that it is too easily defiled. When they commit an act not really wrong in itself, but wrong by their own inadequate standards, pain and even self-destruction may result. On the question of meat offered to idols, no amount of argument on the part of the strong—those whose consciences have been educated to know better—can convince them that an "idol has no real existence."

[37] Cf. Rudolf Bultmann, "Gnosis," *Bible Key Words from Gerhard Kittel's Theologisches Wörterbuch zum Neuen Testament* (New York: Harper & Bros., 1958), II, 41 ff.

[38] On the use of "conscience" in this passage, cf. C. A. Pierce, *Conscience in the New Testament,* "Studies in Biblical Theology, No. 15" (Naperville, Ill.: Alec R. Allenson, 1955), pp. 75 ff.

However, the strong are responsible for the effect of their example. Suppose the weaker brother sees the enlightened Christian, whose conscience permits him to eat meat indiscriminately, sitting in the temple clubroom or enjoying a feast at his pagan neighbor's house. The weaker brother, following the precedent of the strong, may indulge with the result that his own conscience is violated. As a consequence, warns Paul, "By your knowledge this weak man is destroyed" (8:11). He concludes, "Therefore, if food is a cause of my brother's falling, I will never eat meat, lest I cause my brother to fall" (8:13). As he says to the Romans, "If your brother is being injured by what you eat, you are no longer walking in love" (Rom. 14:15).

It may be that a third principle is also implied—the principle of *freedom*. Note, for instance, that the strong brother is addressed here. He is the one who can freely make the decision to indulge or refrain. He can buy what is sold in the marketplace without concern of conscience. He can attend a pagan's party and eat whatever is served without raising questions. Obviously, the weak cannot; his conscience prevents a free decision. The strong, therefore, need not deny his strength; his conscience, Paul agrees, is correct. He must not surrender his freedom, for then he could make no responsible decision.

Suppose, however, the strong Christian is sitting at a pagan dinner party freely eating what is set before him without raising questions. When someone slips up behind him and whispers that "this has been offered in sacrifice" (10:28), he must pass up the beefsteak "out of consideration" for the man who informed him, that is, providing the informant is really weak. It is possible that this alert table critic is not actually weak at all; his conscience will not be defiled by eating meat since he never touches the stuff. He is not weak, but super-strong. He uses his own overscrupulousness to bolster his own self-righteousness and to beat his liberal brother over the head. It is of these fastidious brethren that Paul complains, "Why should my freedom be judged by another man's scruples?" (10:29.) [39] The pressure of the super-strong to curb Christian liberty must be staunchly resisted. As Paul

[39] Héring, *First Corinthians*, p. 99, interprets this to mean that just as the strong cannot judge the weak, so Paul forbids "the weak to judge the strong, or . . . to insult them."

says to them elsewhere, "Why do you pass judgment on your brother?" (Rom. 14:10.) Therefore, as eating meat cannot be a tin badge of undisciplined liberty, neither can abstinence be a cudgel of scrupulous authoritarianism.

IV

Paul's answers to the questions of idolatry and meat offered to idols imply basic ethical principles. It is obvious that relativity and responsibility are again involved. On the issue of idolatry, an absolute can be declared: There can be no compromise with paganism; absolutely no worship of idols is to be tolerated. On the matter of eating meat, however, no definite answer is consistently offered. Sometimes the Corinthians are told to eat without question, while on other occasions they are required never to eat meat. As we have seen, the difference of demand rests on different situations. When the strong brother is alone or in the company of like-minded Christians, he may eat whatever is served. When he is in the presence of the weak, he must refrain from fear of causing these unenlightened to stumble. He makes this decision on the basis of the principles of knowledge, love, and freedom—principles which contain no absolute, but require free and responsible decision. It is implied that the weak Christian can eat pagan food under no circumstances; he is not able to make a real decision in this matter.

Those who are free, however, must make a decision and one which is responsible to their Christian commitment. We have seen this implied in Paul's answer to the problem of sexual morality in chapter 7 and the question of civil justice in chapter 6. Here, however, the necessity of responsibility is explicitly demanded. Paul even goes so far as to suggest that an act not inherently evil—like eating meat offered to idols—is sin (8:12). Such an act, though not wrong in itself, is viewed as sin because it is in clear violation of the principle of the love of the brother. However, this principle rests on still more profound motivation. Paul does not urge his readers to respect the weakness of their brethren for humanistic reasons—because they have some special value as men, true though that may be. For Paul, the brother has value because of what God has done for him; he is the "brother for whom Christ died" (8:11).

This principle of relatively responsible decision on the basis of God's revelation in Christ is also illustrated by Paul's discussion of his ministry in chapter 9. There he insists on his freedom, but acknowledges that such freedom demands responsibility. "Am I not free? Am I not an apostle?" he asks (vs. 1). If he is so recognized, then his rights as an apostle must be respected. He has the right to be accompanied by a wife, as do the brothers of the Lord and Cephas (vs. 5). He has a right to financial support for his mission, just as a soldier, a vine keeper, and a shepherd deserve a share of the fruits of their labor (vs. 7).

Actually, Paul's argument in defense of his ministerial rights is not as good as the point itself. He tries to argue, for instance, that his conclusion has scriptural support. "Do I say this on human authority?" he asks. "Does not the law say the same?" (9:8.) Then he proceeds to quote Deut. 25:4, "You shall not muzzle an ox when it is treading out the grain." The point of the ancient code, of course, was to allow the working beast the privilege of a small share in the produce. Paul's exegesis, however, comes as a shock to the modern animal lover. "Is it for oxen that God is concerned? Does he not speak entirely for our sake?" (vss. 9-10.) [40] The answer to the first question, in spite of Paul, is "yes"; it *is* for oxen that God is concerned, as he is for all his creatures. The answer to the second is "no"; he does not speak for our sake, and the law didn't even have the apostles in mind. Thus when Paul concludes, "It was written for our sake," he engages in a form of "existential exegesis" which has no justification.

Despite the flimsiness of Paul's argument it is no doubt true that an apostle has a right to financial support from the church. "The plowman should plow in hope and the thresher thresh in hope of a share in the crop." "If we have sown spiritual good among you," Paul continues, "is it too much if we reap your material benefits?" (9:10-11.) Thus,

---

[40] Hermann L. Strack and Paul Billerbeck, *Kommentar zum Neuen Testament*, III, 385, give illustrations of the application of this text to man, and of the use of other allegorical devices on the part of the rabbis.

his argument from analogy carries weight, so that when he concludes, "If others share this rightful claim upon you, do not we still more," (vs. 12) most of the Corinthians would be compelled to answer "yes."

But the striking thing is that after he has argued at such length defending his rights, Paul refuses to request them. "We have not," he says, "made use of this right" (9:12). He has not made use of it even though the "Lord commanded that those who proclaim the gospel should get their living by the gospel" (vs. 14). When he refers to a command of the Lord, the apostle may have in mind traditions about Jesus' commission of the twelve, where the master urged his men to enter a house and stay there until they moved on to the next village (cf. Mark 6:10). This ideal also has the support of Old Testament analogy, for "those who are employed in the temple service get their food from the temple, and those who serve at the altar share in the sacrificial offerings" (9:13)—a statement which presupposes texts like Deut. 18:1. Yet, in spite of Old Testament authority and even a word from the Lord, Paul continually refuses to accept Corinthian contributions. He says, "I have made no use of any of these rights, nor am I writing this to secure any such provision" (vs. 15).

When we read this adamant statement, it is easy to assume that Paul universally refused financial support. Yet anyone who has studied his epistle to the Philippians knows that the apostle had received offerings from them not only once but twice (Phil. 4:16). How is it that Paul would accept financial aid from one church and refuse it from another? Obviously, his principle of relativity is again involved. Financial support, like meat offered to idols, is not wrong in itself. It may be refused or received depending on the situation in response to the revelation of God.

What is this absolute by which the relative judgment must be responsibly made? In the context of this discussion of the ministry, it is the gospel. As Paul says in vs. 12, "We endure anything rather than put an obstacle in the way of the gospel of Christ." Apparently acceptance of financial aid from the Corinthian church would have distracted attention from the purpose of the mission—proclamation of the word of God. Perhaps passing the plate would have led to an identification of Paul as one of the many "peddlers of God's word" (II

Cor. 2:17). The gospel, indeed, is proclaimed by no human choice; it is preached in response to the divine demand. "For necessity is laid upon me," says Paul. "Woe to me if I do not preach the gospel!" (9:16.) [41] The reward which the apostle receives, then, is no gift of Corinthian coin; it is the free proclamation of the gospel with all its divine power (vs. 18).

Paul performs his entire ministry in this sort of responsible relativity.[42] "Though I am free from all men," he writes, "I have made myself a slave to all" (9:19). Absolutely free, Paul puts himself under obligation. This servitude is in turn responsible to God's commission; he makes himself a slave to all, in order that he "might win the more" (vs. 19). His freedom allows him to become a Jew to the Jews; to establish a rapport with the children of Israel, Paul can even take the stance of one under the law. He does this in order to win those who are under the law, but not so as to jeopardize his own freedom. He is not himself under the law (vs. 20); he does not submit to Jewish legalism.

On the other hand, "to those outside the law" (vs. 21) Paul assumes the stance of an ordinary Hellenistic man. His obligation to proclaim the gospel to the Gentiles—his purpose of winning those outside the law—drives him out into the forum and into the marketplace. However, his freedom from the law does not release him from divine obligation. Paul is not "without law toward God but under the law of Christ" (vs. 21). His freedom and responsibility are measured in relation to an absolute—the will of God, the commission to the gospel. Thus the apostle can confess, "I have become all things to all men, that I might by all means save some. I do it all for the sake of the gospel" (vss. 22-23).

Most important, Paul implies that a responsible decision in all these ethical matters must be made. He sees himself, therefore, as standing constantly under the demand of moral discipline. To illustrate this idea, Paul reminds his readers of a familiar sight—the training for the

[41] For an incisive exegetical study of this passage, cf. Ernst Käsemann, "Eine paulinische Variation des "amor fati,'" *Zeitschrift für Theologie und Kirche*, LVI (1959), 138 ff. Käsemann points out (p. 151) that since the proclamation rests on necessity, the idea of reward is an impossibility.

[42] Cf. H. Chadwick, "'All Things to All Men' (I Cor. IX. 22)," *New Testament Studies*, I (1954-55), 261 ff.

celebrated Isthmian games which were held at Corinth every second year. "Every athlete exercises self-control in all things." (9:25.) So must even an apostle. The Corinthians were familiar, too, with the bouts of the arena; their theater had been equipped in recent times to accommodate such gladiatorial contests. So Paul remarks, "I do not box as one beating the air" (vs. 26). Even a minister of the gospel must be responsible to the restrictive discipline of God. "I pommel my body and subdue it, lest after preaching to others I myself should be disqualified." (vs. 27.)

Of course, when Paul suggests that the authority for these decisions is grounded in the gospel, he really asserts that the locus of authority is Christ. The gospel, as we have seen, is the dynamic proclamation of Christ; it is the powerful event in which God's redemptive work in Christ is reenacted. Just as the principle of love for the brother is qualified by the identification of the brother as the one "for whom Christ died," so all ethical decisions must be made in response to God's revelation in Christ. The character of love is measured against the Cross; the quality of holiness is exposed in the light of the living Lord. The motivating force behind all Christian action must be the mind of Christ—the mind which moves the disciple to take on the form of a servant, becoming obedient unto death (Phil. 2:5 ff.).

Yet, beyond the revelation in Christ stands God himself. Though Jesus Christ is Lord, there is the "one God, the Father, from whom are all things and for whom we exist" (8:6). Christ is only the one through whom his creative power and ultimate lordship is manifest. In the end God will be all in all (15:28). The final principle for determining action on these ethical questions is praise to the Almighty. "So, whether you eat or drink, or whatever you do, do all to the glory of God." (10:31.) Thus, one can eat what is set before him, for "the earth is the Lord's, and everything in it" (10:26). This text is the benediction which Jews of Paul's day were required to offer over every meal. That Paul has this kind of grace at meals in mind is seen in vs. 30: "If I partake with thankfulness, why am I denounced because of that for which I give thanks?" But the whole Christian life is this sort of thanksgiving—giving honor to God in response for his grace unto us. As Paul writes to the Romans:

He who observes the day, observes it in honor of the Lord. He also who eats, eats in honor of the Lord, since he gives thanks to God; while he who abstains, abstains in honor of the Lord and gives thanks to God. None of us lives to himself, and none of us dies to himself. If we live, we live to the Lord, and if we die, we die to the Lord; so then, whether we live or whether we die, we are the Lord's. For to this end Christ died and lived again, that he might be Lord both of the dead and of the living (14:6-9).

It is in Christ that God's glory is revealed. Apart from him we know neither God's glory nor how to glorify God. "For it is God who said, 'Let light shine out of darkness,' who has shone in our hearts to give the light of the knowledge of the glory of God in the face of Christ." (II Cor. 4:6.) "And we all, with unveiled face, beholding the glory of the Lord, are being changed into his likeness from glory to glory." (II Cor. 3:18.)

V

Can Paul's advice be useful today? It is simply trite to suggest that the contemporary society is plagued by secularism. Some fifteen years ago a symposium seriously considered "Christianity's challenge to the secular spirit of our age." [43] According to that analysis, the real problem of our culture was its divorce from faith. "Secularism," wrote Leroy E. Loemker, "is our failure to let God be God in our lives. Its nature is neither to affirm nor to deny religious faith, but to live indifferently to it." [44]

In the meantime, however, America has become interested in religion. Prominent citizens have written of their faiths, a revival has swept the country, church membership has been on the rise, church buildings have been erected. The resulting "religion in general" has lacked depth. Though four fifths of all Americans acknowledge the Bible to be the "revealed word of God," when asked to name the first four books of

[43] J. Richard Spann, ed., *The Christian Faith and Secularism* (New York and Nashville: Abingdon-Cokesbury Press, 1948).
[44] "The Nature of Secularism," *ibid*, p. 11.

the New Testament, over half of these same faithful folk could not even mention one.[45] "I Believe" was a popular song, but the object of belief remained the unknown god—the "man upstairs," a "living doll," or ghost riders in the sky. We knew the tune, but had never really learned the words.

But just when the world was getting superficially interested in religion, the church was becoming increasingly conformed to the world. Will Herberg points out that "every aspect of contemporary religious life reflects this paradox—pervasive secularism amid mounting religiosity." [46] At just the time the revival was most successful, the advocates of the return to religion themselves criticized our culture as becoming increasingly secular. The forces which were shaping contemporary culture invaded the church—the pressure of the organization, the push to conform. Paul Harrison has suggested that one of the minor organizations of one of our major American denominations offered a structural chart which "resembles closely the bureaucratic plan of Standard Oil of New Jersey." [47]

When these forces invaded, the church surrendered without firing a shot—in fact, without even recognizing that there was a battle. Thus, the church soon took on the shape of many other social organisms. Whyte writes of the little girl who is said to have become dissatisfied with the church. "I don't want to hear about how Christian people live," she told her mother. "I want to learn about God." [48] Some, on the other hand, had learned so much about him that the God of Abraham, Isaac, and Jacob seemed to be a really nice fellow.[49] Such a cozy sort of God would be interested in doing all kinds of things for his people, so that "religion has been made ulterior to almost every conceivable human need from nationalism and free enterprise to business success and 'praying your fat away.'" [50]

Little wonder that such a religion would find followers. The religious

---

[45] Will Herberg, *Protestant, Catholic, Jew*, p. 14.
[46] *Ibid.*
[47] Paul M. Harrison, "Church and the Laity Among Protestants," *Annals of the American Academy of Political and Social Science*, November, 1960, p. 42.
[48] *The Organization Man*, p. 372.
[49] Marty, *The New Shape of American Religion*, pp. 31 ff.
[50] Sydney E. Ahlstrom, "Theology and the Present-Day Revival," *Annals of the American Academy of Political and Social Science*, November, 1960, p. 26.

revival was popular.[51] Why not? It used the same techniques as Madison Avenue; its prophets wore gray flannel and chatted with the president. It had all the answers and none of the questions. Indeed, that was the striking feature of the recent return to religion. Rather than challenging some cultural evil of the day—white slavery or the liquor traffic—as had the older revivals, this new resurgence of piety challenged nothing more specific than sin.[52] It propagated the religion of what Peter Berger has called the "OK world" [53]—a world in which everything was coming up roses, and religion was cultivating the garden.

Worse than this, religion can be the very force which supports the evils of the culture.[54] Thus, in the South, a primary defender of a demonic racial injustice is often the church. The minister not only prays at football games, he may open the meeting of the white citizens' council. The very society which is plagued by an empty activism finds sanction in the busy church. Here women, who hire all of their housework done, do penitential acts in the church's kitchen to atone for their sins of omission in society.[55]

As well as this superficial interest in religion on the part of society, and the captivity of the church by secular forces, there has been a cleavage between religion and culture. Religion has been relegated to one phase of life, secular values to another. This is especially true in the suburbs. "When our typical church member leaves suburbia in the morning," writes Berger, "he leaves behind him the person that played with the children, mowed the lawn, chatted with the neighbors—and went to church. His actions now become dominated by a radically different logic—the logic of business, industry, politics, or whatever other sector of public life the individual is related to. In this second life of his the church is totally absent." [56]

Some theologians, bothered by this split between church and society, have called for a more secular Christianity. Thus Bonhoeffer has raised

---

[51] Cf. Eckardt, *The Surge of Piety in America.*

[52] Cf. Marty, *New Shape of American Religion,* pp. 6 ff.

[53] *The Noise of Solemn Assemblies* (Garden City, N. Y.: Doubleday & Co., 1961), p. 93.

[54] Cf. Peter L. Berger, *The Precarious Vision* (Garden City, N. Y.: Doubleday & Co., 1961), pp. 111 ff.

[55] Cf. Winter, *The Suburban Captivity of the Churches,* pp. 97 ff.

[56] *Noise of Solemn Assemblies,* p. 37.

the question: "How do we speak . . . in a secular fashion of God?" [57] Van Buren has recently asked, "How can the Christian who is himself a secular man understand his faith in a secular way?" [58] This point of view, to use Bonhoeffer's terminology, believes the world has "come of age." The old religious forms and phrases are no longer meaningful to modern man. What is needed in our time is a "religionless Christianity," since man has glossed over his irreligion with a thin veneer of religiosity. The man of faith must recognize the essential "worldliness" of Christianity, or as Paul admonished us in chapter 5, the church must remain in the world. Bonhoeffer's view, of course, is not motivated by an endeavor to make faith easy for modern man. Rather, worldliness is of the essence of Christianity. "Later I discovered and am still discovering up to this very moment," he writes from prison, "that it is only by living completely in this world that one learns to believe." [59]

But how is one to live *in* the world without becoming *of* the world? How can Christianity be secular without becoming secularized? Paul's answer may still be relevant. For one thing, the root problem is polytheism. As H. Richard Niebuhr has shown, modern man is plagued by a plethora of gods.[60] He worships society, the nation, his social group; but the one beyond the many, the God of radical monotheism, is remote and rejected. True enough, man may suppose that he worships the one God of Jesus and Paul, but his life of divided loyalties and easy pluralism belies the creed he recites on Sunday. As in Paul's day this henotheism or outright polytheism takes the form of idolatry. Man really imagines that he worships something, but what he adores is the work of his own hand or the creation of his own mind. He builds gods in his own image, erects their shrine in his suburban den, and bows down nightly to do obeisance. What he worships is at base himself,

[57] Dietrich Bonhoeffer, *Prisoner for God—Letters and Papers from Prison,* ed. Eberhard Bethge, tr. Reginald H. Fuller (New York: The Macmillan Company, 1954), p. 57.

[58] Paul M. van Buren, *The Secular Meaning of the Gospel* (New York: The Macmillan Company, 1963), p. 2. Van Buren's attempt to restate the gospel in terms of linguistic analysis, however, takes a line quite different from that suggested by Bonhoeffer.

[59] *Prisoner for God,* p. 169.

[60] *Radical Monotheism and Western Culture* (New York: Harper and Row, 1960).

116

and this sort of egocentrism is the essence of sin. Paul's demand is clear: "Shun the worship of idols" (I Cor. 10:14).

Of course, one of the real problems of the modern Christian is to recognize an idol when he sees one. One of the first things to be done in clarifying the issue is to move the idols out of the church. As Paul warns:

You cannot drink of the cup of the Lord and the cup of demons.
You cannot partake of the table of the Lord and the table of demons (I Cor. 10:21).

But so long as the church measures her success by the standards of the world, so long as it confuses activity with service, so long as it mistakes organization for divine commission, the believer will not know whether he has come to the church of the living God or to the shrine of human achievement.

In the latter, meat is offered to idols. That is, man is called to partake of things not essentially wrong in themselves but potential stumbling blocks to the brother. Man, for instance, is asked to vote where no clearcut choice is possible. He needs Paul's principle of knowledge— a comprehension of the issues involved, a cognizance of the power structures of this age, an understanding of how justice works in power. Or, the Christian man may be invited to the boss's cocktail party, and is tempted to heed the scriptural admonition to take a "little wine for the stomach's sake" (I Tim. 5:23, KJV); but notices his brother sitting by—a chronic alcoholic who drinks only to the damage of his conscience, not to mention his job and family. "And so by your knowledge," says Paul, "this weak man is destroyed, the brother for whom Christ died" (I Cor. 8:11).

It is the Christocentric principle which is basic to all our ethical action in the secular society. Christ has come to us in the flesh to show that God works in the world for the redemption of man. In the world the church must remain to do his work. Christ has come to set us free —free to make decisions, free from the bondage of the overscrupulous, yet under obligation to decide, under demand to make responsible decisions even over the trivial, even about meat offered to idols. All our actions, no matter how small, stand under the call of God. The

117

character of that demand is revealed in Christ, who emptied himself to take on the form of a servant, becoming obedient unto death. In that death we see the love of God—a love which demands our obedience, which drives us out into the world to express that love. This is the love which judges all our actions when they fall short of the glory of God. Nothing judges us so severely as the cross of Christ. Nothing so demands our discipline as the demand of the suffering servant of God. Yet, the Cross which judges us is the Cross which redeems us; the love which compels us is the love which forgives us. The Cross is the symbol of the intersection of God's judgment and God's mercy; before it we confess.

> For us there is one God, the Father,
>   from whom are all things
>   and for whom we exist,
> and one Lord, Jesus Christ,
>   through whom are all things
>   and through whom we exist. (I Cor. 8:6.)

V
THE PROBLEM OF WORSHIP

It is not surprising that men who are tempted to return to the adoration of dumb idols would have difficulty in knowing how to worship aright the living God. So it has ever been with men. As the humble peasant stands embarrassed in the presence of the great king, so men stand mute before the almighty God. How should they praise and adore him? What could their empty hands offer to him who has made all things? What sort of prayers should they send up to him who knows what they need before they ask? Even the disciples who had walked with Jesus were moved to ask their master, "Teach us to pray" (Luke 11:1).

I

The church at Corinth was especially troubled by problems of worship. This was in part due to the variety of religious backgrounds among its members. Some were accustomed to the simple yet stately services of the synagogue.[1] There Holy Scripture was read and thoughtful discourse offered. There praises were hymned and antiphonal responses intoned. True, the service preserved flexibility, but in the main it moved in a formal and liturgical direction. Thus Philo says that the synagogues were places where the "people sit in order, keeping silence and listening with the utmost attention out of a thirst for refreshing discourse."[2]

Those who came out of Hellenistic religions, on the other hand, were familiar with other kinds of thirst. Devotees of Dionysus, the god of intoxication, were given to bacchanalia—wild orgiastic feasts where food and wine were devoured in quantity.[3] Some of these rites were faintly reminiscent of more primitive ritual in which enthusiasts, mostly women, whipped themselves into a frenzy, leaped upon a hapless animal, tore him limb from limb and drank the blood, still warm and living.[4] Although the Hellenistic age had softened much of this savage sort of worship, some of the old practices—frenzied revels, sensualism, and self-castration—still continued.[5] Greco-Roman religion was no more bloodless than its precursors. The cult of Mithras, which was so popular with the Roman troops, initiated its converts in the taurobolium —a pit in the ground over which a bull was slaughtered. As the blood poured over him, the new devotee eagerly let it immerse his eyes, nose,

---

[1] Cf. George Foot Moore, *Judaism in the First Centuries*, I, 291 ff., Ch. Guignebert, *The Jewish World in the Time of Jesus*, tr. H. S. Hooke (New York: E. P. Dutton & Co., 1939), p. 75; Frederick C. Grant, *Ancient Judaism and the New Testament* (New York: The Macmillan Company, 1959), pp. 41 ff.

[2] *De Specialibus Legibus*, ii, De Septenario. Loeb Classical Library, VII, 346.

[3] Cf. Martin P. Nilsson, *The Dionysiac Mysteries of the Hellenistic and Roman Age* (Lund: C. W. K. Gleerup, 1957), pp. 15 ff.

[4] Cf. Erwin Rohde, *Psyche*, p. 257.

[5] Cf. Nilsson, *Greek Piety*, p. 158.

and tongue.[6] This sort of thing makes it pretty clear that many of the Corinthians would not be satisfied with silent prayer.

As a matter of fact, the church at Corinth suffered from a variety of liturgical problems. Some of these had to do with matters of current social custom. For instance, the question was being asked, "What role should women play within the worshiping life of the church?" In Judaism, of course, they played no major part. They were restricted to certain sections of the synagogue, and were not allowed to recite the lessons of the service. For the most part Jewish women were neither to be seen nor heard. Thus Philo insists that a "woman should not show herself off like a vagrant in the streets before the eyes of other men, except when she has to go to the synagogue, and even then she should take pains to go, not when the market is full, but when most people have gone home." [7]

Nevertheless, the Hellenistic age was generally a time of the emancipation of women. Jerome Carcopino observes that the "Roman woman of the epoch . . . enjoyed a dignity and an independence equal if not superior to those claimed by contemporary feminists." [8] Some of the ancient critics satirize this new-found freedom. Juvenal, for example, derides the "woman who talks of literature and philosophy at dinner," so that "no one can get in a word edgewise, not even a lawyer." [9] He remonstrates the woman who

> Bold as a man, attending the meetings of men, with
> her husband
> One of the throng, while she holds forth, hard-faced
> and dry-breasted,
> Talking with all the High Brass.[10]

But, in spite of the opposition, women in Paul's day had considerable freedom of movement, rights in marriage and divorce, and in some

[6] Cf. A. D. Nock, Conversion—The Old and the New in Religion from Alexander the Great to Augustine of Hippo (Oxford: Clarendon Press, 1933), pp. 69 ff.
[7] Quoted by Salo Wittmayer Baron, A Social and Religious History of the Jews (2d ed. New York: Columbia University Press, 1952), II, 241.
[8] Daily Life in Ancient Rome, p. 85.
[9] Satires, p. 81.
[10] Ibid., p. 80.

places and in some cults the right to hold public and religious office.[11]

The question of the place of women in Corinth was raised by certain ladies who came to church bareheaded. This would have been scandalous in the synagogue, and even in some Greek sanctuaries women were supposed to appear only veiled. The significance of the veil, however, seems to have varied throughout the Hellenistic world. Some considered its absence to be a mark of immodesty, or even a symbol of prostitution. Short hair, too, was viewed by some to be a sign of dishonor. Nevertheless, most Greek women had abandoned the veil, and were experimenting with countless styles of coiffure.[12]

The women of the Corinthian church, consequently, were simply following some of the more daring styles of the day. It is possible, of course, to find evidence of a feminist party in Corinth, or even to suppose the neglect of the veil bears some relation to the factions of chapter 1. No doubt Cephas would have been shocked by such feminine exposure in the assembly, while Apollos might have considered it a matter of course. It is also possible that Paul's idea that "there is neither male nor female" (Gal. 3:28) within the body of Christ had led some of his partisans to support a doctrine of the equality of the sexes. Unfortunately, there is no evidence for such exegesis. Paul is probably not dealing with a movement for the rights of women in Corinth; rather, he is discussing a matter common to Corinthian customs. At any rate, the question for the apostle was: Should a woman wear a veil during Christian worship?

Much more serious were problems which had to do with *the observance of the Lord's Supper*. This was the central act of the church's worship, and anomalies in its practice greatly distressed the apostle. "In the following instructions," he writes, "I do not commend you, because when you come together it is not for the better but for the worse" (11:17). For one thing there were factions about the table of the

[11] Cf. Gerhard Delling, *Paulus' Stellung zu Frau und Ehe*, pp. 2 ff.; William Tarn and G. T. Griffith, *Hellenistic Civilization* (3rd ed. London: Edward Arnold, 1952), pp. 98 ff.

[12] W. G. Kümmel's note in Lietzmann's commentary, "Handbuch zum Neuen Testament" (pp. 183 ff.) argues that the interpretation of the unveiled head as a sign of prostitution is not correct, since Greek women in this period could wear the veil or not depending on shifting styles.

Lord. It is unlikely that Paul is speaking here about the same sort of party strife which he had discussed in the early part of the epistle. Some scholars, noting his more tolerant spirit here when he says, "I partly believe" that such schisms exist (11:18), suppose that this section of First Corinthians belongs to an earlier letter; later, when I Cor. 1 is written, Paul has no doubt about the reality of dangerous divisions.[13]

However, such conclusions need not be drawn if we agree that Paul is talking here about another sort of division. This is probably the truth of the matter. In chapter 1 the crux of separation is inordinate loyalty to leaders; here the basis of division seems to be social and economic. In vs. 21 the apostle observes, "One is hungry and another is drunk." Such a situation could only result from that fact that the Eucharist at this time involved a common meal. Later in the epistle Paul says that the service began with the breaking of bread, and only *after supper* was there participation in the cup (11:25). In between was a full meal, either provided "pot luck" by the members, especially the more affluent, or by the common funds. In any case, some in Corinth began to eat before the others arrived, gorging themselves, consuming most of the provisions, and letting the others go hungry. The former were probably the wealthy—those who had the leisure to come early and whose provisions were the most generous. The hungry, perhaps, were the slaves and common laborers, foundry workers and tired dock hands, who of necessity came late; these needed the most, they received the least. It is a scandal to become drunken at the table of the Lord; it is even worse to be drunk with a false sense of superiority and an indifference to the needs of the brethren.

Paul insists that this breaking of the fellowship destroys the true character of the Supper. He says, "When you meet together, it is not the Lord's supper that you eat" (vs. 20). They eat a meal, all right, but they do not eat the Supper of the Lord. Not that their meal was without religious trappings, for probably the early eaters said their own blessings individually, as was common in some informal religious meals of Judaism. Yet no amount of ritual can make up for a lack of love.

Indeed, where love is lacking there is no church, let alone Supper.

[13] Cf. Schmithals, *Die Gnosis in Korinth*, pp. 12 ff.

The bread of the Supper has its meaning in part as a symbol of the one body permeated by the power of divine *agape*. "Because there is one loaf," declares the apostle, "we who are many are one body" (10:17). Of course, when he says that "there must be factions among you in order that those who are genuine among you may be recognized" (11:19), Paul is probably speaking with irony. There is no necessity for factionalism; its appearance displays distortion of the gospel message. Yet where it exists, as in Corinth, it serves to identify the true Christians—the genuine, the approved, those who hold themselves aloof from petty strife. Those who foster factionalism, on the other hand, are false disciples—men who "despise the church of God" (vs. 22) and eventually destroy it. This destroying of the church and its primary act of worship arouses the ire of the apostle. "Shall I commend you in this? No, I will not." (11:22.)

Other problems in Corinth have to do with *exercise of spiritual gifts* within the worshiping life of the Christian community. As a matter of fact the Corinthians were not "lacking in any spiritual gift" (1:7), yet certain individuals considered particular gifts, especially those of highly demonstrative nature, to be of highest honor. This may have resulted partially from the individualistic and emotional character of much Hellenistic religion. Personal religion among the Greeks was private;[14] the Parthenon or the magnificent temples at Paestum housed gods, not congregations. Even the more intimate mystery associations failed to provide the sort of social participation which was central to the church; Apuleius' hero Lucius is thrice initiated into Oriental cults, but is never moved by close association with his fellow initiates.[15] He is, however, moved by the emotional power of the mysteries, as so many others were moved to excess by the wanton worship of Dionysus or Adonis.

It may have been this emotionalism and individualism which moved some of the members of the church to give expression to their possession of the spirit by means of "speaking in tongues." Something similar to

[14] Gerhard Delling, *Worship in the New Testament*, tr. Percy Scott (Philadelphia: Westminster Press, 1962), p. 172, says that "on the whole, pagan worship in New Testament times was a private matter."

[15] *The Golden Ass*, pp. 235 ff.

this bizarre phenomenon of speech is discussed by Plato; its occurrence is evidenced in some mystery cults, and perhaps in the veiled speech of the honored oracles.[16] The precise character of "speaking in tongues," or as it is technically called, *glossolalia,* cannot be ascertained. Scholars for a time believed that it might have been a miracle of linguistics, whereby the untutored were enabled to speak in foreign languages.[17] But now most specialists suppose that the phenomenon in Corinth defies the sort of interpretation given the pentecostal events by the author or editor of Acts 2 in which a variety of visitors to Jerusalem were able to hear the apostolic message spoken in their native dialects. The fact that speaking in tongues is actually contrasted with intelligible languages in I Cor. 14:10 seems to establish this interpretation. The "interpretatation of tongues," then, was something different from an exercise in grammar.

On the contrary, speaking in tongues is usually interpreted as emotional babbling. "The nature of genuine glossolalia," says a recent interpreter, "is therefore frenzied, inarticulate jargon with a sprinkling of coherent ejaculations whose inflections and tonal qualities have the characteristics of speech." [18] However, the attempt to understand the phenomenon exclusively in psychological terms as some sort of egocentric emotional disorder appears to know more about the moving of the Spirit than is actually warranted. These detractors, who look down on the primitive practice from the vantage point of a more reserved time, are quick to quote Paul's censure of its excesses. They often ignore the apostle's boast, "I thank God that I can speak in tongues more than you all" (14:18). As Delling observes, Christian glossolalia did not involve many of the orgiastic features of its pagan parallels.[19] Perhaps God had chosen that even in this strange speech men should praise him. The real question for Corinth was whether such praise belonged to public worship.

[16] Cf. Behm in Gerhard Kittel, ed., *Theologisches Wörterbuch zum Neuen Testament,* I, 46 ff.

[17] This view is still maintained by J. G. Davies, "Pentecost and Glossolalia," *Journal of Theological Studies,* III (1952), 228 ff.

[18] Ira J. Martin, *Glossolalia in the Apostolic Church* (Berea, Ky.: I. J. Martin, 1960), p. 48.

[19] *Worship in the New Testament,* pp. 31 ff.

II

What sort of instructions does Paul suggest for the solution to these problems of worship? On questions regarding the *role of women* in the church and the sort of headgear which is appropriate for worship, Paul appears to follow the best traditions of his cultural heritage. Christianity has not come to create new social customs; it has come to create a new manner of life. As to the former, such peripheral matters may be settled by considering the best in liturgical practice. This is not to be found in the frenzied rites of the pagans but in the solemn assemblies of the Jews. Here God was worshiped in the beauty of holiness, and here the church should look for its cultural patterns. When it does, it will discover that women ought to play a subordinate role symbolized by their wearing of the veil.

Unfortunately, Paul offers some reasons for his answer. Women, for one thing, occupy an inferior position in the church. "The head of every man is Christ," says Paul, "the head of a woman is her husband, and the head of Christ is God" (11:3). In other words, the apostle finds an order of rank within the divine economy—God, Christ, man, woman. Man was created in the image of God, but woman's glory is only reflected; she bears the glory of man. Indeed, woman was a secondary order in creation; she was created to serve the needs of man.[20] This subordinance should be symbolized by the wearing of a veil and long hair upon the head. When Paul says that nature teaches that man should wear short and women long hair, he no doubt reflects this notion about created order. Surely, he knows that short or long hair is mostly a matter of style depending on the will of man. Long hair, however, like the veil, is a sign of the subordination of woman that God has ordained.

How is this to be squared with the apostle's statement elsewhere that "there is neither Jew nor Greek, there is neither slave nor free,

[20] Else Kähler, *Die Frau in den paulinischen Briefen*, pp. 45 ff., argues that I Cor. 11:3 ff. presents two lines of argument: (1) following the order of creation seems to present woman as subordinate, but this is in part due to Paul's antignostic polemic; (2) following the order of redemption (vss. 11 ff.) where woman is presented as equal.

there is neither male nor female; for you are all one in Christ Jesus" (Gal. 3:28)? Of course, being one is not necessarily the same as being equal; or perhaps Paul is stating one of his famous indicatives which involves an imperative. Women are equal; now treat them as such! But when it comes down to cases, as in Corinth, Paul himself appears to deny their equality. Later in the epistle he even declares that the "women should keep silence in the churches" (14:34).[21] But had they been entirely without expression in the life of the community? We are told in Acts 18:26 that Priscilla joined with her husband in expounding the way of God more accurately to Apollos, and surely Chloe (I Cor. 1:11) and Phoebe, the deaconess of the suburban church at Cenchreae (Rom. 16:1), occupied places of leadership within the Christian community. Perhaps Paul's negative view of women is provoked by special problems at Corinth—problems that have to do with the temptation to emotional excesses in worship.

To answer these problems he falls back on a Jewish interpretation of Gen. 2. Yet even Paul feels that he must modify his harsh conclusions. "Nevertheless, in the Lord woman is not independent of man nor man of woman; for as woman was made from man, so man is now born of woman." (11:11-12.) But in the end it depends on the divine ordering: "And all things are from God."

The details of the argument are even more complex. Paul says that since man is a direct recipient of the divine image, he ought to wear short hair; if he covers his head in worship, he hides the heavenly image. Woman, on the other hand, whose glory is reflected, should be covered at all public occasions. If she refuses the veil she dishonors her head; "she might as well have her hair cut off" (vs. 6, NEB), and this is a disgrace to any woman. One might suppose from this that a lady's long hair would itself serve as a veil, for after all, Paul asserts in vs. 15 that "her hair is given to her for a covering." Yet if she refuses to wear a second covering over the natural veil, she might as well have no cover at all; let her shave her head and bear the shame! Nevertheless, the apostle says approvingly that "if a woman has long hair, it is her glory"

[21] Eduard Schweizer, "The Service of Worship—An Exposition of I Corinthians 14," *Interpretation*, XIII (1959), 400 ff., argues that this verse is a later interpolation; it is actually contradicted by I Cor. 11:5 where Paul speaks of "any woman who prays or prophesies."

(vs. 15), using the word *doxa*—the precise term which was used in vs. 7 for the glory of God and the glory of man. But why should the glory of woman, meager as it may be, be hidden under a veil?

Maybe it is because of the angels (vs. 10). Over the meaning of this verse scholars continue to be baffled. Could Paul mean that the beauty of unveiled women so distracted the heavenly beings that as in Gen. 6:2 "the sons of God saw the daughters of men were fair; and they took to wife such of them as they chose"? Was Paul, like so many rabbis, intrigued by the veiled meaning of this ancient text, so that he seems to be saying, "Girls, when you go to church, watch out for the angels"? Probably not, even though the idea that the angels are present during services of worship is not lacking in the Jewish sources (cf. Isa. 6:2; Ps. 137:1, LXX). This fact may indicate that Paul's meaning is as follows: "Since angels are present, shun all shameful conduct; if men are shocked by your unveiled appearance, how much more the beings of heaven!" [22] Most likely, however, the key to interpretation here is to be found in the word *exousia*, translated "veil" in vs. 10. The term actually means "authority" and stands for the authority symbolized by the wearing of a veil—not that women exercise authority, but that they recognize their subordination to it. This authority is seen in the divine order of creation, and over this order the angels, the heavenly beings of Jewish apocalyptic and the principalities and powers of gnostic speculation, preside.

Finally, even Paul acknowledges the weakness of his argument. Not without visible agitation he crys, "If any one is disposed to be contentious, we recognize no other practice, nor do the churches of God" (11:16). That is, when the apostle comes to the end of the thread of his argument, he grasps at the rope of his own authority and the tradition of the church which was before him. In the phrase, "the churches of God," he no doubt includes the congregations of Jewish background. Their worship was modeled after the conservative practices of the synagogue. To assert that Paul's view is primitive by modern standards is

[22] J. A. Fitzmyer, "A Feature of Qumran Angelology and the Angels of I Cor. XI. 10," *New Testament Studies*, IV (1957-58), 48 ff., indicates that the Dead Sea Scrolls (1QSa ii. 3-7) disallowed the presence of persons of any defect in the assembly of worship because of the angels. His article also gives an excellent summary of the main lines of the interpretation of this Pauline text.

simply to validate his conclusion. In secondary concerns of the conduct of worship the finest products of contemporary culture should be employed.[23]

In regard to the more central concern of the *Lord's Supper*, Paul offers a more profound answer. The Supper, for one thing, is not an ordinary meal. Even though it involves an actual common meal eaten between the breaking of bread and the blessing of the cup, it is not at all common. If one is drawn to the service simply by his hunger for food, "let him eat at home" (11:34). "What!" cries Paul. "Do you not have houses to eat and drink in?" (11:22.) The fact that the Lord's Supper is more than eating and drinking is seen in the drastic results of its abuse. "Many of you are weak and ill, and some have died." (vs. 30.) Such consequences are due to more than overindulgence and indigestion; they are due to the special nature of this Supper. Nevertheless, it was the destruction of the fellowship which eliminated the possibility that an ordinary supper might become the Supper of the Lord.

The true nature and practice of the Lord's Supper has been handed down through the liturgical tradition of the church. When Paul writes, "I *received* from the Lord what I also *delivered* unto you," he is using technical terms for the receiving and handing on of tradition.[24] What he received from the Lord, then, was probably not the product of special inspiration but the deposit of traditional doctrine whose ultimate source was Jesus himself. This assumes that Paul practiced and understood the Lord's Supper in the same fashion as his predecessors in the faith—an assumption which denies the identification of Paul as a eucharistic innovator.[25] This assumption need not deny some variety

[23] As well as support from Jewish practice for his idea of hair styles for worship, Paul also could have found parallels in pagan practice. An inscription giving the rules for initiation into the mysteries at Lycosura states: "Women are not to have their hair bound up, and men must enter with bared heads." (Quoted by Grant, *Hellenistic Religions*, p. 27.)

[24] Cf. Joachim Jeremias, *The Eucharistic Words of Jesus*, tr. Arnold Ehrhardt (New York: The Macmillan Company, 1955), pp. 127 ff.

[25] The theory of Hans Lietzmann, *Mass and Lord's Supper*, tr. Dorothea H. G. Reeve (Leiden: E. J. Brill, 1953), pp. 195 ff., which is taken up by Oscar Cullmann, "The Meaning of the Lord's Supper in Primitive Christianity," in Cullmann and Leenhardt, *Essays on the Lord's Supper* (Richmond: John Knox Press, 1958), pp. 5 ff., that there were two types of Supper in the early church: (1) a fellowship meal seen in the Jerusalem practice of breaking bread, and (2) a Hellenistic memorial meal which was instigated by Paul, is not convincing.

of practice within the early church, as the descriptive phrase, the "breaking of bread" (Acts 2:42), may indicate for the primitive community in Jerusalem. However, this terminology may be only a type of expression for a service similar to Paul's; the author of Acts uses almost the same words to describe what is no doubt an observance of the Lord's Supper under Paul's leadership at Troas (Acts 20:7; cf. I Cor. 10:16). Moreover, the Synoptic accounts, although written after First Corinthians, rest on early, independent sources. Their similarity to Pauline practice indicates that, at least in the Hellenistic church, a likeness in eucharistic practice existed.

At the basis of the tradition was a historic event. Paul begins by speaking about "Jesus on the night when he was betrayed" (11:23). The tradition of the Supper goes back to the happenings of the Upper Room. The question as to whether or not the events which took place there involved a Passover meal cannot occupy us here.[26] Suffice it to say that little of the ancient Israelitic ritual is explicit in Paul's account of the Supper itself. For him, the Passover symbolism is fulfilled primarily in the death of Christ; "For Christ, our paschal lamb, has been sacrificed" (I Cor. 5:7). Yet, it is precisely to this event, the crucifixion, that the events of the Upper Room point. The Last Supper presents the meaning of the happenings of the morrow; the Last Supper is a dramatic presentation of the atoning death of Jesus Christ.

[26] The attempt to identify the type of meal which Jesus and the disciples observed in the Upper Room has led to considerable debate. The Synoptics refer to the supper as a Passover meal (cf. Mark 14:12), while the Fourth Gospel appears to deny this identification (cf. John 18:28). Other Jewish meals which have been suggested include the *haburah* (an ordinary meal of religious associations) and the *kiddush* (a prayer which was said over a cup in the sabbath ritual or which was a part of Passover practice). A good summary of the various theories is presented by A. J. B. Higgins, *The Lord's Supper in the New Testament*, "Studies in Biblical Theology, No. 6" (Naperville, Ill.: Alec R. Allenson, 1952), pp. 13 ff. A generation ago, it was typical for scholars to reject the Passover identification for some other Jewish meal, usually the *haburah*; cf., for instance, Dom Gregory Dix, *The Shape of the Liturgy* (2d ed. Westminster: Dacre Press, 1945), pp. 50 ff. In more recent times, new stress has been placed on the Passover by such works as Jeremias, *Eucharistic Words*. Attempts have also been made to find parallel elements in the cult meals of the Qumran community; cf. Karl Georg Kuhn, "The Lord's Supper and the Communal Meal at Qumran," in Krister Stendahl, ed., *The Scrolls and the New Testament* (New York: Harper & Bros., 1957), pp. 65 ff.; Matthew Black, *The Scrolls and Christian Origins* (New York: Charles Scribner's Sons, 1961), pp. 102 ff.

This drama had two acts.[27] In the first, Jesus "took bread, and when he had given thanks, he broke it, and said, 'This is my body which is for you'" (11:23-24). In the second, he took a cup after the supper saying, "This cup is the new covenant in my blood." Only Jesus can play the title role in the drama, for it presents what he has done for us, or, ultimately, what God has done in him for our salvation. This is the meaning of the new covenant envisioned by Jeremiah: "I will put my law within them, and I will write it upon their hearts; and I will be their God, and they shall be my people" (Jer. 31:33). The Lord's Supper presents a new divine-human agreement, a new way of dealing with man from God's side, a way which writes not law on stone but love on hearts. The Lord's Supper makes real in the church what God has done on the Cross.[28] "God shows his love for us in that while we were yet sinners Christ died for us." (Rom. 5:8.)

The observance of the drama makes God's action again vital in the life of the church. However, the presence of Christ in the Supper has too often lost this dynamic and eschatological sense in favor of some mystical or material meaning. It is certainly true that Paul had made the statement,

> The cup of blessing which we bless,
>   is it not a participation in the blood of Christ?
> The bread which we break,
>   is it not a participation in the body of Christ? (10:16.)

Of course, the word rendered "participation" here can also mean "communion" or "fellowship," so that even here the stress is upon the oneness of the people of God united in worship with the one Lord. Those who insist on locating the presence of Christ exclusively in the elements of the Supper, a presence which is imputed through the bless-

[27] The emphasis on the Eucharist as action is made by Dix, *Shape of the Liturgy*, pp. 1 ff., 48 ff. Jeremias' idea of the Supper as acted "parable" (*Eucharistic Words*, pp. 145 ff.) is also provocative.

[28] Alan Richardson, *An Introduction to the Theology of the New Testament* (New York: Harper & Bros., 1958), p. 369, suggests that "the whole Gospel, in fact, is re-presented, is made present, in all its saving power" in the Eucharist.

ing or the eating of bread and wine, attribute to Paul theological notions of a later age.[29]

The only real evidence of a mystical presence in the elements is seen in Paul's idea that some have become sick and others died from improper participation, as if, in contrast to Ignatius' idea of the Eucharist as the medicine of immortality,[30] Paul is advocating in the elements the presence of a mortal poison. Such a view is hardly worthy of the apostle, and the passage is open to other interpretation.[31] Moreover, in discussing the elements Paul does not make the simple equations: bread equals body, wine equals blood. Instead of bread and wine Paul's parallel is bread and *cup*; the notion of drinking blood would probably have been as repulsive to Paul as to any other Jew, and the idea that in eating and drinking the elements he was consuming Christ, somehow really present, would have been quite as distasteful to the apostle.

No, the presence of Christ is not primarily in the elements but in the dramatic act of the Supper—the breaking of bread, the emptying of the cup. These acts reenact the events of the passion—the breaking of Christ's body, the pouring out of his blood. Indeed, it is not amiss to call this action symbolic, if we understand the term "symbol" in a Semitic sense.[32] When Jeremiah appears before the powers of the world with a heavy yoke upon his shoulders, his action is not a mere symbol; his action, like the dynamic prophetic word, brings about the very thing it symbolizes—the submission of all to Babylon (Jer. 27:1 ff.). So the symbolic act of the Supper accomplishes the very action it portrays—the redemptive action of God. This is why it should be repeated in remembrance of Christ; not as a simple memory of a past event but an act of remembering which makes the past event

[29] It should be noted also that 10:16 is using the Lord's Supper in contrast with pagan cultic meals. In the latter, the presence of the deity was not located in the food which was consumed but in the fellowship of the table. Cf. Nilsson, *Greek Folk Religion*, p. 74.

[30] *Epistle to the Ephesians* xx, 2.

[31] For example, the drastic result may be due to their sin of destroying the life of the church, not from their eating of some magically contaminated food.

[32] Cf. H. Wheeler Robinson, "Prophetic Symbolism," in Society for Old Testament Study, *Old Testament Essays* (London: Charles Griffin & Co., 1927), pp. 1 ff.

of his death present and real for the man of faith in our day.[33]

But the Lord's Supper is not only a drama whereby God's saving action of the past is made present, it is also a proclamation and a hope. Paul says, "For as often as you eat this bread and drink the cup, you proclaim the Lord's death until he comes" (11:26). The fact that it is a proclamation helps us to understand both the nature of preaching and the character of the Supper. Preaching is re-presentation of Christ; it is so proclaiming what God has done in him that men may respond with faith. The center of that divine action is seen in the Cross, so that the Supper which presents Christ's death is a sermon in action, the gospel in drama. This also indicates that the Supper is supremely action, fundamentally an action of God in which the church is called to share. Here every man of faith, regardless of gifts of speech, proclaims in a clear and unmistakable fashion the gospel to which he is committed. Here the Christian can publicly portray Christ as crucified (Gal. 3:1).

Of course, in his thought of the crucifixion of Christ Paul always assumes the resurrection. This is clearly implied in his proclamation of the hope of Christ's return. Thus, in spite of the seriousness of the events "on the night when he was betrayed," and the usual Pauline stress on the death of Christ, the proclamation sounds a trumpet of victory, of hope, of joy. The exact nature of the future coming of the Lord may be better discussed in connection with I Cor. 15, yet it is already clear that his return will involve no shocking surprises. "This Jesus, who was taken up from you into heaven, will come in the same way as you saw him go into heaven." (Acts 1:11.) When stripped of its apocalyptic paraphernalia, this text seems to suggest that Christ's return will mean the accomplishment at the end of history of the redemptive purposes revealed in history in Jesus Christ. Thus, the church in the radiant light of this "already, but not yet," must celebrate the Supper in gladness and expectation, crying, *"Maranatha"*—"Our Lord, come!" (16:22.)

Therefore, at the center the Lord's Supper is an eschatological event. It is God's saving action, continually reenacted in the life of his

---

[33] Cf. Brevard S. Childs, *Memory and Tradition in Israel*, "Studies in Biblical Theology, No. 37" (Naperville, Ill.: Alec R. Allenson, 1962).

133

people. Its traces of Passover observance remind the faithful that God has led them out of Egypt. Its stress upon the Lord's death makes real God's supreme redemptive act in the midst of history for all men. Its continual repetition provides men of ongoing history with the opportunity to confess the crucified Christ. Its pointing to the future grants hope to the world, joy to the faithful, trust in the victory of God. Indeed, participation in the Supper of the Lord illuminates the whole history of salvation. After they had supped with the risen Christ, the two pilgrims of Emmaus marveled, "Did not our hearts burn within us while he talked to us on the road, while he opened to us the scriptures?" (Luke 24:32.)

In the light of this idea of the Supper, what instruction could be offered to the Corinthian errors? These errors first deserve further analysis. Paul warns his hearers against eating the bread and drinking the cup in an unworthy manner; such conduct would make one guilty of profaning the body and blood of the Lord (11:27). Actually, the Revised Standard Version gives a misleading translation here; the word "profaning" is not to be found in the Greek text. There we simply read that he who partakes of the Supper unworthily is "guilty of the body and blood of the Lord." That is, he has failed to recognize the Supper as an act of God, as seen in his going ahead with his own supper in reveling and drunkenness. Such conduct, rather than sharing the benefits of the Supper, makes one a guilty participant in the event which the observance reenacts. He who is not for Christ is against him. He who would partake of the Supper must first examine himself (vs. 28) to see if he is a confessor or a crucifier of the Christ. Man's existence was put to question in the Cross, and now that same existential question is encountered in the Supper.

In analyzing the Corinthian errors the real problem is to understand the meaning of Paul's phrase "discerning the body" (vs. 29).[34] The word *diakrinō* means "to make a distinction or to differentiate, to judge correctly or to recognize." To eat and drink without discerning the body, then, must mean to ignore the true character of the body, to

---

[34] A brief summary of the various interpretations of this text is given by Higgins, *Lord's Supper in the New Testament*, pp. 70 ff. Cf. also Ernest Best, *One Body in Christ* (London: S.P.C.K., 1955), pp. 107 ff.

fail to distinguish it from what it is not. But what is meant by "body" here? The fact that Paul has just depicted Jesus as breaking bread and saying, "This is my body," has led many to conclude that the body mentioned in vs. 29 refers to Christ's body present in the elements. When the Christian partakes of the bread, he must recognize that he is actually handling the body of Christ.

Such a conclusion would not be entirely consistent with the line of interpretation adopted above. If discerning the body means recognizing the presence of Christ in the Supper, then that presence is to be seen in the whole drama of the meal, not exclusively in the elements. After all, the failure to discern involves both eating and drinking, whereas the body metaphor in 11:24 refers specifically only to eating, to the bread. Moreover, the bread-body metaphor has been used earlier with little ambiguity. "Because there is one loaf," Paul has written, "we who are many are one body" (10:17). In that statement bread stands for body, and body means church. This is precisely the meaning Paul presents at length and with clarity in chapter 12; the body of Christ is the church. Is it possible to conclude that discerning the body means recognizing the reality of the church in the service of the Supper?

Actually the only barrier to such an interpretation is I Cor. 11:24. When Jesus is quoted as saying, "This is my body," it is difficult to suppose that he is talking about the church. Of course, there are some who so identify the Christ and the church that even in the Eucharist it is the church as well as Christ which is continually being broken, continually being crucified anew.[35] But if any identification is to be supposed, it must be with the risen Christ and not the Jesus of the Upper Room. To understand how the church can offer itself "for you," for itself, demands a sort of exegesis which is more at home in Delphi than in Athens. Rather, it is better to notice that the words of Jesus in 11:24 come from the traditional eucharistic formula; they are not distinctively Pauline.[36] Paul's special use of the body metaphor is to be found both before (10:17) and after (12:27) the Lord's Supper passage (11:23 ff.). The words, "This is my body," which are

[35] Cf. Neville Clark, An Approach to the Theology of the Sacraments, "Studies in Biblical Theology, No. 17" (Naperville, Ill.: Alec R. Allenson, 1956), pp. 49 ff.

[36] Cf. Jeremias, Eucharistic Words, pp. 127 ff.

too readily distorted into an undue stress on the elements, belong to the tradition which Paul had received from the Hellenistic church and which he had delivered to the church at Corinth.

"Discerning the body," therefore, means to recognize that God's redemptive action in the Supper occurs in the church. That redemptive action re-presents the crucifixion of Christ as the revelation of God's love. But if the church turns its back on that love, if it acts without love of the brethren, it displays ignorance of the true character of the Supper. If some of its members go ahead with their own meal with the result that "one is hungry and another is drunk," they have undermined the basis of the church's life. The attempt to celebrate the Supper without recognizing the church grounded in the love of God is to eat and drink without discerning the body.[37] This results in the destruction of the Lord's Supper and, ultimately, in the destruction of the church.

Support for this interpretation can be found in Paul's final words. "So then, my brethren, when you come together to eat, wait for one another." (11:33.) After recounting the traditional understanding of the Lord's Supper, does the apostle censure the Corinthians for their failure to comprehend some complex doctrine of the real presence in the Eucharist? Quite to the contrary, he berates their denial of the Christian fellowship. The fact that he both begins (11:21 ff.) and ends (11:33 ff.) this discussion on the same theme makes it evident that God's *agape* working in the church and in the sacrament has been the main melody of the whole composition. When Paul says that neglecting to wait for one another may have the result of coming together "to be condemned" (vs. 34), it is obvious that even the guilt of vs. 27 and the judgment of vs. 29 have to do with violations of the church's character. The consequence that some have fallen sick and some have fallen asleep is not due to poison in the cup but poison in the heart. The church is a body, a living organism; the disease of one member spreads to the others so that illness and death result. Before the whole body is mortally infected, the members must be cleansed. "But when we are judged by the Lord, we are chastened so

---

[37] Cf. Günther Bornkamm, "Herrenmahl und Kirche bei Paulus," *New Testament Studies*, II (1955-56), 202 ff.

that we may not be condemned along with the world." (11:32.)

Paul takes up the problem of *spiritual gifts* in the twelfth chapter. He states basic principles at the outset. For one thing, the Corinthians must be wary of trusting their own emotions. "You know that when you were heathen, you were led astray to dumb idols, however you may have been moved." (vs. 2.) Certainly men's feelings were aroused by paganism; anyone who had observed the stirring rites of the mystery cults would have to admit that. But now that they had become Christians, it was clear that pagan worship was wrong, and thus that their emotions were not always dependable. So also in the church, emotional excess is no evidence of superior piety—no proof of exclusive possession of the Spirit's gifts.

What, then, is the true criterion of the Spirit's presence? The simple confession which every member makes. Paul says that "no one speaking by the Spirit of God ever says 'Jesus be cursed!' and no one can say 'Jesus is Lord' except by the Holy Spirit" (vs. 3). Obviously, no true Christian would want to curse Christ. Is Paul, therefore, talking about abuse which is heaped upon the church by its opponents, pagan or Jewish? Probably not, for what would such a curse uttered perhaps in the synagogue have to do with the question of spiritual gifts in the church? Possibly some Christians, in the emotional excesses of Corinthian worship, have actually cried, "Jesus be cursed," quite without knowing what they were doing. More likely, Paul is pointing out that in speaking in tongues, with its emotional abandon, its intellectual poverty, a worshiper might say almost anything; his nonsensical syllables could even add up to a curse of Christ.

When Paul says, "No one can say 'Jesus is Lord' except by the Holy Spirit," his argument appears weak. Anyone can say, "Jesus is Lord." Paul, however, is not talking about mouthing words; he is describing the basic Christian confession. In contrast to the mystery religions in which one might cry, "Serapis is Lord," or in the imperial cult where one might shout, "Caesar is *Kyrios*," the Christians quietly acknowledge the risen Christ to be Lord of all things and especially of themselves. This confession was one of the earliest public confessions of faith. It was announced at baptism, and perhaps used spontaneously within the worship service. In no case, however, could it be validly

137

confessed apart from the Spirit's activity. To make the confession is to acknowledge the lordship of Christ—a lordship which is exercised in the life of the Christian by the Holy Spirit. Thus, the real test of the Spirit's presence is the total commitment of life—a commitment fundamental to Christian existence.

Within this basic life in the Spirit, there are a variety of spiritual gifts. There is no one exclusive gift, for instance the gift of spiritual speech, but many gifts distributed among those who have made the basic commitment.

> Now there are varieties of gifts,
>   but the same Spirit;
> and there are varieties of service,
>   but the same Lord;
> and there are varieties of working,
>   but it is the same God who inspires them
>   all in every one. (12:4-6.)

These couplets stress the conviction that the manifestations of the Spirit in the members of the church are gifts. They are not achieved by the piety of men; they are granted by the grace of God. Some interpreters are quick to find in these verses a full-blown doctrine of the Trinity,[38] and it may be there by implication. However, Paul's idea of the Father, Son, and Holy Ghost is at best functional. His three statements here say essentially the same thing; the varieties of gifts are varieties of service; the varieties of service are varieties of working. The Spirit and the Lord are simply different means through which God accomplishes his purposes. The threefold statement, nevertheless, makes it "triply" clear that God is the ultimate source of all the benefits of the Christian community.

Indeed, those who parade their spiritual possessions show that they do not understand the Spirit's purpose. Different gifts were given to different individuals, but not for the religious aggrandizement of the few. They were given for the common good. The recipient who hoards his gift, who does not share it for the upbuilding of the church, renders

---

[38] For example, cf. Robertson and Plummer, "International Critical Commentary," p. 262.

his gift impotent. It is as if he had lost the gift; his treasure has been corroded by his own selfishness. Such selfishness is in evidence whenever an individual supposes his gift offers him a superior status in the life of the church.

In 12:8-10 Paul proceeds to list gifts of the Spirit. Usually these gifts are classified into three groups: the pedagogical gifts, including the utterance (*logos*) of wisdom and the utterance of knowledge; the supernatural gifts, such as the gift of faith, the gift of healing, the working of miracles; and the gifts of special communication, including the gift of prophecy, the ability to discern spirits, the gift of tongues, and the gift of interpretation. The difference between the *logos sophias* (word of wisdom) and the *logos gnōseōs* (word of knowledge), if existent, is difficult to determine. No doubt these gifts have to do with the intelligible communication of the gospel and its implications. The wisdom of God is grounded in the crucified Christ (1:24), and the knowledge of God is received through personal commitment to him (8:3).

It is equally difficult to differentiate among the gifts of power. The gift of faith, of course, should not be confused with the response of faith through which man accepts justification (Rom. 3:27). That experience was basic to every Christian, while faith here is a special manifestation of the Spirit granted to particular members of the body of Christ. Faith, like the gift of healing or the working of miracles, is a power given by the Spirit which makes possible such unusual acts as curing the sick and casting out demons. Strange as these phenomena may seem to our more prosaic age—an age in which there seem to be no demons to cast out—to the world of the New Testament, populated by dangerous spiritual powers, they seemed the very sort of things the Spirit of God should perform. Although the "man in Christ" did not boast of his special powers (II Cor. 12:2 ff.), nor anywhere describe them in detail, he did insist that his work all the way from Jerusalem around to Illyricum was accompanied "by the power of signs and wonders, by the power of the Holy Spirit" (Rom. 15:19).

The gifts of speech are listed last, probably because of their importance for the discussion. The nature of prophecy in the early church is not quite clear. It is evident from 14:1 ff. that the prophet speaks a rational, intelligible message. Although the element of predicting the future may not have been entirely absent, the prophet here, as in the Old Testament, was more concerned to make the word of God relevant to the present, to the situation of his listeners.[39] The prophet is less a football forecaster and more a weather analyst who studies carefully the signs of the times. Yet even the careful student can read them in error. This is why there must be those who discern or distinguish between spirits; there must be other prophets who can weigh the worth of the various prophecies. As Paul says later, "The spirits of prophets are subject to prophets" (14:32). These prophets who speak and discern are primarily eschatological messengers of God; prophecy is a phenomenon of the end time, as the prophet Joel had declared (2:28).[40] The prophet heralds the end of the old aeon; he proclaims the word of the One who makes all things new.

The gift of speaking in tongues has already been identified—an emotional outburst of unintelligible utterance. It can be made intelligible, however, if someone in the congregation is given the power to interpret. Indeed, if there is interpretation, glossolalia is equivalent to prophecy (14:5). That is why Paul can say, "I want you all to speak in tongues" (14:5). Perhaps this gift is something like modern abstract art; to the normal eye it is but a jumble of color, but to the gifted interpreter the painting carries meaning, usually in terms of feeling and emotion. So speaking in tongues is to the untuned ear but a clamor of sound, yet to the one who possesses the gift of interpretation it contains a moving message. It, too, is a sign of the end time—a sign that old forms are broken down, that God's Spirit captures the inarticulate, that God chooses new ways that men may praise him.[41] But, for all of this, speaking in tongues is the major cause of trouble in Corinthian worship. The point of the passage before us is to indicate that glossolalia is only one of a variety of gifts. "All these are inspired by one and the

[39] Cf. Friedrich in Kittel, *Theologisches Wörterbuch zum Neuen Testament*, VI, 856 ff.

[40] Cf. H. Greeven, "Propheten, Lehrer, Vorsteher bei Paulus," *Zeitschrift für die Neutestamentliche Wissenschaft*, XLIV (1952-53), 14 ff.

[41] Cf. Delling, *Worship in the New Testament*, pp. 35 ff.

same Spirit, who apportions to each one individually as he wills."
(12:11.)

Since one Spirit has granted all the gifts, each is involved in a relationship with the others. To illustrate the nature of this relationship
Paul introduces his well-known metaphor of the body (cf. Rom.
12:4 ff.). "For just as the body is one and has many members, and all
the members of the body, though many, are one body, so it is with
Christ." (12:12.) This introductory statement already makes it clear
that the body figure portrays the unity of those who receive the various spiritual gifts. It is also clear that the body represents the church.
"For by one Spirit we were all baptized into one body—Jews or Greeks,
slaves or free." (vs. 13.) Entrance into the church is by way of baptism, and within its membership social distinctions, like those errone-
ously drawn by the worshiping Corinthians, are completely erased.
When he goes on to say that "all were made to drink of one Spirit"
(vs. 13), Paul probably does not refer especially to their participation
in the Lord's Supper but to their sharing of spiritual benefits within
the life of the community; the water of baptism suggests the figure.

Paul begins the analogy by saying, "The body does not consist of
one member but of many" (12:14). For one thing, each member is a
part of the body whether it likes it or not. "If the foot should say, 'Because I am not a hand, I do not belong to the body,' that would not
make it any less a part of the body." (vs. 15.) The same is true of
the eye. Secondly, the whole body is not to be equated with one member. "If the whole body were an eye, where would be the hearing?"
The same thing can also be said of the ear, or of any other organ. "If
all were a single organ, where would the body be?" (vs. 19.) Since
there is a body, however, there must be a variety of members. So,
"there are many parts, yet one body" (vs. 20).

In the third place, the members of the body are interdependent;
each part is needed by the others, and every member is necessary to
the healthy function of the whole organism. "The eye cannot say to
the hand, 'I have no need of you,' nor again the head to the feet, 'I
have no need of you.'" (vs. 21.) All are necessary because "God ar-
ranged the organs in the body" (vs. 18). Of course, all are not equally necessary; man can get along better without a hand than without

141

a head. This fact leads Paul to his fourth point. The weaker parts are indispensable, and because of their inferiority, deserving of higher honor.

In illustrating this point the analogy becomes a little shaky. When Paul talks of investing the less honorable members with greater honor, he is referring to covering certain parts of the body with a greater amount of clothing. Thus the unpresentable parts—he means the sexual organs—are at great effort made presentable through the proper sort of dress. But when Paul attributes these customs in clothing to the ordering of God, the analogy has wandered astray. How can he say that "God has so adjusted the body, giving the greater honor the inferior part" (vs. 24)? It could more readily be argued that God has given greatest honor to the head, and it is in no sense inferior. But Paul prefers to make a point. The inferior deserve greater honor.

That Paul wants this figure of speech to be applied to the church is again made clear in 12:27: "Now you are the body of Christ and individually members of it." Just how many points of parallel are intended between the analogy and its application cannot be absolutely ascertained. However, the last point—that greater honor is due to the less honorable—indicates that the application is more important than the figure itself. It is the humble members of the Corinthian church who need honoring, and they need it not because of some notion about honoring the body but because they have so little of it. Since even dubious elements of the analogy allow application, we may proceed to list these points in the body metaphor which illustrate the character of the church:

1. The church is a unity—"there are many parts, yet one body" (vs. 20); there should be "no discord in the body" (vs. 25).

2. Every member has an important function to perform—the "weaker are indispensable" (vs. 22).

3. Every functioning member is a part of the church and no member, or group of members, is exclusively the church—the "body does not consist of one member but of many" (vs. 14).

4. The functions of some are more important than others, but those who perform lesser functions deserve greater honor in the church—it

is God's will that greater honor is given to the inferior member (vs. 24).

5. The members are mutually interdependent—they are bound together by an *agape* which transcends ordinary concepts of unity. "If one member suffers, all suffer together; if one member is honored, all rejoice together." (vs. 26.)

It is well to notice that these instructions are directed to Corinthian problems. The unity of the church is threatened; some members are claiming to have exclusive possession of the Spirit, so that those of "lesser" gifts are despised as having no place in the body of Christ; the former attempt to carry on their functions totally independent of their "less fortunate" brethren. To make it worse, all these aberrations are apparent in the heart of the common life—in the worship of the church.

When this practical use of the body metaphor is noticed, the traditional questions of interpretation loom smaller. They are two: (1) From what background does Paul draw the idea of the church as the body of Christ? (2) What theological significance does the use of this concept have for understanding the nature of the church? As to the background, we find a host of ideas about the body of Christ. It comes from Stoicism, Gnosticism, or Judaism; it finds parallels in the Old Testament idea of "corporate personality," or in rabbinic speculation about the body of Adam.[42] The fact that such a variety of answers can be offered to this question makes it evident that no decisive answer is indicated. After all, the figure of the body was used as early as the fifth century B.C., and its widespread traces, all the way from gnostic syncretism to rabbinic speculation, indicate that Paul could have found it in a variety of places. His use of the figure, whereby a social organism is compared to a human body, is not without a certain originality. In

[42] A brief survey of these various views is given by John A. T. Robinson, *The Body—A Study in Pauline Theology,* "Studies in Biblical Theology, No. 5" (Naperville, Ill.: Alec R. Allenson, 1952), pp. 55 ff. For the rabbinic speculation about Adam, cf. W. D. Davies, *Paul and Rabbinic Judaism* (London: S.P.C.K., 1948), pp. 36 ff. For the gnostic speculation about the primal man, cf. Ernst Käsemann, *Leib und Leib Christi* (Tübingen: J. C. B. Mohr, 1933). It is interesting that Käsemann's rather extreme view on gnostic backgrounds has been somewhat softened in his more recent writing. Cf. "Neutestamentliche Fragen von heute," *Zeitschrift für Theologie und Kirche,* LIV (1957), 17 ff.

fact, the essence of Paul's idea is this: The church and its members are like a body and its organs. It is surprising that some of the more romantic scholars have not imagined that the apostle took the metaphor from what he had learned about anatomy through "Doctor Luke." Such romanticizing is discredited on many grounds, of course, and Paul's particular use of the body metaphor may simply come out of personal observation.

We must urge that the "body of Christ" be taken as a metaphor. This brings us to the question about the body and the nature of the church. Some insist on taking the figure literally. J. A. T. Robinson, for instance, writes that the church "is in fact no other than the glorified body of the risen and ascended Christ." [43] One might quip that the church at Corinth has a long way to go, but seriously, this is part of the problem. The church simply does not reflect the glory of God to the degree that it can be seen in the face of Christ (II Cor. 4:6). If Christ and the church are identical, then our concept of Christ must be radically revised, our understanding of the fundamental character of God's revelation in history would have to be altered, and such ensuing doctrines as the church died for the church would demand explanation.[44] But why is one of Paul's figures of speech to be taken literally? Why is it not just as readily urged that the church is literally an olive tree (Rom. 11:17 ff.), a building (I Cor. 3:9 ff.), or a loaf of bread (I Cor. 5:7)? [45] Why not really take the body metaphor literally? If Christ and the body, the church, are one, then some members must be literally hands, or eyes, or feet.

If, on the other hand, the body of Christ is a figure of speech, what does it tell us about the church? Basically, in its context, it tells the church at Corinth how it ought to behave in its worship. Besides that, the body figure seems to call for a functional interpretation. The gifts of the Spirit which have just been discussed all have to do with action which the church performs—teaching, healing, speaking. The organs

[43] *The Body*, p. 51.

[44] The notion that the church is the "extension of the incarnation" is adequately refuted by Best, *One Body in Christ*, pp. 195 ff.

[45] Paul S. Minear, *Images of the Church in the New Testament* (Philadelphia: Westminster Press, 1960), lists, somewhat ambitiously, ninety-six New Testament analogies for the church.

of the body are depicted as having function; the ear, for instance, is necessary because of the need for hearing (vs. 17). Thus, the church as the body of Christ must mean that the church is the means through which the functions of the Spirit are performed. As Eduard Schweizer says, "This usage of the term 'body' would open the way for an understanding of the body-of-Christ concept in which the church would be considered as the instrument by which Christ did his continuing service to the world." [46]

After discussing the body of Christ, Paul proceeds to posit an order of functionaries within the Christian community. "And God has appointed in the church first apostles, second prophets, third teachers, then workers of miracles, then healers, helpers, administrators, speakers in various kinds of tongues." (12:28.) These are the members of the body who perform the functions granted by the Spirit. The functionaries do not exactly correspond to the functions listed in 12:8 ff.; the prophet is no doubt the one who has received the gift of prophecy, but whether the administrator has received the gift of working miracles or the talent of distinguishing between spirits cannot be known. In fact, the list of functionaries in vss. 29-30 does not exactly correspond with that of vs. 28, or to Paul's other list of spiritual functions in Rom. 12:6 ff. This makes it apparent that the apostle has no crystallized notion of clerical rank.

He does, nevertheless, acknowledge a hierarchy of spiritual gifts. The lists in 12:28-29 represent an order of importance. Paul says, "But earnestly desire the higher gifts" (vs. 31). The higher gifts are possessed by those who are listed first—apostles, prophets, teachers. The lowest gift is the ability to speak in tongues—a gift even less valuable than the talent of administering the mundane affairs of the church. Thus, this passage anticipates Paul's criticism of glossolalia which he will take up in chapter 14. Those who possess that gift are the ones who have claimed exclusive possession of the Spirit, who have despised what seemed to them to be the "lesser" gifts. These despisers actually share the lowest gift mentioned and ought to strive for something better. Yet there is a still more excellent way.

[46] "The Church as the Missionary Body of Christ," New Testament Studies, VIII (1961-62), 1 ff.

III

The still more excellent way is described in I Cor. 13.[47] In the description Paul states the basic theological principle on which his instructions for worship are based. That principle, of course, is love; for love, in contrast to all other activities of the Spirit, is the more excellent way. The chapter itself has a hymnic character which makes exegesis seem almost a sacrilege. Nevertheless, interpretation is demanded and, to facilitate it, scholars usually divide the passage into three sections.

First, the chapter speaks of the superiority of love. Love is superior to any of the gifts listed in 12:8 ff.—the gifts of teaching, working, and speaking. Suppose I could speak in all the tongues of men, both emotional and intelligible, and even speak the language of heaven, the language of the angels; if I do not speak with love, my speech would be mere noise like the ringing gongs and the clanging cymbals of pagan worship. Suppose I have received the gift of prophecy so as to know all the mysteries of God—his secret wisdom revealed in Christ did not fully manifest till the future—so as to proclaim the gospel and teach its implications with all truth and all clarity; yet if I do not communicate God's love, my message is robbed of its power. Suppose that I can do mighty works, have faith to move mountains (Mark 11:23), power to heal, courage to brave the fires of martyrdom; if I have no love expressed in the concrete situations of my existence, my deeds profit nothing. In short, no gift which the Corinthians have acquired, or which they in their wildest hopes can expect, is able to be compared with the gift every Christian has received—love.

Secondly, the chapter describes the work of love. In its work love stands in sharp contrast to the activity of the Corinthians. "Love is patient and kind; love is not jealous or boastful; it is not . . . rude." (vss. 4-5.) But these are the very things the Corinthians have displayed with their factions at the Lord's table, their pride in spiritual posses-

---

[47] The argument of Eric L. Titus, "Did Paul Write I Corinthians 13?" *Journal of Bible and Religion*, XXVII (1959), 299 ff., that this chapter is not genuine, although impressive, is not convincing.

sions. "Love does not insist on its own way; it is not irritable or resentful; it does not rejoice at wrong, but rejoices in the right." (vss. 5-6.) But the Corinthians have gone their own way, resentful of the brethren, happy in the midst of their errors, eager to dote on the evils of others. In contrast to the Corinthians, who will put up with very little, who are always ready to believe the worst, whose hopes for the church are too small, whose patience with the brethren is too short, "love bears all things, believes all things, hopes all things, endures all things" (vs. 7). In short, love, since it is God's way of acting, can do anything; it can even give the church the power to overcome its wrongs.

Since love is God's way, Paul can speak in the third section of the hymn about the endurance of love. "Love never ends." (vs. 8.) All the other gifts—for instance, prophecy, tongues, and knowledge—will pass away. These gifts which are given through the Spirit for use in the time between the beginning of the end in the Cross and the culmination of the end in the eschaton have no real use in the age to come. Prophecy makes God's word relevant to the present, but has no use in the time beyond history; it is like tongues, a sign that the end has started to come, but it has no more use when the day of the Spirit dawns in its full radiance. Even knowledge with its clear instruction in the gospel's implications is for the present time; it is grounded in a historical revelation whose limits are no more when God is all in all (I Cor. 15:28). Even if the supposed *gnōsis* of the Corinthians were genuine, it would not endure.[48] "For our knowledge is imperfect and our prophecy is imperfect; but when the perfect comes, the imperfect will pass away." (vss. 9-10.) The perfect (*teleion*), of course, is the eschaton.

Paul illustrates this point in two ways. "When I was a child, I spoke like a child, I thought like a child, I reasoned like a child; when I became a man, I gave up childish ways." (vs. 11.) The main purpose here is to show that the gifts of the Spirit current in the church belong to the present, incomplete time; in the future time, the time of fullness, these gifts are no more adequate. However, the use of the concept "childish" does carry a note of derision, and the term *laleō* for immature speech

---

[48] Although Paul may be refuting Corinthian gnosticism here, it is evident that *agape* is for him an ethical concept. When Käsemann (*Leib und Leib Christi*, pp. 171 ff.) refers to *agape* as "aeon," the Pauline gospel has been gnosticized away.

can mean "to babble," so that the whole illustration may subtly ridicule Corinthian perversion of gifts. This is not so for the other illustration. "For now we see in a mirror dimly, but then face to face." (v. 12.) Corinthian bronze mirrors were treasured throughout the ancient world, and a fine example can be found in the Athens museum today; but their shiny surfaces, no matter how highly polished, could only reflect a relatively imperfect image. In the day to come, even the glory of God seen in the face of Christ will be dimmed, worship will be perfect, God will be seen face to face. "Then I shall understand fully, even as I have been fully understood." (vs. 12.) Now, one does not really know God, but is known by him (Gal. 4:9). Then, man shall know God.

Paul concludes with an exalted statement: "So faith, hope, love abide, these three; but the greatest of these is love" (vs. 13). That is, these things endure even into the age to come. Faith lasts because it is of the essence of man's relation to God; faith is total personal commitment to God, and such commitment exists in the eschaton—in fact, only exists as total there. Hope is Paul's term for the character of eschatological life; that hope which was in history imperfect, unseen, is in the eschaton realized. Why is love the greatest? Probably because it is God's way. God acts by love, not faith or hope. Faith and hope always confess a dependence on God. Love is of the essence of the divine activity. In acting through love, man can act like God; he can become perfect like his Heavenly Father (Matt. 5:48).

This love, of course, is *agape*. As Nygren has shown, it has little to do with *eros*.[49] *Eros* is love for the lovely—the Greek love for the good and the beautiful. *Agape* is radically spontaneous—God's love for the unlovely. *Agape* is not aroused by the object; it is grounded in the nature of the subject. God loves, because it is of his nature to love. "Why, one will hardly die for a righteous man—though perhaps for a good man one will dare even to die"—*eros* at its highest level. "But God shows his love for us in that while we were yet sinners Christ died for us." (Rom. 5:7-8.) Such love is never realized fully by men in this age, yet its power must permeate the life of the church. It demands that no

[49] *Agape and Eros*, pp. 105 ff.

148

offense be given through adopting of novel social customs; it insists that factionalism and despising of the brethren destroy the Supper of the Lord; it demands that all spiritual powers be exercised in humility. Love is ever granted anew in the church's worship; by that love the church's life must be continually renewed.

In chapter 14 Paul applies the principle of love to the specific problems of worship, especially speaking in tongues. He insists that glossolalia is inferior to prophecy. "Make love your aim, and earnestly desire the spiritual gifts, especially that you may prophesy." (14:1.) The reason for his preference is that prophecy like love builds up the church. Indeed, speaking in tongues is not addressed to the congregation. "One who speaks in a tongue speaks not to men but to God." (vs. 2.) Glossolalia is good for praise, but not for proclamation. Such speaking goes unheard by human hearers; its content remains a mystery. "On the other hand, he who prophesies speaks to men for their upbuilding and encouragement and consolation." (vs. 3.) Prophecy builds up the church, while glossolalia builds up the ego—a false construction evidenced in Corinthian pride. Edifying the church means so strengthening its life that God's love revealed in Christ may be manifest in the world.

Such strengthening will occur only if intelligible information is communicated to the church's members. Speaking in tongues cannot benefit the congregation unless it mediates revelation, knowledge, prophecy, or teaching. That is, the church is built up by clear understanding of the manifestation of God in Christ and a profound understanding of the implications of that revelation for current life. If musical instruments do not sound with clarity, no one will know what is played. "If the bugle gives an indistinct sound, who will get ready for battle?" (vs. 8.) So in the church glossolalia is not understood; it is speaking into the air. Naturally, there are many meaningful human languages, but if I cannot translate, they are meaningless to me. Speaking in tongues has no intelligible meaning and, therefore, cannot build up the church.

The true test of ecclesiastical speech is intelligibility. If anyone has the gift of tongues, he should pray for the power to interpret so that some edifying message may be communicated. Actually, glossolalia is

149

emotional speech; it is praying with the spirit and not with the mind. But emotional modes of worship must always be related to the intellectual.

> I will pray with the spirit
> and I will pray with the mind also;
> I will sing with the spirit
> and I will sing with the mind also. (14:15.)

Otherwise, no one else can worship; worship is no longer public. If you pray in unintelligible tongues, how can some novice, sitting by, say, "Amen." You might profit by such worship, but not he. Then, perhaps to the Corinthians' surprise, Paul declares that he can speak in tongues more than any of them. Yet, as valuable as this emotional type of worship may be, it is better practiced in private. For speaking in church intelligibility is the criterion. "In church I would rather speak five words with my mind, in order to instruct others, than ten thousand words in a tongue." (vs. 19.) For the man who can preach and teach the gospel with clarity, glossolalia in the church is a colossal waste of words.

Speaking in tongues will not be able to build up the body by adding members to it. As he begins this line of argument Paul appeals to their maturity. "Brethren, do not be children in your thinking; be babes in evil, but in thinking be mature." (vs. 20.) This hints that the Corinthian troublemakers have actually been childish, especially in their fondness for foolish babbling (13:11). Besides appealing to the maturity of his hearers, Paul buttresses his argument with scripture. He quotes Isa. 28:11, where the ancient prophet announces how God's message is not heard by his people; it is as if the message were declared in some foreign language, some unknown tongue. Paul's interpretation is that "tongues are a sign not for believers but for unbelievers." By this he means a sign which has a negative effect—a sign which contributes to the unbelievers' unbelief. Prophecy, on the other hand, is "not for unbelievers but for believers" (vs. 22). That is, the intelligible message of the prophet will lead men to faith.

Paul illustrates these points with a fascinating description of Corinthian worship. "If, therefore, the whole church assembles and all speak in tongues, and outsiders or unbelievers enter, will they not say that you are mad?" (vs. 23.) This description supports the conclusion that glossolalia is an inarticulate, emotional expression. When a non-Christian hears such babbling, he will not be converted to the faith; he will view the Christians as demon-possessed rather than controlled by Christ (II Cor. 5:14). However, if the members of the church prophesy, the outsiders will be moved by the intelligible proclamation; they will be judged by the powerful message which cuts to the heart; they will fall down in repentance and worship before God, for they will confess that God is really present in the church. The worship of the church, therefore, should be so designed as to move men to faith, not to derision; it should be long on prophecy and short on tongues.

Paul proceeds to describe the actual conduct of a worship service (14:26 ff.).[50] One should not hope to find a divinely inspired order of worship here, yet some of the elements of the early Christian service are listed—a hymn, a lesson, a revelation, a tongue, or an interpretation. The hymn, no doubt, was like the singing of Jewish worship—songs of praise based largely on the Psalms. Expressly Christian hymns are abundant in the book of Revelation (e.g., 5:9 ff.; 15:3 ff., etc.). The lesson probably consisted of Old Testament texts read and explained; the explanation of these texts in their particular Christian meaning was perhaps the father of the sermon. However, the vital proclamation of that day was the revelation—the message of the prophet, which, as we have seen, applied the word of God to the present demands of the Christian faith. Tongues was the practice of glossolalia, and interpretation was the gift of discerning some intelligible message out of this spiritual manner of speech. Besides these elements, early Christian worship probably included prayers, confessions, benedictions, doxologies, and especially the Lord's Supper.

The actual order of worship preserved a large degree of flexibility. Paul says that two or at most three may speak in tongues provided there is someone to interpret. Two or three prophets may speak, but only one at a time. If a revelation is granted to another sitting by, the first should stop speaking. Since the spirits of the prophets are subject

[50] Cf. Eduard Schweizer, "The Service of Worship."

151

to the prophets, the prophet receiving a subsequent inspiration takes precedence over the current speaker. Here Paul is only describing the spoken elements of worship, and it should not be supposed that the entire service was this unordered. The elements of praise and confession, hymn and prayers, grounded in the liturgy of the synagogue,[51] no doubt, had a certain formality. This worship was directed to a God who "is not a God of confusion but of peace" (vs. 33). The seeming informality of the liturgy was restricted by the admonition to "let all things be done for edification" (vs. 26). "All things should be done decently and in order." (vs. 40.) It is evident, however, that no calendar of the order of service was sent out to the printers on Thursday. As Cullmann observes, "It is precisely in this *harmonious combination of freedom and restriction* that there lies the greatness and uniqueness of the early Christian service of worship." [52]

IV

In the end problems of worship find their answer in *agape*. All worship is a response to God's love. That love must be expressed in the common life of the worshipers. That love is the criterion by which all modes of worship must be tested. Paul's answer to the veil question, at first sight, seems to fall below this standard; does he not actually show a lack of concern for the feminine members of the community? But, although his requirement of the veil rests on traditional assumptions, the ideal of *agape* is not lacking. Paul displays a genuine concern for any who may be offended by daring styles—both those who view and those who wear them. His concern is that the church may be edified, and little matters like style in hair and hats should not be allowed to disturb that purpose. The best cultural heritage ought to be

[51] The extreme statement of Delling, *Worship in the New Testament*, p. 42: "The order of synagogue service has obviously not influenced the early Christian one," is given a much needed corrective by C. F. D. Moule, *Worship in the New Testament*, "Ecumenican Studies in Worship, No. 9" (Richmond: John Knox Press, 1961), pp. 9 ff.

[52] Oscar Cullman, *Early Christian Worship*, tr. A. Stewart Todd and James B. Torrance, "Studies in Biblical Theology, No. 10" (Naperville, Ill.: Alec R. Allenson, 1953), p. 33.

followed, since it gives best expression to the principle of edification of the common life.

Agape is the basis for the apostle's instruction about the Lord's Supper. We have seen that the real problem in Corinth was a fracture in the fellowship. Yet, when one remembers that the tradition of the Supper goes back to the "night when he was betrayed," that it remembers the death of the crucified one, then all their selfish reveling, all their lack of love, all their despising of the church is condemned. The Supper is itself a re-presentation of God's *agape,* and it must be celebrated in the *agape* of the brethren. This same love must also be manifest in the exercise of spiritual gifts. Love is the greatest gift of the Spirit; it is the way God himself works. Thus the entire worshiping life of the church—its hymns, prayers, prophecy—must reveal that divine *agape.*

How valid is this answer for the worship problems of the contemporary church? Is it even possible that Paul's more specific instructions will help to solve the liturgical difficulties of our own time? In any case, it is clear that problems exist. Differences in worship are more apparent than many of the doctrines that divide us. What has a Pentecostal healing service to do with a celebration of Eucharist in an Anglo-Catholic cathedral? Some people swing the hymns, and some swing the incense! Moreover, it is not enough to assume that differences of liturgy are simply concerns of personal preference—"nontheological factors" which can be taken care of after the coming great church is united, or when the cultural lag which hinders the weaker brethren is bridged. Yet as long as ecumenical meetings are marred by disunity at the Lord's table, the seriousness of the problems is apparent.

Less serious, of course, are problems which have to do with current cultural questions. What sort of architecture, music, and art ought to be used to accompany Christian worship? This question may even be more significant than the Corinthian concern with hair and hats, since music, for example, is an actual element of worship itself. Following Paul, we may suggest that the divine *agape* be expressed through the finest elements of our cultural heritage. No precise answers are thereby forthcoming, but some general conclusions may be suggested. For instance, the jumpy jive of 1920 "pop" music is not adequate to express the love of God revealed in the cross of Christ. Sweetly sentimental paintings which depict Jesus as the hero of our egocentric aspirations, or plush, theater-chair auditoriums which cater to the comfort of the self-indulgent, remind us of the proud who want to flaunt their daring styles or boast of their spiritual possessions.

Instead, the church should employ the best architecture, music, and art which our cultural heritage affords. Just as the church at Florence utilized the genius of Brunelleschi and Ghiberti, so the church of today should appropriate its vast treasure of aesthetic inheritance. This may mean that traditional patterns will have prominence; the forms of expression go back to ancient symbols like the fish and crosses of the catacombs; Christian art, like the Christian Eucharist, has historically determined content. Nevertheless, the church, like Julius II, must ever be alert to some new Michelangelo or Bramante who comes to express the ancient truth in new forms. Bach and Brahms may remain standard, but other voices will be heard. It is interesting that when one's taste in music or architecture runs exclusively to the baroque or gothic, he is thought to be a little passé in his aesthetic appreciation, yet some of the masters of the liturgical arts are anxious to feed us fully on medieval forms.

Above all, the church must avoid adopting traditional forms simply because they are currently in vogue. The recent "liturgical revival" with its passion for divided chancels and elevated altars can be in some communions only another form of ecclesiastical status seeking. Nevertheless, the burden of guilt must be placed on the free churches. Their worship has usually grown up without rhyme or reason. The Disciples, for instance, have decided, with little biblical or theological ground, that two elders should normally preside at the table of the Lord. The liturgical churches, on the other hand, have tradition and theology undergirding all they do. The revival of liturgy has its value when liturgical forms of the great tradition are used with genuine understanding and vital presentation of the divine *agape*. "Finally, my brethren, whatever is true, whatever is honorable, whatever is just, whatever is pure, whatever is lovely, whatever is gracious, if there is any excellence, if there is anything worthy of praise, think about these things." (Phil. 4:8.)

It would indeed be presumptuous to attempt to solve the complex problems of the Lord's Supper in a few lines. Nonetheless, Paul offers some elementary principles for our consideration. For one thing, historical origins are important. Since God has revealed himself in history, and since his Son is the source of our eucharistic tradition, modern practice ought to be shaped in accordance with the original observance. Thus practices which originated in the Middle Ages or even in the middle of the second century ought to be responsible to the events of the Upper Room. This does not mean that the service has to conform to the original in every detail. Even the different New Testament reports show minor variety, and the inclusion of a full meal between the breaking of bread and the offering of the cup would not add materially to the significance of the Supper as a dramatic symbol. The important thing is that God's action in Christ be re-presented in power and simplicity.

On the basis of this principle other conclusions can be cautiously drawn. The question of who can partake, of course, is not directly answered. However, it is evident that Paul made no distinction between the service of the Supper and the rest of the communal worship. That unbelievers were present is evidenced by their possible reaction to glossolalia (14:23 ff.) and the fact that participation in the Supper involved a proclamation. Perhaps it may be assumed that unbelievers did not partake of the elements, since what meaning could such participation have for them? Yet no formal prohibition is announced. Basically, the participants were to examine themselves. Improper participation provokes judgment—a judgment that God imparts. Some churches who demand "closed communion" have assumed God's role as judge; some churches who practice "open communion" fail to remind the participants of the seriousness of the Supper.

Nowhere does Paul mention those who officiate at the observance of the Lord's Supper. This is particularly significant in light of his discussion of ecclesiastical functionaries in chapter 12. It seems necessary to conclude that no special class of official was designated for this function. Of course, some leaders had to offer the prayers and distribute the food, but these could have come from the helpers or the administrators. Therefore, those who consider presiding at the Eucharist to be a special gift of the Spirit, and one of the highest, need to be reminded that there are a variety of gifts and that their special prerogative is not mentioned by the apostle. This is not to suggest that those who preside at the Supper are without qualifications. They are those who have examined themselves and are able to so lead that God's action will be apparent and man's response appropriate.

It may be assumed, with Cullmann, that the Lord's Supper was the central action of weekly worship (Acts 20:7).[53] Thus, it is encouraging to find many Protestant groups concerned with the frequency of observance.[54] The notion that holding the Lord's Supper every Sunday renders it commonplace is answered by Roman Catholic and Anglican frequency of observance without loss of solemnity. This is not to excuse those whose frequent celebration of the Supper is without understanding, or whose major concern is to so arrange the service that the elements can be distributed in twelve-and-a-half minutes instead of thirteen. Nevertheless, when the Lord's Supper is observed every Sunday, then something really happens in worship. The choir may be flat and the sermon may be flat, but when the Supper is offered, then God has acted.

The question of spiritual gifts is rarely raised in most segments of the church. Those who "speak in tongues" are looked upon as the socially disfranchised, the psychologically disordered. Yet those who make such judgments, failing to discern the unity of the body, may more easily fall under the wrath of God than the weaker brethren whom they disparage. Paul's judgment against those who claim some special baptism of the Spirit is just as valid today as then; speaking in tongues is inferior to intelligible communication and, at best, is to be practiced in private. Actually in our day of more sophisticated anthropological knowledge—a day when expressions like glossolalia are totally foreign—it is a question as to whether speaking in tongues should be encouraged at all. Remember, sheer emotion is no criterion for true worship, "however you may have been moved" (12:2).

In today's church the question is whether anyone is moved at all.

[53] *Ibid.*, pp. 26 ff.
[54] Cf. Max Thurian, *The Eucharistic Memorial*, Part II, tr. J. G. Davies, "Ecumenical Studies in Worship, No. 8" (Richmond: John Knox Press, 1961), pp. 125 ff.

Some have not "even heard that there is a Holy Spirit" (Acts 18:2). The order of service is so formally prescribed that the Spirit has no chance to move. Should a revelation be granted to someone sitting by, he could not offer it to the congregation since his name would not appear on the program. Of course, it is wrong to conclude that the Spirit cannot help in the planning of the service's order, and it should not be supposed that only highly liturgical services lack inspiration. Sometimes a High Anglican can celebrate the Eucharist with more genuine emotion than some Pentecostals have ever known. Some of the less liturgical orders have a deadening formality quite as rigid as any prescribed by the prayer book. In a tiny rural church in Oregon, a rustic Sunday school superintendent led the "opening exercises" with unvaried rigidity: "Now to your hymnals. . . . Now to your leaflets. . . . Now to your classes."

What we need is that balance of order and freedom which characterized the Pauline churches. Worship needs to be formal. It is not a matter to be undertaken carelessly. Patterns of worship help the worshiper to participate meaningfully. Yet, there should be times of informality, too—times when small groups gather for confession and prayer. Evening services which allow spontaneity and stress Christian fellowship ought to be encouraged. Naturally, such informality should not descend into egocentric display or emotional excess; all things must be done in order and for the edification of the church. Although it is bad when an outsider comes in and says you are mad, it is worse when a visitor comes in and says you are dead.

This is the real problem with contemporary worship. It lacks vitality. Even during the height of the religious revival, attendance at worship was nothing to brag about. People were drawn to the church by other inducements—friendly coffee hours and cheery couples' clubs. Worship was often viewed as something unbearably dull which had to be endured. It was not so in the early church. There the Christians broke bread "with glad and generous hearts" (Acts 2:46). The new age had begun to dawn, and the new day was heralded with joy and praise. Over against the powers of darkness, the believers proclaimed "Jesus Christ is Lord" (Phil. 2:11). He was the risen Christ, victorious over death, present in the worshiping community; his way was love, his message good news. To worship him was to look to the future with joy, to anticipate with vital hope the total triumph of the end time. So they prayed with eagerness, *"Maranatha"*—"Our Lord, come!" (I Cor. 16:22.)

VI
THE PROBLEM OF DEATH

Roger Shinn has written that the "modern world is . . .
morbidly preoccupied with death." [1] But so man has always been.
Every philosophy and every religion has had to face this ultimate
problem. And so it was at Corinth. Paul had saved the biggest and
most basic question for the last. If man could answer this question
about the destiny of his life, then many of the lesser problems of his
existence could be resolved in course. This was a problem about his
very nature—a problem in which all other difficulties found their
origin. Paul's answer, of course, states the Christian doctrine of the
resurrection—a doctrine as strange to us as it seemed to men of Athens
long ago (Acts 17:32).

[1] Roger L. Shinn, *Life, Death, and Destiny*, "Layman's Theological Library" (Philadelphia: Westminster Press, 1957), p. 38.

I

What was the nature of the problem at Corinth? Well, for one thing, men in Paul's day had become skeptical about any possibility of life after death. Festugière points out that "in the first century before our era it can be said that beliefs about a life beyond the tomb were regarded by knowledgeable people as no better than old wives' tales." [2] The Stoics suggested a stoical attitude toward death; since all men must die, do not weep but learn to accept it calmly as the natural end of human life. The Epicureans insisted that death should hold no threats for genuine happiness: Since there is nothing after death, death cannot possibly harm you, so why fear it now? Saracophagi and gravestones from the Hellenistic age depict a quiet acceptance of death as a normal or even a happy occasion. Sometimes these ancient coffins are decorated with chubby cherubs whose very presence belies all wailing, or funeral monuments may display noble family scenes to remind the remaining that the life which is gone was good and all that man should expect. Death is here to stay, accept it.

But many were not satisfied. It was just that Epicurean notion that death was the end which really bothered them. Therefore, many of the older beliefs about some future existence persisted. Among the Jews, none of these beliefs were very old. Ancient Hebrew religion simply did not stress life after death. True enough, man might survive the grave in *sheol*—a cold and shadowy existence beneath the earth, almost worse than no survival at all.[3] The idea of a meaningful life after death is scarcely to be discovered in the Old Testament, and where it is found, as in passages like Isa. 26:19, scholars are quick to assign the material to a later time.[4] Indeed, after the failure of the national hope and under the influence of their Persian overlords, ideas of a

[2] *Epicurus and His Gods,* p. 12.
[3] Cf. Pss. 55:15; 116:3; Ezek. 31:15 ff.
[4] Cf. Millar Burrows, *An Outline of Biblical Theology* (Philadelphia: Westminster Press, 1946), p. 204.

future fulfillment were inaugurated into Hebrew religion.[5] If there were no guarantee of victory in this world, and if the hope of achievement in one's descendants were precarious, then the Jews might entertain some notion of triumph in another existence, some survival beyond the grave. As in the Iranian religion of their neighbors, the struggle between the cosmic powers of good and evil would have to be resolved in a struggle transcending ordinary existence.

Of course, not all Jews were convinced. The Sadducees, who held strictly to the books of Moses, considered the idea of resurrection to be both unscriptural and irrational (Mark 12:18 ff.). The Pharisaic idea of life beyond the grave did involve a doctrine of resurrection—a notion that the very body which was laid in the tomb was revived and raised up to life. Quite apart from the fact that acceptance of this notion involved mental gymnastics for some intellectuals, the idea of the resurrection even resulted in debate among its adherents. What was the precise nature of the resuscitated body? Would the wicked be raised as well as the righteous; and if so, what would be their fate? The rabbis liked to debate the question as to whether the resurrected would be raised clothed or naked, sometimes using Cleopatra as their example.[6] Surely, the resurrection was not to be missed, but even the faithful were undecided about its nature.

The reason Judaism posited a doctrine of bodily resurrection was that it could conceive of no other kind of existence beyond the grave. Man was a unity, body and soul, and the concept of a bodiless soul was inconceivable.[7] It was not so among the Hellenists. For them, man was a duad. His body was of the earth, earthly; his soul was from the heavens, divine. As Seneca wrote: "This poor body, the prison and fetter of the soul, is tossed hither and thither; upon it punishments, upon it rob-

---

[5] For an excellent discussion of the foreign influence on Old Testament ideas about life after death, cf. Robert Martin-Achard, *From Death to Life—A Study of the Development of the Doctrine of the Resurrection in the Old Testament*, tr. John Penney Smith (Edinburgh: Oliver and Boyd, 1960), pp. 186 ff. He concludes that "Iranian influence on the formation of the Old Testament belief in the resurrection must be neither exaggerated nor denied" (p. 193).

[6] Babylonian *Talmud, Sanhedrin,* 90b. The translation of this text is, however, disputed.

[7] Cf. E. C. Rust, *Nature and Man in Biblical Thought* (London: Lutterworth Press, 1953), pp. 95 ff.

beries, upon it diseases work their will. But the soul itself is sacred and eternal, and upon it no hand can be laid." [8] The body is bad, the soul good, immortal. This anthropology could find primitive expression in the story of Dionysus.[9] According to the myth, Dionysus, a favorite son of Zeus, was devoured by the Titans. When Zeus learned of their treachery, he destroyed these terrible beings with his thunderbolt. Man, so the legend goes, arose from the smoldering ashes—his body descended from the Titans, utterly evil; his spirit composed of the divine fire, eternally good. The doctrine became almost axiomatic with sophisticated philosophers like Plato. It was based not simply on some mythological or philosophical speculation, however, but on keen observation of the human predicament. It seemed that the body was the place where evil and corruption took their grip on man, where base lusts found their origin. All nobility, all creativity, on the other hand, was located in the mind or spirit—a realm somehow aloof from material contingency.

In this view, death could hold no real threat for man. The body would die, to be sure, but with it would perish all that was evil in man. The soul was eternal in its very nature. With it would survive all that was really good in man. Death was a sort of graduation exercise—an event in which the limitations of the body were to be overcome by the freedom of the spirit, or to quote Seneca again, "Death is a release from all suffering, a boundary beyond which our ills cannot pass—it restores us to that peaceful state in which we lay before we were born." [10]

But what was the "peaceful state"? Had not Plato suggested that the eternal soul of man was continually being reborn into new forms of life? [11] What frightening shape would it occupy in the next existence? The skepticism and fear of death in the Hellenistic age did not result from some sophisticated notion that life without a body is scientifically problematical. It was the product of a pervasive fatalism that clouded the whole age. Perhaps it also reflected a tacit concern with the body after all, for although the dissolution of the husk of man's being was

[8] *Moral Essays*, "Loeb Classical Library," II, 457 ff.
[9] Cf. Frederick C. Grant, ed., *Hellenistic Religions*, pp. 107 ff.
[10] *Moral Essays*, ii, 67, Cf. Nilsson, *Greek Piety*, p. 155.
[11] *Republic*, x, 16.

empirically evident, with it went the hope of individual significance. If a soul was born today as Caesar, and tomorrow as Casear's slave, and day after tomorrow as Caesar's dog, what was the actual identity of the soul? It was just this search for some meaningful existence which plagued Hellenistic man—the man whose old collective securities (the city-state, the ancestral religion) were so rapidly dissolving.

The belief in individual immortality was found by many within the popular mystery cults recently imported from the East. Here a myth was usually basic. The story was told, with countless variations, of some god who somehow died and somehow rose again. Osiris, for instance, had been killed by a jealous rival, his body chopped up and scattered all over Egypt.[12] But his beloved consort, Isis, went wandering about the earth searching for the pieces. When she found them, she put them together, and Osiris came back to life. Devotees of the cult who participated in the reenactment of the ritual drama (no literal chopping up, of course) were guaranteed the same immortality as the god. To be sure, it was an immortality of the soul, not of the body, and in the related gnostic cults the notion of a bodiless eternity was elementary doctrine. Yet the idea of individual survival was assured, so that the members of the cult were freed from any threat of defacing reincarnations. The cults were themselves harbors for derelict individuals, and their rituals offered personal immortality.

Nevertheless, the myth had a basis in nature; the dying and rising of the deity was symbolic of the rhythm of the seasons. As vegetation died in winter only to be raised fertile in the spring, so rose the god and men. Life after death became, as in older Greek religion, a matter of the natural order. But if it is so closely related to nature, as in the mystery cults, how is it so easily freed from the imprisoning cycles of nature itself; how is the body with its problems and involvements so readily disposed?

Are any of these views reflected in the thinking of the Corinthian Christians? If we are to accept the recent attempt to homogenize the Corinthian opposition, the answer would probably be, "no," or at least, "not many." Scholars like Schniewind have insisted that Paul's op-

---

[12] For an ancient account of this myth in its various forms and interpretations, cf. Plutarch, "Isis and Osiris" (Moralia), "Loeb Classical Library," V, 6 ff.

ponents were a particular brand of Gnostics who held that the eschatological benefits had already been appropriated. With the coming of the Spirit the new life had already come; there wasn't any more.[13] Such a view readily accepts the reality of Christ's resurrection, but emphatically denies the possibility of any future resurrection for the faithful. Texts like I Cor. 4:8 certainly witness to the existence of this kind of "realized eschatology" among the Corinthians, while arguments like, "If the dead are not raised, then Christ has not been raised" (15:16), seem to presuppose a belief in the resurrection of Christ on the part of Paul's readers.

However, this presupposition rests on the acceptance of Paul's previous argument. If the opponents had originally acknowledged Christ's resurrection, why does Paul spend the first eleven verses of chapter fifteen arguing for its reality, stressing especially the witnesses of that event whose testimony can be attested? Similarly, in vs. 17, the apostle begins, "If Christ has not been raised," as if the possibility of denial is open to his hearers. If the objectors are limited to gnosticism, one wonders how Paul can quote them as saying, "How are the dead raised? With what kind of body do they come?" Could the Gnostics, whose basic beliefs preclude the possibility of a bodily existence after death, actually ask about the nature of the resurrection body? Of course, it could be maintained that their question is sarcastic, that the very raising of the question with its ludicrous implications is itself a refutation of Paul's ridiculous doctrine of a bodily resurrection. However, the argument which follows takes the question literally and proceeds to talk about the varieties of bodily existence. The question has been raised, no doubt, by men who can conceive of a physical resurrection; that they should be identified as Gnostics is incredible.

It is better to suppose that I Cor. 15, like the rest of the letter, is written to a cosmopolitan community whose views of life after death are varied. Thus when one raises a question about the character of the resurrection body, it is best to assume that he comes into the church out of a background of Pharisaic Judaism, and when Paul answers that question using precisely the same figure of speech (kernel and wheat)

[13] Julius Schniewind, "Die Leugner der Auferstehung in Korinth," *Nachgelassene Reden und Aufsätze* (Berlin: Alfred Töpelmann, 1952), pp. 110 ff.

which the rabbis employed in their discussions of the resurrection body,[14] then that assumption is confirmed. Similarly, when Paul asserts, "Some of you say that there is no resurrection of the dead" (15:12), we may suppose that these are Corinthian Christians subject to the general skepticism of their age. Otherwise, why should Paul cite the typical Epicurean proverb, "Let us eat and drink, for tomorrow we die" (vs. 32)?

It is also possible, as the older commentators like Lietzmann and Moffatt assert, that some Corinthians held to a view of immortality of the soul while rejecting the resurrection. There is no explicit evidence for this in chapter 15. However, Paul's careful handling of the idea of the "spiritual body" may indicate a subtle refutation of the notion of bodiless spirits, as may the phrase, "if there is a physical body, there is also a spiritual body" (vs. 44). At any rate, it is at least possible that the Corinthians had been answering the problem of life after death in three ways, typical of their age—complete skepticism, a belief in immortality of the soul, a doctrine of resurrection of the body. As we have seen, none of these views is without its problems; and as we shall see, none of them, at least in its current form, is for Paul an adequate solution to the problem of death.

II

When we turn to Paul's instruction on this problem, one thing is clear from the outset. Paul posits a doctrine of resurrection; his is in no sense a Greek belief in immortality. This is due, in part, to the Hebrew-Christian idea of man which the apostle readily accepts.[15] Man is a unity. He is not some sort of a metaphysical schizophrenic. Although he consists of body and soul, these are simply his outer and inner beings, not two hostile powers, one essentially evil, the other innately good and eternal. True enough, the inner nature sometimes

[14] Cf. Strack and Billerbeck, *Kommentar zum Neuen Testament*, III, 475.
[15] Cf. Werner Georg Kümmel, *Man in the New Testament*, tr. John J. Vincent (Philadelphia: Westminster Press, 1963), pp. 38 ff.

struggles against the outer, but the latter is not the exclusive locus of evil. The lusts of the flesh include such "spiritual" sins as "enmity, strife, jealousy, anger, selfishness" (Gal. 5:19 ff.). Indeed, the word "flesh" for Paul represents no metaphysical terminology; it belongs instead to the realm of morality and soteriology. To live "according to the flesh" does not mean primarily to possess a physical body but to live under the power of sin, subject to the evil forces who hold sway over this world.[16] The spirit which aids man in the earthly struggle is not a natural attribute of every man but a gift of God, granted to those who respond to his revelation with faith. As for man's essential nature, he was created body and soul by God, and as Paul's Bible clearly said, "God saw everything that he had made, and behold, it was very good" (Gen. 1:31). Man, therefore, does not possess an eternal spirit which is delivered at death from association with a corruptible body. Rather, his whole being has been corrupted by sin; his whole being must be redeemed by the God who made all things good.

Paul's rejection of Hellenistic notions of immortality also rests on his acceptance of the Hebrew-Christian view of death. In contrast to the Greek view that death is a pleasant release from the prison of the body, the Old and New Testaments assert that death is the one great threatening reality. Nowhere is this so graphically seen as in a comparison of the deaths of Socrates and Jesus, as Cullmann reminds us.[17] The Greek sage died a noble death, quietly drinking the hemlock in happy acceptance of the imminent immortality. The man from Nazareth wrestled with death, earnestly prayed that the cup might pass from him, cried in anguish from the cross. As to a noble example for dying, Jesus comes off second best. This may in part result from the Christian view of man. Since man is a unity, the death of man is not simply the sloughing off of some unessential part of his nature but the destruction of his whole being. In dying, man is just like the subject of the little boy's jingle:

> I had a little dog
> His name was Rover,

---

[16] Cf. Bultmann, *Theology of the New Testament*, I, 239 ff.

[17] *Immortality of the Soul or Resurrection of the Dead?—The Witness of the New Testament* (New York: The Macmillan Company, 1958), pp. 19 ff.

> When he lived,
>> He lived on clover.
> When he died,
>> He died all over.

But more than this, anguish on the lips of Jesus means that death stands over against the will of God. As Paul says, "The last enemy to be destroyed is death" (15:26).

With these presuppositions in mind let us proceed to analyze Paul's argument in regard to the resurrection. First, he insists that the resurrection of the Christian is grounded in the resurrection of Christ— the event which is basic to the whole Christian faith (15:1-11). The resurrection of the Lord is the essential element in the church's message. Paul begins by saying, "Now I would remind you, brethren, in what terms I preached to you the gospel, which you received, in which you stand, by which you are saved" (vss. 1-2). Their entire Christian existence is dependent on the message which the apostle proclaimed. Yet this *kerygma* was not exclusively Paul's; he delivered to the Corinthians what he had received. The words which Paul employs to describe this receiving (*paralambanō*) and delivering (*paradidomi*) represent technical terms used to express the reception and handing on of traditional doctrine. Moreover, some of the phrases which compose the following expression of the *kerygma* have a certain un-Pauline ring, as Joachim Jeremias has shown.[18] The message which Paul describes here, then, is essentially the same as the message of the church which was before him.

As to content, the message stresses the events of God's revelatory action in Christ:

> Christ died
> he was buried
> he was raised
> he appeared.

The last two elements are crucial. Not only is the resurrection the topic of discussion here in chapter 15, it is also essential to the formulation

---

[18] *The Eucharistic Words of Jesus*, pp. 129 ff.

of the whole message. Without the resurrection faith no church would have originated which could have announced this gospel. Yet it was just this event, the resurrection, that was causing such difficulty to the Corinthian skeptics. They were apparently Christians who would have readily worshiped on Good Friday but would have been quite uncomfortable on Easter. They were like believers of all generations who, hearing about the resurrection, want to know what really happened.

Theologians like Karl Barth, of course, find this kind of question out of order.[19] To ask about the historicity of the resurrection is already to misunderstand it, and thus to miss it. The resurrection is no event to be put alongside other events; it is unique, the act of God who wholly transcends history. To subject the resurrection to any of the canons of historical investigation is both to deny it by definition and to undermine the radical character of faith which its acceptance demands.

There are elements of truth here. Surely the resurrection is a unique event; it is the great act of God quite unlike other happenings. The resurrection of Christ is different, for example, from any other raising of the dead reported in the Scriptures, since it is the event which announces the lordship of Christ, the triumph of God. It is also true that the truth of the resurrection cannot be established by any arduous effort of historical research. Even if that were possible, it would rob the resurrection doctrine of its essential basis in faith; if belief in the resurrection rests on the results of human investigation, then it depends not on trust in God but on the efforts of men; such faith is no faith.

However, some theologians insist that the historical character of Christianity demands a doctrine of the resurrection which has historical content. Thus, Richard R. Niebuhr says, "When the resurrection of Christ is thought of as a 'sacred event,' transcending the historical continuum that conditions all experiential concepts and perception, it has in fact lost its revelatory quality." [20] Although this charge is actually leveled at Rudolf Bultmann, the question can be raised as to whether

---

[19] *Church Dogmatics, I/2—The Doctrine of the Word of God*, tr. G. T. Thomson and Harold Knight (New York: Charles Scribner's Sons, 1956), pp. 106 ff.; *The Resurrection of the Dead*, tr. H. J. Stenning (New York: Fleming H. Revell, Co. 1933), pp. 134 ff.

[20] *Resurrection and Historical Reason* (New York: Charles Scribner's Sons, 1957), p. 87.

Niebuhr really understands Bultmann's view of history, let alone his notion of the resurrection.[21] Niebuhr himself has insisted that the resurrection cannot be judged by the canons of nineteenth-century historiography, and it is just such a view shaped by the methodology of the natural sciences which Bultmann attempts to avoid. His confession that the resurrection is *the* eschatological event does not necessitate the conclusion that the resurrection is not (in his understanding) historical.[22] But, although we cannot solve the quarrel at this point, we may adopt a historical methodology which may allow both the category of uniqueness (Niebuhr) and the possibility of radical faith (Bultmann).

On the basis of such an understanding of history, what may be said about the historical aspect of the *kerygma* as described in I Cor. 15:3 ff.? No one will deny, of course, that Christ died. However, when the *kerygma* states that "he was buried," some readers imagine that Paul, or at least the gospel which he had received, included a clear implication of the doctrine of the empty tomb. This doctrine, so the argument runs, is the most historical and verifiable of the whole resurrection complex, and therefore the solid ground for understanding the resurrection as an event of history. It must be acknowledged that some heroic support for the empty tomb idea has been enlisted of late by people like von Campenhausen.[23] It is also true that on occasion Paul seems to talk about a transformed body (cf. Phil. 3:21) as if the old body is used in the creation of the new with the result that the tomb would have to have been empty; and it is true, too, that deniers of the historicity of the empty tomb cannot avoid the question, "What happened to the body?"

Nevertheless, all of these questions have been adequately answered by Hans Grass.[24] Von Campenhausen's notion that the disciples waited around in Jerusalem until they received the report of the empty tomb

[21] Cf. Schubert M. Ogden, *Christ without Myth* (New York: Harper & Row, 1961), pp. 86 ff.

[22] Bultmann can even refer to the acts of God as "objective." Cf. "Zum Problem der Entmythologisierung," *Kerygma und Mythos,* ed. Hans Werner Bartsch (Hamburg-Volksdorf: Herbert Reich, 1952), II, 196.

[23] Hans Frhr. von Campenhausen, *Der Ablauf der Osterereignisse und das leere Grab,* "Sitzungberichte der Heidelberger Akademie der Wissenschaften" (2d ed., Heidelberg: Carl Winter, 1958). Cf. Jindrich Maneck, "The Apostle Paul and the Empty Tomb," *Novum Testamentum,* II (1958), 276 ff.

[24] *Ostergeschehen und Osterberichte* (2d ed., Göttingen: Vandenhoeck & Ruprecht, 1962), pp. 138 ff.

from women who as yet had no resurrection faith, and then rushed off to Galilee to receive the resurrection appearances, is simply incredible. Those who stress the transformation of the body need to be reminded of texts like II Cor. 5:1 ff., where the dissolution of the old body is clearly implied. Probably the idea of the empty tomb was introduced late into the tradition for apologetic and polemic reasons. In no case was it an essential element of the *kerygma*. Our text is, of course, the oldest extant formulation of that message, but even the early chapters of Acts report no tours to the "garden tomb," where dubious listeners are convinced of the truth of the resurrection proclamation. Even the first to receive the report of the empty tomb are said not to have believed (Luke 24:11). The empty tomb, even if historical, would have been powerless to elicit faith. The point of the statement, "He was buried," was to stress the reality of Christ's death so as to underscore the certainty of God's action in his resurrection.

But if the empty tomb is of doubtful historicity, what are we to make of the suggestion that the resurrection can be dated—a suggestion apparently expressed in the statement that Christ was raised "on the third day"? Unfortunately, this bit of data also falls before the critic's sharp sickle. If the idea of the third day results merely from the antique notions that three days intervene between important events, or that the soul of the dead hovers around the grave for three days (both of which are improbable interpretations), then no historical data have been revealed anyway. But actually, the resurrection on the third day is without a unanimous tradition. Although similar texts speak of resurrection "on the third day" (Matt. 16:21; 17:23, etc.), others suggest that the Son of man was to remain "three days and three nights in the heart of the earth" (Matt. 12:40)—a statement which not only creates historical difficulties of its own but also lacks precise agreement with the idea of resurrection on the third day. The assumption that early Christian worship on the first day of the week supports the historicity of the third day tradition ignores the probability that the formulation of that tradition antedates the crystallization of Sunday worship in the primitive community. Not even proof of the discovery of the empty tomb or the occurrence of resurrection appearances on the first day of the week could secure the resurrection *event* for Sunday; empty tomb and appearances have to do with the consequences of the event, not with the event itself.

Most likely, the belief that the raising of Christ took place on the third day results from the motif of fulfilled prophecy.[25] As Paul says, this event of the third day was "in accordance with the scriptures" (15:4). The Old Testament text which the apostle (or better, the *kerygma*) had in mind was probably Hosea 6:2. Although that passage appears to us to refer to a contemporary situation and to say very little about the resurrection of the dead, the Jewish rabbis often interpreted it as referring to the resurrection at the last day. Finally, when the *kerygma* employs precisely the same words as the Greek version of the ancient prophet, it is difficult to avoid the conclusion that the whole idea finds its origin here. The concept of the resurrection on the third day is not a matter of history but of theology.

So, too, is the other reference to scripture in our passage. When Paul says that "Christ died for our sins in accordance with the scriptures" (vs. 3), he may have specific texts like Isa. 53 in mind. Nevertheless, the assiduous effort to find precisely what passages he had in view, and to evaluate what they meant in their original contexts, often misses the basic point. Paul's concern is not to cite chapter and verse in support of his theology or to prove that the prophets of the past were the peerless predictors of the future. Rather, his intent was to witness to what God had done. The crucifixion-resurrection is the realization of the scriptures' concerted witness; the scriptures which testify to the whole drama of God's redemptive act in history find their culminating message in this—that God has raised Christ from the dead.

Yet, if both the empty tomb and the third day are of questionable historicity, what is left to be said about the historical manifestations of this divine action? This question can be answered only on the basis of a consideration of the resurrection appearances. Paul presents a list:

> he appeared to Cephas
> then to the twelve
> he appeared to more than five hundred brethren at one time

[25] Cf. Grass, *ibid.*, pp. 127 ff. Against this, cf. B. M. Metzger, "A Suggestion Concerning the Meaning of I Cor. XV. 4*b*," *Journal of Theological Studies*, VIII (1957), 118 ff.

then he appeared to James
then to all the apostles
last of all, he appeared also to me (vss. 5-8).

The analysis of this record of the appearances of the risen Christ is fraught with all sorts of difficulties. It is generally felt that the traditional material contained in the pre-Pauline *kerygma* included only the first two members of the list, although some scholars find evidence of two or three different lines of tradition underlying the whole text.[26] In any case, it is clear that all of these appearances could have been confirmed by the personal experience of Paul (cf. Gal. 1:18-19.) quite apart from any intervening tradition. The fact that Paul asserts that most of the five hundred brethren are still alive affords the possibility of the same sort of confirmation to his readers as well.

We need not be long occupied with some of the related questions. What relation does "the twelve" have to "all the apostles"? At least, the latter may be assumed to be a larger group. What relation do these appearances have to those recorded in the Synoptic tradition? Actually, only the appearances to the five hundred,[27] to James, and to Paul are lacking there, and in all three cases the testimony of the apostle is indubitable; the accounts in the Gospels are secondary, and where they include appearances missing in Paul, he is to be preferred as probably listing all the appearances of the resurrection known to him. Although the New Testament is not wholly clear on the matter, Paul's argument is without ambiguity. Christ has appeared to certain witnesses whose testimony can be verified—a testimony sufficient to demonstrate to the Corinthians that God had raised Christ from the dead.

But if the testimony rests simply on the confession of witnesses, is not the resurrection a purely subjective phenomenon? How are we justified in assuming that the resurrection is an event with historical mani-

[26] Cf. Paul Winter, "I Corinthians XV 3b-7," *Novum Testamentum*, II (1958), 142 ff.; Ernst Bammel, "Herkunft und Funktion der Traditionselemente in 1. Kor. 15, 1-11," *Theologisches Zeitschrift*, XI (1955), 401 ff.

[27] The attempt to identify the appearance to the five hundred with the events of Pentecost which was suggested by E. von Dobschütz, *Ostern und Pfingsten* (Leipzig: J. C. Hinrichs, 1903), pp. 31 ff., and which has recently been advocated by S. MacLean Gilmour, "The Christophany to More than Five Hundred Brethren," *Journal of Biblical Literature*, LXXX (1961), 248 ff., is unconvincing.

festations? Admittedly, the word which Paul uses for the appearances (ōphthē) is often employed to describe visionary experiences, but it can have a more mundane meaning as well. The problem with describing the resurrection appearances as visions, of course, is that some scholars wish thereby to psychologize away the resurrection event as a mere hallucination, the product of strain and stress, the result of exaggerated expectation. Quite apart from the fact that such suppositions cannot adequately explain the vitality of the resurrection faith, the definition of vision which ensues is too narrowly conceived. Is it not possible, as Grass suggests,[28] that God can actually act in a vision and who, except those who attempt ill-advisedly to force the movements of history into the categories of natural science, can deny that a vision may actually be a phenomenon of history?

The real evidence for the resurrection event, however, is to be found in the testimony of Paul himself. "Last of all . . . he appeared also to me." (vs. 8.) Here is the confession of an eyewitness of the resurrection. Is his witness to be denied? Surely, his whole existence is proof of its validity. Though formerly a persecutor of the church of God (vs. 9), the experience of the resurrection led him to propagate its faith to the ends of the earth (vs. 10). Paul's new existence is a phenomenon of history, and, he says, "By the grace of God I am what I am" (vs. 10)— a grace granted the apostle through God's action in the revelation of the risen Christ. The entire New Testament, the whole history of the church, the total movement of Christendom within history is dependent on the resurrection faith of Paul and the rest of the apostles.

But, one may object, we are talking here of the resurrection faith, not proving the reality of the resurrection fact. Although the resurrection is not a fact which can be proved,[29] nor the solid proof on which a faith can be built, and although the event of the resurrection was perceived only by the eyes of faith, it may be argued that the resurrection faith is itself a phenomenon of history, since its overt expression shaped the course of historical events.

Can we go farther? Is it really possible to accept the resurrection

[28] *Ostergeschehen und Osterberichte*, pp. 189 ff.; 233 ff.
[29] The effort to prove the resurrection is still maintained by some theologians; cf., for instance, Michael Ramsey, *The Resurrection of Christ* (2d ed. London: Geoffrey Bles, 1946), pp. 33 ff.

faith and deny the resurrection event? Can the faith that God raised Christ from the dead have any meaning if God did not actually raise Christ from the dead? Paul, surely, would have answered "no." Hint of his belief in the genuine historical character of the resurrection can be seen in his phrase, "last of all." By this, he probably does not mean that the appearance to him was simply the last of a continuing series. Considerable time has elapsed since his own experience of the resurrection, yet he knows of no other appearances. He must conclude that the appearance of Christ to him was last of all; there would be no more. The appearances are not to be confused with ordinary visions or continuing perception of the glory of God in the face of Christ (II Cor. 4:4-6). The resurrection appearances are unique—the manifestations of a virtual act of God—an act which, though it cannot be limited to the third day, had its boundaries set in history. Among all the transiencies of history, Paul is certain of one event: God hath raised Christ from the dead!

III

If the resurrection of Christ is established, then the rest of Paul's argument seems to follow logically. He goes on to consider the consequences of denying the resurrection (vss. 12-19). He is answering the objections either of those who accept the raising of Christ while denying the resurrection of the dead (Gnostics), or of those who had doubted any life after death until being moved by the force of Paul's argument (vss. 1-11) to acknowledge the resurrection of Christ (Skeptics). In any case, Paul is speaking to Christians; basic elements of the faith are taken as presuppositions to his discussion. Thus the fundamental point of his argument is that acceptance of the proclamation of the risen Christ precludes denial of the raising of Christians. Paul begins, "Now if Christ is preached as raised from the dead, how can some of you say that there is no resurrection of the dead?" That Christ has been preached as raised has just been established; that denial of the resurrection is an impossibility is about to be demonstrated.

In developing his argument Paul actually follows two lines of reasoning. They are quite similar, although the first (vss. 13-15) places a slight emphasis on the witnesses to the gospel, while the second (vss. 16-18) puts a subtle stress on the recipients of the resurrection message. In structure each of the lines of argument consists of three elements. First, he employs two "if-then" clauses followed by a general conclusion. The first line may be outlined as follows:

> If there is no resurrection of the dead,
>   then Christ has not been raised.
>
> If Christ has not been raised,
>   then our preaching is in vain and your faith is in vain.
>
> We are even found to be misrepresenting God,
>   because we testified of God that he raised Christ.

The argument is quite clear. The first point is almost syllogistic:

> No men are raised from the dead.
> Christ is a man.
> Therefore, Christ is not raised from the dead.

The Corinthian Christians, of course, cannot accept the conclusion. They believe in the resurrection of Christ. The major premise is, therefore, put into question.

The second point takes up the false conclusion of the first and shows that it has still more incredible consequences. If Christ has not been raised, the preaching of the apostles is in vain, or as the New English Bible says, "null and void." As his readers have seen, the resurrection of Christ is an essential element of Paul's proclamation—"no resurrection, no gospel!" comments Moffatt.[30] The Corinthians know, however, that Christ is the content of the gospel—a gospel which is not simply a recitation of kerygmatic data but a vital presentation of the living Christ (Gal. 3:1; II Cor. 4:4 ff.). They know that this gospel is not empty or in vain, for through their response of faith they have been empowered with the divine Spirit (I Cor. 1:7). Their faith

[30] *Moffatt New Testament Commentary*, p. 236.

is not in vain; it is the very ground for the working of God.

Yet deny the gospel of the resurrection and you abuse its heralds—you abuse those whose daily dying for the gospel has made possible your new life in the power of God (II Cor. 4:7 ff.). If you deny the resurrection, you affirm that these apostles of God are false prophets; the resurrection is the very word which they proclaim. If you deny the truth of their proclamation, you assert that Paul and his colleagues are fraudulent witnesses to the work of God; they declare that God raised Christ from the dead. Blasphemy of even the "least of the apostles" (vs. 9) is bad enough, but the Corinthians appear to have done more. They have stood in the very presence of the power of God and said, "I do not know him."

The second line of argument can be similarly summarized:

> If the dead are not raised,
>   then Christ has not been raised.
>
> If Christ has not been raised,
>   your faith is futile and you are still in your sins.
>
> Then those who have fallen asleep in Christ have perished.

The first point is practically identical with its parallel statement in the earlier line of argument—absolute denial of resurrection necessitates denial of the resurrection of Christ. There is a slight change in construction, however. Whereas in vs. 13 Paul spoke of the resurrection of the dead (*anastasis nekrōn*), here he refers to the dead as subject (*nekroi*); the former discusses the principle of resurrection; the latter depicts people who are to be raised.

In any case, the second point focuses sharply on the plight of men who lack the resurrection faith. Their response to God has been futile, since they are still in their sins. Thus denying the resurrection means rejection of the gospel which "is the power of God for salvation" (Rom. 1:16). But surely the Corinthians have not done that; surely most of them have submitted to the folly of the Cross which saves those who believe (I Cor. 1:21). Yet they need to be reminded that salvation cannot be based exclusively on the crucifixion, but demands also the doctrine of the resurrection; that he who carried the cross also wears the crown; that we worship not only the dead Messiah but also the living Lord who calls the living to come forth from the dead.

If God does not do that, says Paul, "Then those who have fallen asleep in Christ have perished." The verb *koimaō* ("to fall asleep") is used by both classical and Hellenistic authors to describe death. In no case, however, is Paul suggesting a euphemism; for him, death is to be taken seriously; it is the last enemy (15:26). Although he may be simply taking up contemporary usage, Paul seems to have a special idea for the death of the Christian. The key phrase is "in Christ." For those who die *in the Lord,* death maintains its seriousness but loses its sting (vs. 56). Dying for them is different; they are held in a special relationship with the risen Christ as they await the putting on of their incorruptible bodies at the end of time (II Cor. 5:8; Rom. 14:8). Those who perish, on the other hand, are those who are utterly cut off from the presence of God; their life is imprisoned in the crumbling walls of this world whose form is passing away (I Cor. 7:31), whose end is destruction.

Hence, Paul can conclude, "If our hope is grounded solely in this life, we are the most pitiable of all men" (vs. 19, WB). The Christian lives in this life with hope, but his hope is not directed toward the present. "Who hopes for what he sees?" (Rom. 8:24.) Instead, the Christian points his hope toward the God who raised Christ from the dead, who makes all things new (II Cor. 5:17), who will grant us his kingdom in the eschaton (I Cor. 4:8). The interpreter of this verse, however, must be wary of supposing that the future hope is the reason for the faith, that the Christian man directs his faith toward God because some future reward is to be received. That would be to walk by sight instead of faith, to *hope* for what one *sees.* On the contrary, hope is a consequence of the whole faith—a faith which embraces the scandal of the Cross, and hopes where there is no hope, hopes for life out of death.

That is why the Christian man, if he forfeits the resurrection faith, is of all men most to be pitied. When that faith trembles, the whole structure of his existence totters. When that faith falls, his whole life crumbles. Take away faith in the future, and there is no faith in Christ;

177

take away faith in Christ, and there is no faith in the God who raised him from the dead. Take away faith in God, and the Christians are but ordinary men (I Cor. 3:3)—"foolish, faithless, heartless, ruthless" (Rom. 1:31). But the Christians have thought it was other; they have put their trust in the God who revealed himself in Christ; they have committed their lives to him who reconciled them to himself. They have known faith, hope, love. But if their hope rests in a God who cannot triumph over the principalities and powers of this earth, who cannot renew the cosmos and triumph over the ultimate enemy, death, then their hope is nothing. It is better never to have hoped at all. Oh, pity these Christians who have *hoped* for the *seen;* they have hoped for nothing.

But the Christians have not hoped in vain. "Christ has been raised from the dead." (vs. 20.) Paul introduces this shift in argument with the phrase *nuni de*—words which he often uses to stress an important affirmation (cf. Rom. 6:22); the Revised Standard Version reading "in fact" is appropriate. The discussion which follows describes the inevitable consequences of that fact. First, Christ's resurrection is not an isolated event; it inaugurates the raising of the Christian. Christ is the "first fruits of those who have fallen asleep." Here the apostle employs a figure from Hebrew cultic practice (Lev. 23:9 ff.); when a crop was reaped, the first fruits of the harvest were offered to God. This showed that the whole crop was dedicated to the Creator. Thus, a few sheaves of grain could be lifted up to the Lord as a symbol of the whole harvest. So the resurrection of Christ is the beginning of a larger act of God—the raising of all who were one with the Messiah (cf. Rom. 11:16).

Indeed, the Christians are one with the risen Christ, just as all men are one with their ancient ancestor, Adam. "Adam" means "man," and all the descendants of this original man inherit the mortality which results from his sin (cf. Rom. 5:12 ff.). Christians, however, belong to the new humanity. Just as Adam introduced death into history, so the new man, Jesus Christ, brought resurrection of the dead. Paul's idea may be influenced by Hellenistic speculation about the primal man— a superhuman figure of whom all men are but an earthly shadow. However, the apostle's use is different. He does not speak of Christ as the first man, but as the last Adam; his idea is not mythological, but historical and eschatological. The defeat of death results from the acts of God—an action begun in Christ and to be consummated in the future. "For as in Adam all die, so also in Christ shall all be made alive." (vs. 22.) The second "all," of course, is qualified by the phrase "in Christ"; the point of the Adam-Christ figure, as that of the first fruits, is to depict the unity of Christ and those who call him Lord.

These followers of Christ, however, have not yet been raised. The events of the eschaton have only begun to unfold, and they shall proceed according to the divinely appointed order. That Paul conceives of this sequence in a chronological fashion is clear from his use of *epeita* ("then," vs. 23) and *eita* ("then," vs. 24). The actual order will be as follows:

> Christ the first fruits
> those who belong to Christ
> then comes the end.

The first event, the resurrection of Christ, has already occurred; the rest is future. Of this, Corinthians who suppose that the eschaton has already come need to be reminded. The character of the raising of the Christians is not described until later in the chapter. Here it is merely said that it will take place "at his coming," that is, at the *parousia* of Christ. The coming of the triumphant Lord heralds the resurrection of the dead.

About "the end" more is said, but the details are baffling. The key sentence seems to be: "Then comes the end, when he delivers the kingdom to God the Father after destroying every rule and every authority and power" (vs. 24). The rest appears to be explanation of this consummation of God's purposes. The end, of course, does not mean termination but fulfillment; it refers to the completion of God's creative intention. Thus, Christ, his reigning Messiah, must conquer all the forces which resist divine control—the principalities and powers, the demonic beings who have subjected the cosmos to their bondage.[31] These ideas Paul has not only borrowed from gnostic speculation; he finds them in scripture. Citing Ps. 110:1 and Ps. 8:6, he confesses that

---

[31] Schlier, *Principalities and Powers in the New Testament*, pp. 46 ff.

all things must be put into subjection to Christ. In "all things," of course, God himself is not included, and Christ, in turn, will be subjected to the Almighty. The New English Bible is helpful in unraveling these sentences: "But in saying 'all things,' it clearly means to exclude God who subordinates them; and when all things are thus subject to him, then the Son himself will also be made subordinate to God who made all things subject to him, and thus God will be all in all" (vss. 27-28).

The character of this consummation is nowhere clearly defined. However, the idea that God is "all in all" (*panta en pasin*) has nothing to do with the mystical notion that in the end all things are absorbed into the divine. Paul's eschatology is too historical and his doctrine of creation too objective to foster that sort of Oriental mysticism. What he means instead is that, in the end, God is really God. It is to this idea that the rather easily misunderstood rendering of the Revised Standard Version points: "That God may be everything to every one." In the end, every knee will bow and every tongue confess that God is Lord. To those who request a more precise picture of the end, Paul could only reply, "You foolish man!" (15:36.)

He would offer the same answer to those who might suppose that his own descriptions of the eschaton were to be taken literally. How could the new age possibly be described in terms of the old? In Paul's descriptions of the end he employs terminology readily at hand in contemporary literature. That he does not intend these expectations to be prosaically understood is apparent from his lack of consistency in their use. Compare, for example, the order of events listed here with the account of the end offered in some other Pauline texts:

I Thess. 4:16 ff.
the Lord will descend from heaven
a cry of command
the archangel's call
the sound of the trumpet of God
the dead in Christ will rise
we who are alive . . . shall be caught up together with them
to meet the Lord in the air
so we shall always be with the Lord

Rom. 8:21 ff.

the creation itself will be set free from its bondage to decay
and obtain the glorious liberty of the children of God
we wait for adoption as sons,
the redemption of our bodies

Rom. 11:25 ff.

the full number of Gentiles come in
all Israel will be saved
God has consigned all men to disobedience,
that he may have mercy on all

I Cor. 15:52 ff.

the trumpet will sound
the dead will be raised imperishable
we shall be changed
death is swallowed up in victory
God . . . gives us the victory through our Lord Jesus Christ

II Cor. 5:1 ff.

we have a building from God . . . eternal in the heavens
what is mortal may be swallowed up by life
we are . . . away from the body and at home with the Lord
we must all appear before the judgment seat of Christ

II Cor. 5:17

if any one is in Christ, he is a new creation
the old has passed away . . . the new has come

Phil. 1:23

my desire is to depart and be with Christ

Phil. 3:20-21

we await a Savior, the Lord Jesus Christ
who will change our lowly body to be like his glorious body

It must be admitted, of course, that some of these passages do not purport to present an orderly picture of the eschatological events, and it must be acknowledged, too, that harmonization of these texts may be possible. However, all the texts have an eschatological reference, and the effort to weave them into some new order will result in a patchwork quilt of unintelligibility. One wonders, too, how Paul's hearers who presumably had only one or two of his epistles could have made sense out of the eschaton at all; only the Thessalonians, perhaps, would have known about the glorious meeting in the air.

The truth of the matter is that Paul presents different descriptions of the eschaton. Some of these are not entirely consistent with others. The idea that life after death begins with a future act of resurrection (I Thess., Rom. 8, I Cor. 15) does not support Paul's notion that he can "depart and be with Christ" at the time of death (Phil. 1:23). The view that the Christians will be changed at the sound of the trumpet (I Cor. 15:51) is not exactly the same as the belief that the old has already passed away, that the new has already come, and that anyone who is in Christ is a new creation now (II Cor. 5:17). The suggestion that God will show mercy to all (Rom. 11:32) is not fully in harmony with the implication of I Cor. 15:22 that only those who are in Christ will be raised.

Actually, consistency is not intended. Paul uses a variety of figures in different contexts to express the significance of the eschatological element under discussion. The trumpet and archangel are found in Jewish apocalyptic. The "house not made with hands, eternal in the heavens" (II Cor. 5:1) sounds Platonic, but probably comes to the apostle by way of Hellenistic gnosticism. Rom. 8 is concerned with the cosmic aspects of eschatology, while Rom. 11 focuses on the historical question; Phil. 1 is occupied with the individual character of the resurrection life, while I Cor. 15 stresses the corporate character of the Christian resurrection. Paul himself does not know all the details of the future, and will not pretend to portray them in the paltry terms of the present. He uses the poetic symbols of his contemporaries to depict "what no eye has seen nor ear heard" (I Cor. 2:6)—to declare that God's purpose in history and creation will surely be fulfilled. "O the depth of the riches and wisdom and knowledge of God! How unsearchable are his judgments and how inscrutable his ways!" (Rom. 11:33.)

In context, Paul is insisting that the resurrection of the Christian—an event of the future—is the inevitable consequence of the resurrection of Christ. "The last enemy to be destroyed is death." (vs. 26.) Indeed, death, in contrast to Greek and modern notions, is contrary to the will of God. As Karl Barth says, "Death is the peak of all that is contrary to God in the world, the last *enemy*, thus not the natural lot of man, not an unalterable divine dispensation." [32] But Christ has already defeated this foe in decisive battle. The future triumph is sure. "Thanks be to God, who gives us the victory through our Lord Jesus Christ." (vs. 57.)

In I Cor. 15:29-34 Paul presents further arguments in support of his belief in the resurrection of the dead. He begins with a cryptic reference to the "baptism for the dead."

> Otherwise, what do people mean by being baptized on behalf
>   of the dead?
> If the dead are not raised at all, why are people baptized
>   on their behalf?

The practice has been interpreted in four major ways: (1) baptism for the dead is nothing more than ordinary baptism which always anticipates the resurrection; (2) the practice under discussion is a baptism out of respect for the dead whereby the candidate submits to the rite in response to the persuasive efforts of a friend who in the meantime has died; (3) it is a baptism for the sake of the dead, that is, for the purpose of being united with the departed friend or relative in the resurrection; (4) baptism for the dead is a vicarious ritual in which a living representative undergoes a baptism on behalf of a dead person who had never been baptized. [33]

No certainty is possible, but some suggestions may be made. For one thing, the practice does not seem to be a regular baptism, but a special ritual observed presumably at Corinth. This would rule out the first interpretation. [34] Moreover, the "dead" under discussion appear

---

[32] *Resurrection of the Dead*, p. 169.

[33] Bernard M. Foschini, *Those Who Are Baptized for the Dead, I Cor. 15:29—An Exegetical Historical Dissertation* (Worcester, Mass.: Heffernan Press, 1951), lists some thirty-five different interpretations of the passage, but some of these, like the "immersion of divers after the bodies of the shipwrecked" (p. 24) are not worthy of discussion. For an excellent survey of the history of the exegesis of the text, cf. Mathis Rissi, *Die Taufe für die Toten* (Zürich: Zwingli Verlag, 1962), pp. 6 ff. After his historical discussion, Rissi concludes (p. 57) that some view of vicarious baptism is assumed by Paul.

[34] It also rules out Foschini's conclusion (*Those Who Are Baptized*, pp. 91 ff.) that "baptism is not 'for the dead,' but unto life," which he defends with an ingenious but unconvincing method of punctuation.

to be people other than the candidate himself. The second interpretation would seem to add little to Paul's argument, since baptism in respect for the dead could be practiced without believing in the resurrection at all. The third seems impossible as a practice of Corinthians who denied the resurrection; to observe the ritual in this sense would have necessitated acceptance of the resurrection.

Actually there is no objection to the fourth interpretation except the notion that vicarious baptism contradicts Paul's doctrine of faith.[35] A ritual of this type was actually practiced in Judasim, Hellenism, and early Christianity, and it certainly fits the construction and context of Paul's argument. That Paul approves the practice is nowhere said. That the dead man represented had given no evidence of faith need not be assumed. That the motive for vicarious baptism is inferior to that necessitated by the second and third interpretations is debatable. That baptism effects the resurrection of the dead is not essential to Paul's argument. He is simply saying that the practice of vicarious baptism, which may have been observed by the Corinthians merely as an act fulfilling "all righteousness" (Matt. 3:15), or signifying the unity of the faithful dead with Christ,[36] has no validity unless the person represented will actually be raised; baptism has no effect upon the dead, and is therefore meaningless, unless the dead will really live.

Paul turns to his own experience.

> Why am I in peril every hour? . . .
> I die every day! . . .
> I fought with the beasts at Ephesus. (vss. 30 ff.)

By the latter phrase Paul probably does not mean that he was literally thrown into the Ephesian arena. He tells of no such incident in his

---

[35] So the argument against vicarious baptism by Maria Raeder, "Vikariatstaufe in I Kor. 15:29?" *Zeitschrift für die neutestamentliche Wissenschaft*, XLIV (1955), 258 ff. It is also true that the objection to vicarious baptism assumes a sacramental view of baptism—that the rite of baptism really effects salvation; this view is not necessary, as Rissi, *Taufe für die Toten*, pp. 68 ff., shows.

[36] Rissi, *Taufe für die Toten*, pp. 85 ff., convincingly argues that the dead under discussion were Christians who had expressed their faith but had died before they were able to be baptized. Since Paul's view of baptism is only a sign of the believer's oneness with the crucified and risen Christ, not a magically operative sacrament, a substitute could receive baptism to give expression to this symbolism.

long register of sufferings listed in II Cor. 11:23, and his Roman citizenship would have protected him from such a sentence. However, his reference here is to more than a mere theological quarrel with his opponents; he refers to a situation where his very life was endangered (cf. Acts 19:23 ff.).

The real problem of the passage is to decide how the apostle understands these experiences as supporting belief in the resurrection. Surely he does not mean that his mission is undertaken in order to receive some eschatological reward; his motive for preaching, as we have seen (I Cor. 9:16), rests on other ground. Perhaps he is suggesting that just as baptism can be for the benefit of another, so his ministry is for their benefit—their patricipation in the hope of the resurrection. He does speak of "my pride in you" (vs. 31), and elsewhere he says, "Death is at work in us, but life in you" (II Cor. 4:12). Nevertheless, he does raise the question here: "What do I gain?" (vs. 32.) This seems to mean that the whole life of the ministry presupposes the resurrection; death can be endured, since it is not the ultimate answer. The gain to Paul is the experience of life continually perceived in the struggle against death. "I die every day." (vs. 31.)

Paul continues the argument by citing a couple of ancient proverbs.

> If the dead are not raised,
> "Let us eat and drink, for tomorrow we die."
> Do not be deceived:
> "Bad company ruins good morals." (vss. 32 ff.)

The first was a pagan slogan which had already found its way into the Old Testament (Isa. 22:13), and was typical of the Epicurean skepticism of Paul's day. The second, a quote from Menander, in no way discloses the apostle as a savant of classical literature, for it had become proverbial and could have been cited without forethought about footnotes.

Again, it is unwise to suppose that Paul is offering the resurrection as a reward for high ethics. For him, morality is always grounded in faith. Ethics are involved in the discussion, however, since Paul can command: "Sin no more" (vs. 34). It is difficult to conclude that the sin he has in mind is the denial of the resurrection; such an idea seems without support in the context. Similarly, one is reluctant to identify the "bad company" as Christians who deny the resurrection of the dead. They have not been presented as sinful, but pitiable; they are not to be shunned, but convinced. The "bad company" are pagans who deny the resurrection—those who say, "Let us eat and drink." To deny the resurrection is to become one with them, to forfeit the entire Christian life; it is to be like the pagans without hope in the future and without ethics in the present (cf. Rom. 1:18 ff.). To the shame of the Corinthians, some are dangerously near this denial of their faith. "For some have no knowledge of God." (vs. 34.) Belief in the resurrection is essential to the Christian faith.

IV

Having answered the denial of the resurrection of the dead, Paul deals with a question from another quarter: "How are the dead raised? With what kind of body do they come?" (I Cor. 15:35.) This query, as has been suggested, is probably raised by a Corinthian of Jewish background. It was the very question which the rabbis had been debating for decades. It can be found in the pseudepigraphic II Baruch: "In what shape will those live who live in Thy day?" (49:2.) Paul replies sharply, "You foolish man!" or as the New English Bible reads, "A senseless question." The point is simply this: You cannot describe life after death in terms of the present existence. What, then, is the nature of the resurrection?

Obviously, it is different from life in this world. Paul illustrates this with an analogy drawn from the rabbinic debate—the seed and the plant. The seed must die before there can be a plant, and the former, a bare kernel, is not at all like the plant which succeeds it. Indeed, God gives to it a new body which he has chosen, so that there are all sorts of bodies in creation—bodies of men, animals, birds, fish. And if this does not make it clear that God can create bodies radically different from the rest, consider the heavenly bodies—the sun, moon, and stars.

"So is it with the resurrection of the dead." (vs. 42.) This application of the analogies, of course, does not recommend a literal interpretation. For instance, Paul does not mean that the resurrection is parallel to the natural processes of growing seeds, nor that those raised from the dead become like the astral deities who inhabit the heavens. His point is single: The resurrection body is not the same as the body of the earthly existence.

This is made evident in the series of contrasts which follows:

> What is sown is perishable,
> what is raised is imperishable.
>
> It is sown in dishonor,
> it is raised in glory.
>
> It is sown in weakness,
> it is raised in power.
>
> It is sown a physical body,
> it is raised a spiritual body.

The difference is determined by the act of God. There is a dualism here, but not in the nature of man. The contrast is between the old and the new being. The old man is subject to an inherited mortality; the divine image has been dishonored by sin; man is infected by a persistent weakness. But the new man is incorruptible, a being of glory and power. The old man could be called an animate body; the new being is spiritual *sōma*.

Before discussing the nature of the spiritual body, it will be well to look further into the text. Paul insists that, "If there is a physical [animate] body, there is also a spiritual body" (vs. 44). This would be admitted, of course, only if one is convinced by Paul's doctrine of the resurrection. If man is really raised from the dead, and if his existence after death is in complete contrast to the present, then that existence has a reality which can be called spiritual. That there actually is such a spiritual existence, Paul knows from his own experience of the resurrection; in that experience, the risen Christ appeared to him as the "life-giving spirit" (vs. 45).

187

Therefore, there are two men—the first Adam and the last Adam. From his Bible Paul knew that the first man had become a "living being" (*psychē zōsan*, Gen. 2:7); from his own experience he knew that the living Christ was radically other. Just as we are one with the first Adam, so we shall be one with the man of heaven and bear his image. The idea of the man of heaven, again, may reflect gnostic speculation about the *Urmensch* in whose image all men are patterned. Yet for Paul, the man of heaven is not the first man but the second; the image of the first man which all men bear is inadequate, and it must be changed into the image of the second. Among other things this discussion makes it evident that the resurrection body of the Christian will be similar in nature to the body of the risen Christ.

Within this discussion Paul employs two contrasts. The first has to do with the difference between the physical and spiritual body; the second, with the distinction between earth and heaven. The latter is not intended to suggest some dualistic metaphysics whereby the earthly man is composed of dust while the man of heaven consists of some spiritual substance. Neither does it suggest a localizing of the eschatological existence, as if the old life continues here, while the new being is to be found in "heaven." Rather, the two ages are of different nature; the form of this world is passing away (I Cor. 7:31); God makes all things new (II Cor. 5:17).

The first contrast confronts us directly with the problem of the spiritual body. The word *psychikon* (translated "physical" by the Revised Standard Version) simply indicates a body which has life—an animated body. The term *pneumatikon*, on the other hand, describes a body which is vitalized by the Spirit of God. The phrase "spiritual body," therefore, does not suggest a body composed of a substance called spirit, just as the words "physical body" do not denote a body which consists of a material called soul (*psychē*). Hellenistic anthropology did contrast body and soul as two conflicting elements in the nature of man. Paul affirms a new contrast. There are not two warring substances within man, but two men—the old man with an animated body; the new man with the Spirit of God. The term "body" can stand for the whole being, so that "spiritual body" may be translated "spiritual person."

The term "spiritual body," of course, defies definition and perhaps intends a certain ambiguity. To ask for something more precise would be a "senseless question." The phrase simply points to a new being, wholly responsive to the power of God. Paul hopes, however, to avoid two inadequate definitions of the life after death. On the one hand, the spiritual body is not to be identified as the immortal soul, some bodiless specter, but a spiritual reality, a whole person who has continuity with the old. On the other, the spiritual body is not to be identified with the physical frame which has been placed in the tomb, for "flesh and blood cannot inherit the kingdom of God" (vs. 50).[37] Paul thus avoids the Greek doctrine of immortality and the Jewish notion of the resurrection. Instead, he speaks from the radical ground of Christian faith. Death is taken seriously as the total destruction of the old, but hope is grounded in the creator God, who calls the living forth from the dead.

In the end, then, the resurrection remains a wonder. "Lo! I tell you a mystery." (vs. 51.) Some questions remain unanswered. What will happen to the nonbelievers? Paul has no knowledge, only hope (Rom. 11:32). What is the time of the resurrection? No one can know, and Paul is ambiguous; the end is surely future, yet the new creation has already begun (II Cor. 5:17), and Paul can desire "to depart and be with Christ" (Phil. 1:23). In the great resurrection of the eschaton (surely Paul's emphasis in I Cor. 15), will men be raised as individuals or as some new corporate reality? The notion of particular persons recognizable by the structures and associations of this life is surely construed along the lines of the world which is passing away and in conformity to the modern cult of individuality. Yet those who participate in the old Adam do not lose their identity, and life in the new humanity is created by the God of Abraham, Isaac, and Jacob (Mark 12:27).[38]

[37] Lynn Boliek, *The Resurrection of the Flesh* (Grand Rapids, Mich.: Wm. B. Eerdmans, 1962), p. 134, makes a valiant effort to interpret this verse in a manner consistent with traditional theology. Thus, the "resurrection of the flesh," like the "resurrection of the dead," refers to the *terminus a quo* of the resurrection; just as the dead are not dead after they are raised, so also flesh and blood is no longer flesh and blood after the resurrection. But this view is a denial of the traditional view of the physical resurrection which Boliek hopes to defend—the very view which he quotes Luke 24:39 to support (p. 117).

[38] The view of M. E. Dahl, *The Resurrection of the Body*, "Studies in Biblical Theology No. 35" (Naperville, Ill.: Alec R. Allenson, 1962), pp. 93 ff., that the resurrection involves a *somatic identity* based on a view of the "semitic totality" (pp.

Nevertheless, in the end time, the body of Christ will be perfectly formed, united in obedience and in fulfillment of the purposes of God.

The rest is poetry. It can scarcely be translated, let alone interpreted.

> All of us will not sleep,
> All of us will be changed,
>   in a moment,
>   in the flash of an eye,
>   at the last trumpet.

> For the trumpet shall sound,
>   and the dead shall be raised,
>   and even we shall be changed.

> This corruption must be clothed with incorruption,
> And this death must be clothed with life. . . .

> Then will be fulfilled the word which is written,
>   Death was swallowed up into victory.
>   Where, O death, is your victory?
>   Where, O death, is your sting?

> The sting of death is sin,
>   the power of sin is law;
> But to God be thanks,
>   he gives victory to us
>   through our Lord Jesus Christ. (I Cor. 15:51 ff., WB)

V

After that poetry, however, Paul concludes with practical advice. "Therefore, my beloved brethren, be steadfast, immovable, always

---

59 ff.) is suggestive. It is important to note that Dahl describes the Pauline presentation of the resurrection as a "parable" (p. 93), and that he insists that the resurrection cannot be literally understood (p. 95), so that an explication of the doctrine of resurrection demands a "remythologization" (pp. 85 ff.). On the implications of the unity of man for the concept of resurrection, cf. also, James J. Heller, "The Resurrection of Man," *Theology Today*, XV (1958), 217 ff.

abounding in the work of the Lord, knowing that in the Lord your labor is not in vain." (I Cor. 15:58.) The doctrine of the resurrection is to be applied to their daily tasks. Just as denial of the doctrine disturbs their faith, so its affirmation undergirds their life with power. Life is not without meaning; history is not without purpose. God is at work there—the God who raised Jesus from the dead; his goals shall be attained. Therefore, those who work in response to his power share the divine destiny—the destiny "which God decreed before the ages for our glory" (I Cor. 2:7).

But granted that Paul's answer to the problem of death was found to be relevant by the early Christians, what validity might it have today? Can the doctrine of the resurrection of the body have any meaning for modern man? One thing is certain—the problem of death is still with us. This does not mean that modern man is eager to face the question. On the contrary, he hopes to avoid it. His concerns are centered on the living. He has no desire to depart and be with Christ. He is quite at home here. He does not sing the old song:

> I am a stranger here, within a foreign land.

It may be, however, that in his frenzied effort to forget death, modern man has become a victim of what Roger Shinn calls a "gigantic conspiracy" [39]—a conspiracy which hopes to convince us that there really is no death. Cosmetics salesmen, for example, offer lipstick and hair oil which guarantee eternal youth. The mortician measures his art by his ability to make the corpse look as if it were not dead at all. Some mourners have wondered if they came to the right funeral; the dead person has not looked so good in the last twenty-five years. As Peter Berger has said, "The procedures, terminology, and professional ideology of the mortician's trade in this country all revolve around one fundamental aim—the camouflage of the reality of death." [40] Then there are the new-style cemeteries, or rather, memorial parks, which shun tombstones like the plague. A recent newspaper article is headed, "The Happy Graveyard," and the subtitle continues, "Cali-

[39] *Life, Death, and Destiny*, pp. 37 ff.
[40] *The Noise of Solemn Assemblies*, p. 48.

fornia's Forest Lawn is for the living; has a third as many weddings as interments; doing well financially, too, if you please." [41] This popular tourist attraction boasts gigantic works of art, piped music, sleeping rooms for the departed, a souvenir shop, Babyland, Lullabyland, Slumberland, and Vesperland. After all, its only a little way to Disneyland. What a nice place to be married.

The more serious prophets of our time, however, find death less enjoyable. Tennessee Williams writes drama which throbs with the pangs of death; the *Sweet Bird of Youth* has flown away forever; *Suddenly Last Summer*, death came with horror. Albert Camus' *Stranger* begins his story with his mother's funeral and ends with his own execution for a senseless crime. William Faulkner's *Sound and Fury* is the sound of death; his halting character of the Negro servant, Dilsey, speaks the prophetic word, that she has seen the beginning and the end. Miller's *Death of a Salesman* is the death of every urban man. Many people prefer fairy tales in which knights and princesses marry and live happily ever after. But what happens after that?

The answers which Paul found in the Hellenistic age prevail. In general, there is skepticism about any life after death. Since the scientists have found no evidence for it, there is no reason to believe in it. Death, when it is faced, is viewed as simply the natural end of life. Face it stoically. Eat and drink. Take out plenty of insurance. Maybe go to church, just in case. Skepticism, of course, is the admission that there is no answer.

More popular is belief in the immortality of the soul. This is seen in funeral rituals where the body is consigned to the earth, while the soul is committed to God. Actually, the funeral industry, whose efforts to promote the "high cost of dying" have been adequately assessed,[42] reflects a confused picture of the meaning of death. The recent stress on "grief therapy," whereby the viewing of the remains is supposed to have some therapeutic value for the bereaved, is mitigated by the effort to make the corpse appear alive. The old custom of pronouncing

[41] The Louisville *Courier-Journal*, August 6, 1961.

[42] Cf. Jessica Mitford, *The American Way of Death* (New York: Simon and Schuster, 1963).

Ashes to ashes,
Dust to dust

has all but disappeared, while the idea of a "spiritual" immortality is maintained in the notion of the "beautiful memory picture." But if life after death consists merely in memory, why all the attention to the body? One mortuary has published an attractive advertising calendar with the inscription, "Beautiful Bodies by Chambers," [43] while hosts of more sensitive morticians have been pushing foam-rubber mattresses for the departed, airtight, hermetically sealed caskets, and leakproof vaults which will last through eternity.[44]

Nevertheless, the notion that man has an immortal quality about his being—his personality, his creativity, his mind, his ideals—has persisted. But in support of such beliefs there is little convincing evidence.[45] The view falls, as it did in Paul's day, due to its doctrine of man and its idea of death. Man is not a dualism but a unity, as modern anthropology, biology, and psychology know. The belief that some part of man, his spirit or soul, can endure apart from the body is without scientific support. Death, therefore, is the end of the whole man. How then can man pretend that death is not real? It is the one great reality which threatens his existence. One of the main lessons to be learned from Paul is the seriousness of death.

Strange as it may seem, there are still some who expect the resurrection of the flesh. Their view can be seen in hope for a life after death construed in terms of this world's aspirations. When a group of movie stars were asked about their views of heaven, William Holden is reported to have said, "It's where a fellow can lead a dog's life: just eat, sleep, have a good time, take a short run every day, and be waited on hand and foot by people silly enough to work for a living." Olivia de Havilland is quoted as describing a place "where there are thirty hours to every day, four days to every weekend, three men to

[43] *Ibid.*, p. 226.
[44] *Ibid.*, pp. 56 ff.
[45] Cf. Corliss Lamont, *The Illusion of Immortality* (3d ed. New York: Philosophical Library, 1959). Lamont's argument is often extreme. Correctives may be supplied by A. E. Taylor, *The Christian Hope of Immortality* (New York: The Macmillan Company, 1947); John Baillie, *And the Life Everlasting* (New York: Charles Scribner's Sons, 1933).

every woman, and two hundred cents to the dollar." [46] Others, more seriously, wish for a mansion in the sky, while some, more modest, will be satisfied with a quaint little cottage with picket fence and no domestic strife.

> If you get there before I do,
> Tell all my friends I'm coming, too.

Such a view misses the flower for the seed, focuses on the present, hopes too small. What a poverty of vision to pattern the new world according to the old! What little faith in the presence of the God who spoke and all things came into being.

The Christian, of course, has faith in this God who raised Jesus from the dead. His resurrection is the cornerstone of our doctrine about life after death. As we have seen, historical evidence may be offered in support of the vitality of the resurrection faith, and denial of the resurrection event might involve difficulties greater than its acceptance. Nevertheless, belief in the resurrection of Christ is open today, as it was in the beginning, only to the eyes of faith. A resurrection which is subject to the research of man cannot be the work of God; a faith which rests on human proofs is not faith in the God whose ways are not our ways. Yet the Christian sees by faith, and at the center of his vision is the living Christ. He knows the Christ who lives; therefore, he knows that Christ was raised.

It is difficult to overestimate the significance of this faith. Yet many modern preachers avoid the resurrection even on Easter. Instead of praise to the living Lord, many congregations are urged to engage in the rites of Spring. Some chancels are crowded with memorial lilies, while one California sanctuary was traditionally lined with singing canaries on Easter Sunday. No doubt they could praise the glories of nature better than the preacher. But if he had been about his real business, some hearers, like the men of Athens, would have mocked.

Indeed, the resurrection has become the stumbling block of the modern church. Whereas the early auditors of the gospel tripped over the Cross, today's listeners cling to the Cross as if Christ were still hanging there. Expositions of justification, atonement, reconciliation,

---

[46] The Louisville *Courier-Journal*, January 31, 1962.

the revelation of the suffering God, have been central to the contemporary theological discussion, while the resurrection has sometimes been treated as an embarrassing appendage. We need to be reminded that early Christian interpretation of the death of Jesus followed the resurrection faith and was dependent upon it. The primitive *kerygma* stressed the death of Jesus as the act of man and spoke of "this Jesus whom *you* crucified" (Acts 2:36), while the supreme revelation of divine action was seen in the resurrection of Christ "whom *God* raised from the dead" (Luke 24:5, KJV).

The resurrection, of course, is more than an event which preceded the preaching of the church. It is a primary element of the Christian faith, as theologians like Richard R. Niebuhr have shown.[47] Rudolf Bultmann is surely right in supposing that the resurrection makes the meaning of the Cross clear.[48] Through the resurrection faith the disciples came to know that God had redeemed them in the crucifixion of Christ, that the lowly one was their Lord, that God chose suffering love as his route to triumph. It is also true that no interpretation of the resurrection can be entertained which removes the reality of the death of Jesus, so that the crucifixion becomes simply a temporary detour on the smooth road to success; no understanding of the resurrection faith permits an easy bypass of the scandal of the Cross.

However, the recognition that the resurrection is the clue to the Christian interpretation of the Cross need not reduce the resurrection faith to mere subjectivity. This, of course, is what Bultmann has been charged with doing.[49] His linking of crucifixion and resurrection is, in any case, Pauline;[50] while his view of the latter as *the* eschatological event, in his interpretation of history, does not reduce but enhances its reality.[51] Regardless of the validity of that view, our own analysis of I Cor. 15 has resulted in a concept of the resurrection as having clear historical manifestations. It has been argued that the visions through which the risen Christ was revealed can be understood as historical phenomena. It has also been suggested that the resurrection faith has had

---

[47] *Resurrection and Historical Reason*, pp. 14 ff.
[48] *Kerygma and Myth*, I, 38 ff.
[49] Cf. R. R. Niebuhr, *Resurrection and Historical Reason*, pp. 50 ff.
[50] *Theology of the New Testament*, I, 292 ff.
[51] *Kerygma and Myth*, p. 40; Ogden, *Christ without Myth*, p. 87.

historical expression which has founded the church and shaped the course of history.

We must agree, however, that the resurrection in essence remains *the act* of God which transcends history; it cannot be reported as simply an event within the course of ordinary occurrences.[52] It is unique; it is the end of history. Only this sort of an event can do what the Christian faith confesses the resurrection to accomplish. It is the event which shows God to be God. Of course, God's revelation does not conclude with the crucifixion. How can one say that suffering love is the way to God's triumph if the action of God stops at the Cross? How can one confess that Jesus Christ is Lord if he is really only dead? How can one even suppose that God's purposes are being fulfilled in history if the evil forces of history have been able to overcome his Christ? Indeed, is the God revealed exclusively in the crucifixion of Jesus really God? As Paul so cogently argues, denial of the resurrection of Christ is to undermine faith in the gospel "which you received, in which you stand, by which you are saved" (I Cor. 15:1-2).

There are those today, however, who can accept the resurrection of Christ without belief in the future resurrection of Christians. After all, Paul's view of the raising of the dead in the eschaton appears to be nothing more than apocalyptic symbolism. Just as one cannot accept literally the sound of the trumpet or the meeting in the air, so one is not able to put his faith in the resurrection of the last day. When such mythological wrappings are stripped away one can perceive that the new life is granted to the man of faith now, at the moment of radical decision. Thus Bultmann's existentialist eschatology[53] and the realized eschatology of C. H. Dodd,[54] in their efforts to eliminate or

[52] The argument of Eric C. Rust, "Interpreting the Resurrection," *Journal of Bible and Religion*, XXIX (1961), 25 ff., that the resurrection has two essential elements: the public "fact of the Empty Tomb" (p. 27), and the private experience of the resurrection faith, hardly makes his point that the resurrection is historical in some literal sense, since neither of these elements is of the essence of the resurrection event.

[53] Cf. Günther Bornkamm, Rudolf Bultmann, and Friedrick Karl Schumann, *Die Christliche Hoffnung und das Problem der Entmythologisierung* (Stuttgart: Evangelisches Verlagswerk, 1954), pp. 19, 56 ff.

[54] Cf. especially *The Parables of the Kingdom* (New York: Charles Scribner's Sons, 1936), pp. 50 ff. In his more recent writings, Dodd has more correctly referred to an "inaugurated" eschatology; cf. *The Interpretation of the Fourth Gospel* (Cambridge: University Press, 1954), pp. 6 ff.

de-emphasize the futuristic elements of eschatology, are reminiscent of Corinthian gnosticism.

However, the future aspect is essential to biblical eschatology. As John Knox says, "The eschatological expectation in some literal, temporal sense is implicit and essential." [55] The elimination of the future hope is not an interpretation of New Testament "mythology" but its eradication. When one interprets the apocalyptic language of Paul, he should not conclude that the use of mythological terminology precludes belief in a literal end of history and the cosmos. Rather, mythological language is employed to express the meaning of that end for the man of faith. That meaning is that God's purposes in history and in his creation will be fulfilled; that the forces which stand against that fulfillment will be overcome. Otherwise, is God really God? Is he really the Creator of heaven and earth and the Lord of history? Yes, confesses the Christian, for he knows the living Christ of the new creation, the Lord before whom every knee must bow. "Thanks be to God, who gives us the victory through our Lord Jesus Christ." (I Cor. 15:57.) Paul is quite right; the resurrection of Christ says something significant about the end.

Another serious objection to belief in the resurrection of the dead is the notion that expectation of life after death involves a certain egocentric motivation which is antithetical to the Christian faith. Roger Shinn mentions those who seem to say, "If you will just stop being self-centered for a few more years, you can enjoy self-centered delight forever." [56] There are no doubt people who look to the resurrection as a reward for services parsimoniously offered here. As we have seen, Paul opposes such views. Besides, if the Christian hopes to arouse interest in the resurrection in terms of this-worldly rewards, he will surely come off second best in relation to the Moslems, who can offer good food, wine, and dancing girls.

But all these notions of reward arise from the error of construing the new in terms of the old. They reflect the petty question of the Sadducees. "In the resurrection whose wife will she be?" (Mark 12:23.) But, as Jesus pointed out, there is neither marriage nor giving in marriage in

[55] *Christ and the Hope of Glory* (Nashville: Abingdon Press, 1960), p. 32.
[56] *Life, Death, and Destiny*, p. 86.

the life of the resurrection. Yet wherever men talk about the infinite worth of the human personality which God will surely want to preserve, they show that they are not yet ready for the spiritual body. The new being stands in judgment on the old.

This is why death must be realistically accepted. It is the end of the old. It cancels out the possibility of trust in human values. It shows that the securities of this age are futile. Indeed, in death radical faith is for the first time really possible. Here trust in nothing else is possible. Man's pride and prestige, his wealth and possessions, his petty defenses against his foes are all overcome by the last enemy. At death, nothing else is possible but faith in God.

This faith in God, radically conceived, is the ground for all belief in the resurrection. What the resurrection life will be like, the Christian cannot fully know. It must, however, be in some way like the new life which he has already experienced through oneness with the risen Christ—a life of obedience and fellowship with God, a life of perfect love toward the brethren, a life which seeks not its own but its neighbor's good. Thus the Christian can face death seriously yet unafraid, for the sting of death is sin and from the power of that sin he has been redeemed. He has no fear of the destruction which destroys the old; he has faith in the God who makes all things new. The resurrection remains an act of God—a totally new creation.

Yet, although the Christian can accept death, he can never be satisfied with it. Death is not the natural end of man but the final enemy of God. God does not will death, but life; he does not work destruction, but new being. As long as death reigns, God's lordship stands in limitation. But God has already wrestled with this primal foe and dealt him a mortal blow. The struggle is yet to be, but God's triumph is sure. Death will be consumed in victory; God will be all in all.

198

CONCLUSION

In comparison with what has gone on before, chapter sixteen of First Corinthians seems mundane. It does show, however, that the high theology of the epistle is addressed to ordinary people, plagued by the practical problems of the church in an urban society. Paul begins the chapter with a reference to the "contribution for the saints" (vs. 1). By this he means an offering which he has promised to collect from his Gentile churches for the poor Christians of Jerusalem (Gal. 2:10). Perhaps he hopes to remind the Corinthians, who are all too concerned with their own affairs, that they have a share in the health of the whole body of Christ. At any rate, the members of the congregation are to set aside a portion of their weekly income so that no emergency collection need be announced when the apostle arrives. It may be that the "first day of every week" (vs. 2) is payday in Corinth, but the reference could be to Sunday—the day when Christians met together for the breaking of bread (Acts 20:7). That the Corinthians needed prodding on this matter is clear from the fact that Paul later had to occupy two chapters with it (II Cor. 8–9). That his efforts finally met with success is evident from Rom. 15:26.

Next, Paul informs the church of his travel plans (vss. 5-9). He hopes to return to Corinth by way of Macedonia. That is, he expects to come to them by the slower overland route rather than by the more direct course across the Aegean. The Corinthians might very well have been upset by this, since Paul's delay in coming had already given rise to disappointment (4:18). But surely the churches at Philippi, Thessalonica, and Beroea deserve a visit, too. The real reason for the delay, however, is the situation in Ephesus, "for a wide door for effective work has opened to me" (vs. 9). Therefore, Paul has decided to "stay in Ephesus until Pentecost" (vs. 8). At a later date these travel plans would be radically revised. A "painful visit" would be made to Corinth (II Cor. 2:1), and a severe letter, written "out of much affliction and anguish of heart" (II Cor. 2:4), sent to the Corinthians before Paul would finally make this journey to them by way of Macedonia (Acts 20:2). The problems of their church would continue to occupy the apostle.

In the meantime, he is sending Timothy to Corinth. Although it might seem that this young co-worker would actually carry the epistle, Acts 19:22 indicates that Timothy, along with Erastus, will travel the longer route via Macedonia also. Paul seems to expect that the Corinthians will not be satisfied with a substitute. He reminds them, therefore, that Timothy "is doing the work of the Lord, as I am" (16:10). The Corinthians are urged to accept the ministries of this young emissary, and speed him on his way back to Paul. It would be Timothy's report which would give occasion to the troublesome events about to transpire.

Paul had also been urging Apollos to visit Corinth (16:12). Apparently that eloquent preacher had been working with him in Ephesus. However, "it was not at all God's will for him to go now" (vs. 12), which no doubt meant that some door had opened up for Apollos, too. Paul's reasons for wanting Apollos to make the trip are evident. He knew that the problems at Corinth required a theological heavyweight. What would young Timothy mean in comparison with this homiletical master from Alexandria—a man whose effectiveness had already been tested in Corinth? Perhaps Paul also wanted support for his own argument. Everything he had said, Apollos could say better.

Although Apollos cannot come now, other leadership will be available for the Corinthian community soon. Paul commends the household of Stephanas, the "first converts in Achaia" (16:15), who are with him now in Ephesus. Perhaps a congregation of the church actually meets in their house in Corinth, but more important, "they have devoted themselves to the service of the saints" (vs. 15). Paul may have in mind their liberality in regard to the collection, but more likely he refers to their continual service of the Corinthian church. It is not clear whether Fortunatus and Achaicus are a part of this household (perhaps its slaves) or not. Actually, a certain Fortunatus is mentioned in Clement's epistle to Corinth (I Clem. 65:1), but he seems to be a resident of Rome rather than Achaia. At any rate, these three men have brought news from Corinth and will probably serve as the bearers of First Corinthians to its readers back home. Paul has been refreshed by their presence, since they tighten the bond which unites all Christians; "they have made up for your absence" (vs. 17).

That bond is also evidenced in the greeting of the Asian churches (16:19 ff.). Paul wants to point out to the Corinthians that they are part of a larger fellowship. The special greeting from Aquila and Priscilla will remind them of this. This devoted couple had worked in their midst, and just as they no doubt hosted a church in their shop at Corinth, so now a congregation meets in their house in Ephesus. The intimacy of that fellowship is recalled by a symbolic act which has its background in a custom of the Hellenistic home: "Greet one another with a holy kiss" (vs. 20).

Then, while the amanuensis stretches his weary fingers, Paul picks up the stylus and pens a quick greeting of his own (16:21 ff.). How much it is like the man from Tarsus—how abrupt, how terse, how compact! He hurls an anathema at anyone who "has no love for the Lord" (vs. 22). He utters the eschatological hope: "Our Lord, come!" (vs. 22.) He offers a simple benediction:

The grace of the Lord Jesus be with you.
My love be with you all in Christ Jesus. Amen (vs. 23).

These liturgical elements may indicate that Paul expects his letter to be read in a service of worship. Into some ordinary room, dimly lighted by oil lamps, will crowd the common folk to hear the word of the apostle, to break the hallowed loaf, to await the coming of their Lord.

I

When we look back through First Corinthians, what do we see that is relevant for the church of yesterday and today? We said at the outset that Corinth and the modern city offer certain parallels. These parallels, however, may be merely superficial. Today's city is situated amidst the complex machinery of a technological age; its towers are built by the principles of a scientific method; its future is predicted by barometer and computer, its tomorrow is the effect of causes graphically plotted. Yesterday's city was at home in a world of mystery; its columns were shaped by sacred hands; its future foreseen by an intoxicated prophetess, its tomorrow the destiny of a ruthless fate. Perhaps this is why the Christian religion flourished in the ancient city; perhaps this is why the church is facing such grave difficulties in the modern metropolis.

Yet, for all these obvious differences, Corinth and Cleveland are not really so far apart. Man in the contemporary city faces the same problems as his ancient ancestors—the problem of seeking security in a world of transiency, the problem of finding freedom in a social structure of fateful forces, the problem of man's ultimate destiny, of death, destruction, nonbeing. The church which valiantly attempts to answer these questions is not essentially different from that founded in Corinth nineteen centuries ago. Its message is the same—Christ and him crucified, a stumbling block to scientists and foolishness to the philosophers; its mission is not different—to be the body of Christ in the world, to do the work of God; its ethic is the same—to secure undivided devotion to the Lord; its hope has not changed—that God will be all in all.

But, if the world of yesterday was superficially different, we might expect the problems of the ancient church to vary in externals from those of today. Thus the problem of division in the church was actually a struggle of petty factions within the Christian community, not a complex conflict of denominational doctrines and polities. These factions, however, contained the germ of division, and the causes of the ancient struggle—false wisdom, pride, and inordinate loyalty to leaders—are not unlike the roots of division in the church of today. Beneath these causes was a subsoil of self-centeredness. Such soil produces small sprouts which boast of belonging to Paul, Apollos, or Cephas, or which speak with undue pride of their special heritage, their distinctive witness. The latter may even dare to acclaim, "I belong to Christ."

The problem of morality has changed little. The immorality of the Roman world is legendary, and even Hollywood has turned it to profit. Yet the latter may be worse than the former; one gets the impression that the actors may be less moral than the drama. The loose living of the stars is, of course, a constant target of the contemporary critic, but those who throw stones need to be reminded that the glass houses were built by the public. Of course, a case of incest within the church seems pretty bad, but tastes in immorality these days run in other directions. Polygamy has been replaced by a series of marriages and divorces; the monotony of monogamy has been modified by the promiscuity of extramarital sex relations. At base, morality is the problem of man who turns his back on the Creator to worship the creature, who treats men who are made in the image of God as if they are tools for his egocentric aggrandizement.

The problem of secularism takes different forms. In fact, the term "secular" is without exact equivalent in Paul's vocabulary. His world could never be conceived apart from supernatural forces—the principalities and powers, the many gods and many lords which inhabited the cosmos. These strange forces controlled the stars in their courses, bringing seedtime and harvest, visiting men with sickness and health. Thus, what we have called secularism, Paul faced as the problem of idolatry. This problem was forced upon the apostle by his insistence that the church remain in the world. There the streets were decorated with pagan shrines, and from these shrines came the main supply of meat for the marketplace. Paul's question was twofold. Could a Christian worship an idol? Could a Christian eat meat which had been offered to an idol? Remote as these matters may seem to the modern mind, the ethical motifs which underlie them are still operative. The similarity is due to the demand that the church stay in the world; this demand is essential to the church's destiny. Thus the question is, fundamentally, how can the Christian live in the world? The problem is not unlike Paul's. Can a Christian share some of the values of contemporary society without submitting to that culture's control? Can the church fulfill its essential mission as a secular institution without being secularized?

The problem of worship is distinctively a problem of the church. Here we may expect to find the greatest relevance of Paul's analysis. Here, too, will be found the answer to the essential character of the church's life in the world. The church at worship is the church being the church. Of course, some of the particular problems at Corinth are irrelevant to contemporary liturgy. The question of wearing veils, for instance, is not germane to the recent liturgical debate. The ladies will wear their hats to worship quite without need of admonition from the apostle. Orders of worship, the relation of form and spontaneity, are a continual challenge to the clergy; and the Lord's Supper, which is intended to bring all Christians to a common table, is a source of constant debate and division. Basically, the problem of worship is the problem of man who does not fully know God or rightly how to praise him.

The problem of death is not new. Paul, of course, could blame it on Adam, while modern man supposes that it is the natural outcome of his existence. Even of the "immortal" Socrates it could be said:

> All men are mortal.
> Socrates is a man.
> Therefore, Socrates is mortal.

Of course, a few people can be found who expect a physical resurrection. These speak quite correctly of the unity of man, but glory in the majesty of God's creation, meaning themselves. Others, aware that this frail frame is passing into dissolution, concentrate on the grandeur of man's mind or the eternal value of the human personality, meaning theirs. Most men, however, are sheer skeptics. For all their efforts to grasp some straw, they view the grave, whenever they take the courage to face it, as the end. Every minister who has spent those sorrowful moments with the family alone with the dead knows that most of his parishioners consider that farewell to be the last. The problem of death is the problem of facing it; most people have too much fear for themselves and too little faith in God.

The problem of the Corinthian and the contemporary churches is how to live in the world in response to the God who stands outside it. How may the ways of men become the way of a God whose ways are not our ways? The audacity of God consists in this: that he is concerned with the ways of men, that he confronts them with a righteousness which they cannot attain. Though he has created men in his image, that image has been blurred. Men have cut a chasm between themselves and the righteous God. But he has called them out of bondage into freedom, out of Egypt into a land of promise. From this people a righteous remnant has been redeemed—" a chosen race, a royal priesthood, a holy nation. . . . Once you were no people but now you are the people of God" (I Pet. 2:9 ff., WB).

II

Paul's answer in essence is just that—the church should be the people of God; the church should be the church. To the problem of division he offers stern judgment. Factionalism in the church is against its very nature. "Is Christ divided?" Instead of the Corinthian confidence in the wisdom of the world, Paul demands the wisdom of God revealed in the proclamation of the crucified Christ. Rather than the Corinthian pride, Paul calls them to humility; what do they have which is not from God, for "he is the source of your life in Christ Jesus" (1:30)? Instead of inordinate loyalty to leaders, Paul requires a loyalty to God, for "he who plants and he who waters is nothing, but God who gives the growth is everything" (3:7, WB).

It is evident that these demands of Paul afford no easy answer. Of course, the church is essentially one, and everybody knows that the Johannine Christ prayed for its unity. Paul, however, offers no clear blueprint for ecumenical success. The wisdom of God will no doubt help the cause, but who has a special corner on that? Some of the most divisive factions in the church are confident that they are preaching Christ, and even the advocates of some easy unity imagine that their lowest-denominator faith is formed in the image of the tolerant Jesus. Humility will help, but whenever one notices it, it begins to disappear. Loyalty to God is surely necessary, but how can one measure a commitment to an unseen Lord? The transcendent God administers no ordinary loyalty oaths.

Paul is also eager to give advice on ethics. In contrast to the squeamish churchman of today, he is so bold as to write sexual advice into Scripture. His demand in regard to a case of gross immorality is drastic: Put the evildoer out of the church. On other matters, however, the apostle is less severe. Celibacy is good, but hard to find. Divorce is disallowed, but tolerated under certain circumstances. Monogamy is demanded, and the marriage bond provides a mutuality which transcends the simple need of procreation. A mixed marriage even makes possible the operation of the grace of God; through such a union the pagan partner is sanctified and the offspring of this union are recognized as holy.

But the fact that Paul is adamant on such matters as incest and monogamy, while lenient in regard to celibacy and divorce, indicates that he is caught in the ancient circle of relativity. This problem is explicitly stated in I Cor. 6, where Paul suggests that legal disputes between Christians should be settled before the church. Then he announces another principle: You should have no lawsuits at all! This demand of an absolute helps us to understand that Paul's ethic is not simply ensnared in Protagorean relativism; Paul does not say that man is the measure of all things. However, his allowance of the relative does create a problem for Pauline morality. In spite of the fact that Paul always couples his relativity with the declaration of the divine absolute, the resulting ethic remains problematic. When must one obey the absolute absolutely—when must the church invoke excommunication? When can the relative be applied in a manner which is responsible—when can the church allow divorce?

These questions become even more acute in Paul's answer to the problem of secularism. True enough, the apostle does not attempt to avoid the issues. He insists that the church must remain in the world. Its worship, however, must remain pure. The Christian can make no compromise with idolatry; one cannot partake of the table of the Lord and the table of demons. But one can, under certain conditions, eat food which has been offered on that very table, while under other circumstances the Christian can assert, "I will never eat meat."

The principles which contribute to these decisions are derived from the Christian faith. The principle of knowledge, which every intelligent adherent of a monotheistic faith possesses, suggests that an idol is nothing and therefore cannot taint food. According to this principle, the wise Christian can eat whatever is set before him without raising questions. The principle of love of the brethren, on the other hand, may suggest that the intelligent Christian should not touch the idolatrous food; some of the brethren are weak, and this example may invite them to eat, resulting in a painful conscience and destruction of the brother. There is still another principle—freedom—and according to this virtue no one's scruples should be allowed to shackle a Christian into moral bondage. And beyond all this a principle grounded in the character of the absolute makes its elusive demand: Do all things for the glory of God.

It does not take a linguistic analyst to see that Paul's language here is confusing. Nor does he help matters by offering the illustration from his own ministerial conduct in I Cor. 9. No one will doubt his right to support from the churches, nor his right to turn it down. But when he takes it from some and refuses it from others, the reasons are not clear. Apparently, he wants to make it obvious to the Corinthians that proclaiming the gospel is its own reward. But what about the Philippians? Has not Paul descended to a simple situational ethic? This interpretation is supported by his willingness to become all things to all men. To be sure, he does not submit to Jewish legalism, and the law of Christ prevents a descent into license; and to be sure, he does it all for

207

the sake of the gospel. But how far can one go toward law, and to what degree is one free from obligation, and how can one be true to the gospel in an age when eye has not seen nor ear heard what God has prepared for those who love him?

Paul's answer to the problem of worship involves profound theological concepts. Of course, one wonders why he spent time on the question of the veil at all, but even this seemed significant at Corinth. As his instruction on morality and secularism shows, Paul believed that all human affairs, no matter how trivial, stand under the demand of God. This matter of veils, moreover, suggests an important liturgical principle: In matters of secondary importance—music, art, and architecture—the church should employ the best forms of contemporary culture. Actually, Paul would have been quite at home in a more or less formal kind of service. His liturgical life had been nurtured in the synagogue, and there traditional forms and ordered worship had become the pattern. However, Paul wanted vitality in worship, too. The Spirit should not be quenched, and although those who assumed it to be their special possession needed chastening, Paul stresses the dynamic gift of prophecy and does not forbid speaking in tongues.

Worship is, for the apostle, essentially a matter of the Spirit and of tradition. In regard to the former, it must be said that all Christians have received one and the same Spirit. This Spirit is present in the life of the church, and in the church's worship its presence is always evident. Every member of the congregation, then, has received some gift of the Spirit. These gifts have been bestowed for the mutual edification of the membership. Some gifts are higher, to be sure, but the greatest gift of all is the gift every lowly Christian receives—the gift of love. This truly is a gift of the Spirit, since Paul understands the Spirit as the means through which God accomplishes his purposes. Love is the way God works. Faith, hope, and love abide, but the greatest of these is love.

The tradition which is basic to Christian worship goes back to Jesus Christ. On the night when he was betrayed, he took bread. And ever since, the church has met to break this bread and drink the cup which signifies a new covenant. In the drama the event of Christ's death and resurrection is reenacted; the act of God in Christ becomes real in the liturgy of the church. This action is the center of Christian worship. Christ is remembered, Christ is present, Christ is expected to return. Thus the tradition offers nothing to worship which is not also confirmed by the action of the Spirit. Christ is present as the Spirit, and the Spirit bears witness to Christ. The tradition of the church gives worship its content; the Spirit of God gives worship its life.

Of course, Paul's answers are not adequate to solve all the problems which bother us. Who is to officiate at the table of the Lord? Paul does not seem much concerned, and perhaps we should not be either. Yet, someone must offer the elements, and someone must bless them. Surely the celebrants should be responsible to Christ and the Spirit. Who can partake of the elements? Paul implies that only the faithful could partake with meaning, and leaves the question of worthiness to the man of faith. Yet, certainly the modern church needs regulations which are more specific.

The apostle's answer to the problem of death seems most difficult of all. His view of the unity of man, which we have learned from modern science, is convincing, but his notion of the resurrection seems about as relevant as the dinosaur. It wouldn't be quite so bad if Paul had promoted pagan immortality, but his idea of a bodily resurrection is simply incomprehensible. Of course, he has insisted that flesh and blood cannot inherit the kingdom, and that seems to answer all those antiquated, conservative notions. Yet talk about the raising of the body creates problems of its own. Where is the body now? What do we mean by the identity of the old person and the new? To be sure, Paul describes the latter as a "spiritual body," but that seems to be a contradiction in terms. It is better these days to call it a paradox.

Paul's argument in support of his belief in the resurrection is not convincing to the skeptic. The resurrection of Christ, which is basic to everything he has to say, is accompanied by a host of incredibilities— the empty tomb, the third day, the proof from the Scriptures. The insistence that faith in the resurrection is basic to all Christian belief is simply denied by the hosts of the devout who agree that the example and teachings of Jesus are worthy of emulation, but imagine that the resurrection is to be understood as simply the legendary expression of the truth that he envisioned values which are eternal. As to the destruction of the cosmic enemies, the twinkling of the eye, and the sound of the trumpet, all this paraphernalia appears to be borrowed from naïve Jewish apocalypticism. Indeed, much of Paul's ethical advice seems to rest on a view of the end which history has simply shown to be in error. When one looks at I Cor. 15 through the eyes of doubt, the force of the whole argument seems to confirm the very sort of skepticism which Paul hopes to deny. When the apostle proclaimed the resurrection in Athens, the philosophers thought he was mad; when the modern minister announces the resurrection on Easter, his auditors only suppose he is amusing.

At this point it becomes clear that our claim for the relevance of First Corinthians is not made with ease. True enough, we have been able at the end of every chapter to present Paul's argument as having significance for contemporary life. These answers, however, can hardly have been felt to be relevant apart from some participation in the Pauline faith. In no case can Paul's advice be understood as offering easy solutions to the difficult problems of our day. We have just noted that his answers are complex, ambiguous, and for some of our questions, irrelevant. But even to the questions of his contemporaries the apostle's advice offered few clear and easy answers. Perhaps this is why they found it so difficult to follow, for the epistle did not immediately accomplish its purposes. Shortly after its arrival a dispute broke out between the apostle and the church which challenged the validity of Paul's entire ministry (II Cor. 10-13). Later, however, right relations seem to have been restored (II Cor. 1-9). If the church had not returned the apostle to a place of honor, they surely would not have treasured his letter. The fact that they did preserve it, and that it finally made its way into the New Testament canon, indicates that First Corinthians, for all its complexities, was eventually received as relevant for the life of the church.

Perhaps the relevance of the epistle lies not in its answers but in its questions. Paul does not offer an easy solution to the problem of division, but pronounces judgment on Corinthian factionalism and their trust in the wisdom of the world. Paul does not provide a neat code for eliminating the moral problems of the church, but condemns the church's immorality and hypocritical arrogance; he denounces Christian wrongdoing and fraudulent behavior. Paul has no simple solution to the difficulties of life in the world, but demands that the Christians remain there, judging them for their idolatry and condemning their destruction of the brethren. Paul presents no "do-it-yourself kit" for the planning of Sunday worship services, but chastens Corinthian spiritual pride and denounces their pseudocelebration of the Supper of the Lord. Paul does not pacify the Corinthians with some positive thoughts about death, but opposes their skepticism, judges their egocentric hope, and condemns their dearth of faith in God. For some popular preachers the slogan has been: Christ is the answer. For Paul judgment is declared: Christ is the question!

III

Although Christ is seen as standing in judgment on the church, Paul can also confess that the solutions to the church's problems are in some much more profound sense to be found in Christ. Christ is certainly central to the entire argument of First Corinthians. The problem of the church's factionalism is to find resolution in a unity which is Christocentric. Thus Paul declares, "All things are yours . . . and you are Christ's" (3:21 ff.). The problem of morality is answered with reference to Christ. "Shall I therefore take the members of Christ and make them members of a prostitute?" (6:15.) The decision about marriage can be decided by reference to "undivided devotion to the Lord" (7:35). The problem of secularism must also be referred to the confession, "Jesus Christ is Lord," and the fellow Christian whose conscience must be respected is the "brother for whom Christ died" (8:11). The problem of worship should seek its solution in a tradition which goes back to the night when the Lord Jesus was betrayed, and the quarrel over spiritual status may be solved by accepting the gift of love which was publicly portrayed on the next day. The problem of death can be answered by faith in the risen Christ, for what God has done in him is the key to the destiny of human history. It can be concluded without a doubt—the ethic of Paul is Christocentric.

But what does it mean to posit a Christocentric ethic? When Paul confesses that Christ is the measure of all human conduct, he surely does not mean that the essence of Christian morality is to be found in following the ethical example of Jesus. Paul has very little to say about the life of the man from Nazareth, and nowhere presents it as a model for moral conduct. To be sure, Paul does say, "Be imitators of me, as I am of Christ" (I Cor. 11:1), but by this he does not mean asking the question, "What would Jesus do?" Rather, he is suggesting that the Christian ought to be absolutely responsible to the will of God as was the Christ. The Christian should have the mind of Christ, who emptied himself, humbled himself, and became obedient unto death (Phil. 2:5 ff.).

By the same token a Christocentric ethic does not mean following the teachings of Jesus. Paul seems to have little interest in the ethical instructions of the Master and prefers to distill the content of his ethic primarily from the Old Testament. He makes no mention of the Sermon on the Mount, but shows great concern for the law of Moses. It must be acknowledged, of course, that he does know a few traditional words from Jesus, and in I Cor. 7 employs some of these in his instruction on marriage. But in the main, Paul's morality is grounded in his response to the Christ of faith, not in the teachings of the Jesus of history.

It might also be said that a Christocentric ethic does not demand a complex metaphysical Christology. Nowhere does the apostle suggest that Christians ought to be good because they follow a Christ who is of one essence with the Father or who is fully God and fully man. Not even a notion of the incarnation is offered in support of his ethic; it is not suggested, for example, that God has come as man, so that mankind can no longer be viewed as the same, but must be seen as the very being in whom God can reside and therefore man must be treated with a holy respect. Paul does suggest, nevertheless, that the Christian is in Christ and Christ is in the Christian, and seems to give evidence for what has been termed a "Christ mysticism." His terminology, however, has its meaning in the community and in relation to the Spirit. Rather than suggesting that man is somehow permeated with the divine essence, these expressions emphasize the oneness of the new humanity and the action of God in the eschatological age.

As we have argued, Paul's Christology is essentially functional. His

212

concern is not with the nature of Christ but with the action of Christ, or rather with the action of God for man through Christ. Thus, a Christocentric ethic begins with a concept of revelation. The God who is revealed in Christ is the righteous God of the Old Testament. He is righteous, and he demands righteousness of his people. He is also the God who acts, and apart from his revelatory action God cannot be known. The problem of man is not his ignorance but his sin. The problem of revelation is a problem of ethics. God, in spite of or because of man's sin, has acted to reveal his righteousness. The act of righteous revelation has also declared sinful man to be righteous, not with a righteousness of his own, but by the righteousness of God to every man who has faith (Rom. 3:22). The revelation of that righteousness God has accomplished in Christ; he is the object of faith, the once-for-all revelation of God to whom an absolute commitment is demanded. "All the promises of God find their Yes in him." (II Cor. 1:20.)

Thus it is clear how closely a functional Christology is related to ethics. Yet, the righteousness of God is by faith, not by works of the law. Faith, however, is the means by which God's grace is appropriated; it does not cancel out God's claim. Nowhere does Paul suggest that the righteous demands of God have been repealed. Instead, he offers a new way to righteousness; it is by God's grace and man's faith. The old way, the way of works, cannot produce genuine righteousness; it results either in a tragic sense of guilt or in a beguiling sense of self-righteousness. Those who seek a righteousness of their own do not submit to the righteousness of God (Rom. 10:3). The righteousness by faith, on the other hand, involves the commitment of the whole person. Thus it involves an ethical response—a response which is not grounded in egocentric effort but in gratitude for God's graciousness, a response which does not concentrate on the achievement of man but which takes seriously the demand of God.

It is in this demand of God that Paul's ethic finds its absolute. Although he agrees that decision is always made in the human situation, his ethic is not simply situational; its real focus is on the demand of God. The decision is made in history, for there the righteousness of God has been revealed, and the transiencies of history make absolute obedience

213

elusive. Yet God's will is absolute, and man's failure and his faithfulness stand under the judgment of God.

The content of God's will is revealed in Christ, and for Paul the crucial element in that revelation is the crucifixion-resurrection. He conceives of these as one event—the act of God. The crucifixion shows that the demand of God is radical *agape;* the resurrection reveals that this demand is really God's. The demand of love is both herald of judgment and bestowal of mercy. It insists that man's meager love be measured by the absolute love of God; it declares forgiveness for man's inevitable lack of love. Forgiveness does not cancel judgment, since both are revealed in the same event—the crucifixion of Christ. The essence of that event is the love of God, and it is love that both judges and forgives. Nothing judges so severely as the love of God, nothing forgives so completely as the love of God. Judgment and mercy intersect in the cross of Christ. Yet, the resurrection, which is so closely linked with the crucifixion, shows that this love is God's, that judgment and mercy are absolute, that God exercises his sovereignty in love, that when God is all in all, love still abides.

God's judging and redeeming love has been revealed in history. The love of God has been manifest absolutely in the one who knew no sin. This is how God's claim is made upon us; in Christ man is encountered with a decision to absolute obedience. Since God's love has been radically revealed, man can offer no excuses—no claims to ignorance, no retreat into relativity. Since the demand of God is in essence absolute, only he who accepts it absolutely can understand what it means at all. He who has been called knows what the Lord requires of him. Though we pray for mercy, our very prayer is a confession of conscious disobedience. Though we see in a mirror dimly, we have seen the glory of God in the face of Christ.

> Who has known the mind of the Lord,
> Who can comprehend his will?
> Yet, *we* have the mind of Christ. (2:16, WB.)

INDEX OF SUBJECTS

216

217

INDEX OF SCRIPTURE